New Zealand
in the Pacific War

ALSO BY BRUCE M. PETTY
AND FROM MCFARLAND

---

*At War in the Pacific: Personal Accounts
of World War II Navy and Marine Corps Officers* (2006)

Saipan: Oral Histories of the Pacific War (2002)

New Zealand in the Pacific War

Personal Accounts of World War II

BRUCE M. PETTY

McFarland & Company, Inc., Publishers
Jefferson, North Carolina, and London

LIBRARY OF CONGRESS CATALOGUING-IN-PUBLICATION DATA

Petty, Bruce M., 1945–
    New Zealand in the Pacific War : personal accounts of World
War II / Bruce M. Petty.
        p.   cm.
    Includes bibliographical references and index.

    ISBN 978-0-7864-3527-2
    softcover : 50# alkaline paper ∞

    1. World War, 1939–1945 — New Zealand.   2. World War,
1939–1945 — Campaigns — Oceania.   3. World War, 1939–1945 —
Personal narratives, New Zealand.   4. World War, 1939–1945 —
Personal narratives, American.   I. Petty, Bruce M., 1945–
D767.85.N44   2008
940.54'8193 — dc22   2007049748

British Library cataloguing data are available

On the cover: "Mapping Unit" (detail) painting by P.G. Navarro 2nd
Marine Division WWII; map of the Solomon Islands

Manufactured in the United States of America

McFarland & Company, Inc., Publishers
  Box 611, Jefferson, North Carolina 28640
  www.mcfarlandpub.com

For my children, Anne-Marie,
Beatrice, and Faris

Acknowledgments

If I know what is good for me, trust that the first person I will thank is my wife Daniele, who has made it possible for me to write all of my books, including this one. Next, I have to thank my good friend Beret Strong, who can best be described as my mentor and teacher in so many ways. I should also mention Mr. Gates, my freshman-year high school history teacher at Fremont High School in Sunnyvale, California, who, like my father, thought I was hopeless. I also would like to thank the following, who have helped me in invaluable ways, big and small: Lynne Hepworth, Don Taylor, Karen Baker, Justin Taylan, John Leith, Noel Garland, John McCullough, John Innes, Peter Flahavin, Reg Wellington, Ewan Stevenson, Jock Phillip, Megan Hutching, Reg Newell, John Grausz, Wally Ware, Bill Howard and Ron Lambert at the Puki Ariki Library in New Plymouth, Graem Black, Joe Alexander, Michael Wehi Mailetonga Walsh, Bill Williams, Helen McDonald, Joan Love Ellis, Donna and Paul Garner, Diane Ladame, Wheturangi Walsh-Tapiata, Mackenzie Gregory, Samuel McPhetres, Patrick Bronte, Ian McGibbon of the Ministry for Culture and Heritage in New Zealand, and Steve Statharos. Also to be thanked are Paul Wilderson and Mark Gatlin — wherever you may be. And last but not least my mother-in-law, Mary Magdalene Lonchamp, whose interest in my writing career can best be summed up by something she said to me a few years ago: "When are you going to get a job?"

Table of Contents

Table of Contents

PART III
Voices of Americans in New Zealand

PART IV
Voices from the Next Generation

Author's Note

Although this book was researched and written in New Zealand, my publisher is in the United States, thus American spelling of English words will predominate. I have also taken the liberty of putting words in [brackets] for a number of reasons. Firstly, in order to stay faithful to the voice and words of interviewees, I have added words that appear to have been left out on the taped interviews. However, in each case I have confirmed with the individuals being interviewed that these bracketed words do not alter the meaning of the intended statement. As a result, syntax and grammar do not have priority, as I think should be the case when transcribing oral history interviews.

Secondly, I have used [brackets] to aid readers in understanding the meanings of New Zealand colloquialisms, as well as Maori words, thus saving the reader the inconvenience of having to flip back and forth to a glossary.

The author invites interested persons to visit his website, http://www.voicesfromthepacificwar.com.

Introduction

The inspiration for this book came in the early part of 2001, when I interviewed Mackenzie J. Gregory, a retired Australian naval officer, living in Melbourne. Mac, as he likes to be called, was trained to do things the British Navy way and had to learn almost overnight how to do things the U.S. Navy way. For example, he said, "The first few times I had to change to a new course while part of a U.S. Navy task force, were an absolute nightmare. It meant literally picking up the fleet formation steaming on a specific course, rotating that force e.g., through fifty degrees, and then putting it down again so that the ship maintained its relative station just as if you had not moved."

It wasn't simply the fact that Mac had to learn to do things a different way — the U.S. Navy way — that inspired me to do this book; it was the realization that most books written about the war in the Pacific, and published in the U.S., give little credit or coverage to contributions made by Allied forces. Certainly Gen. Douglas MacArthur, commander of Allied forces in what came to be known as the Southwest Pacific Theater, gave Australian forces little credit for what they did while under his command. And as I have discovered from the many books that I have read on the subject of the war in the Pacific — almost all of them researched and written by American historians — few give much attention to the contributions made by America's other allies. Names of ships and units are sometimes mentioned almost in passing, such as when a Dutch, British, Australian, or New Zealand ship was sunk in battle or hit by a kamikaze.

Two New Zealand corvettes, *Kiwi* and *Moa*, are given a rare paragraph or two in some histories for their contribution to victory during the Solomon Islands campaign. In early 1943, these two small vessels had an extraordinary and swashbuckling confrontation with a surfaced Japanese submarine —*I-1*— blazing away at it in a surface battle reminiscent of a bygone day, with HMNZS *Kiwi* adding to the drama by brazenly ramming the enemy submarine.

HMAS *Canberra*, one of four heavy cruisers sunk at the Battle of

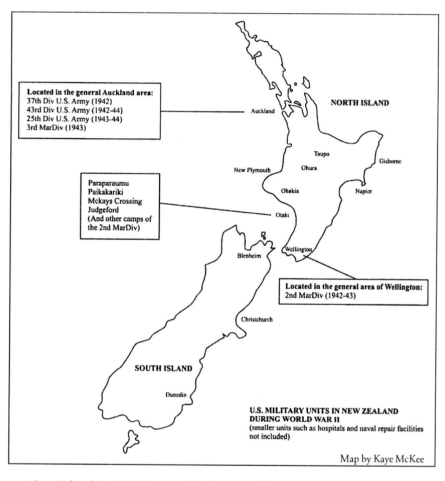

Located in the general Auckland area:
37th Div U.S. Army (1942)
43rd Div U.S. Army (1942-44)
25th Div U.S. Army (1943-44)
3rd MarDiv (1943)

NORTH ISLAND

Auckland

Taupo

Gisborne

New Plymouth

Ohura

Paraparaumu
Paikakariki
Mckays Crossing
Judgeford
(And other camps of
the 2nd MarDiv)

Ohakia

Napier

Otaki

Wellington

Blenheim

Located in the general area of Wellington:
2nd MarDiv (1942-43)

Christchurch

SOUTH ISLAND

Dunedin

U.S. MILITARY UNITS IN NEW ZEALAND
DURING WORLD WAR II
(smaller units such as hospitals and naval repair facilities
not included)

Map by Kaye McKee

Savo Island in the Solomons in August 1942, is an example of where an Allied ship is mentioned simply because it was sunk along with three American cruisers, in what has been described as one of the worst debacles in U.S. Navy history.

Other examples can also be given of other Allied countries, such as the Dutch efforts very early in the war, the British Pacific Fleet later in the war — after Germany had surrendered — the Filipinos throughout the war in which they suffered from Japanese occupation and destruction, and the Chinese in keeping millions of Japanese troops tied down on the Asian mainland and out of combat in the Pacific.

Although the idea for this book was planted more than six years ago, at the time I never thought I would be in a position to write a book on the subject. We were back in California after having lived five wonderful and exciting years on the island of Saipan, where I researched and wrote my first book on World War II in the Pacific. After the fact, my wife and I were less than excited about our decision to return to the bedroom community east of San Francisco where we had started off together, and where two of our three children were born. In the five years that we had been away, the traffic had increased, the air quality had grown worse, and the shopping-mall lifestyle had changed not a whit. We lusted for another shot at the expatriate life.

Almost two years to the day after having arrived back in California we left again, this time for the enigmatic desert kingdom of Saudi Arabia, where my wife took a position at a newly opened rehabilitation hospital outside the ever-growing capital of Saudi Arabia, Riyadh. We had two interesting and exciting years there, but because of the American invasion of Iraq, the car-bombings of four Western compounds — three in May 2003, and one in November 2003 — plus people being shot at and in some cases killed, we felt it was time to move on. We didn't want to return to suburbia, and started looking to the southern hemisphere — Australia and New Zealand. We eventually settled in New Plymouth, New Zealand, a small but beautiful city on the west coast of North Island, with the Tasman Sea and Mt. Taranaki as backdrops.

After finally getting settled, I decided it was time to think again about the idea of writing another book about World War II in the Pacific, the one that Mackenzie Gregory unknowingly inspired me to do when he did his oral history for me in 2001. I spent a lot of time at various libraries and used bookstores in Hamilton, New Plymouth, and even Christchurch on South Island, when I was down there for a history conference.

As I discovered, most if not all books written about New Zealand in World War II were published in New Zealand. That suggested to me that few people outside of New Zealand bought and read any of these books unless they had some dedicated reason for doing so. On the contrary, many books researched, written and published in the U.S. and Britain on the subject of World War II can be readily found in New Zealand libraries and bookstores. Put another way, New Zealanders know a lot more about the U.S. role in World War II than Americans know about New Zealand's role. At the time of America's entry into the war, the population of New Zealand was roughly 1.6 million people. Today, it is just over four million. That also suggested to me that unless an enthusiast on the subject made a dedicated effort, much of what has been written about New Zealand during the war would be difficult to find; at the least, not readily available to the general reader outside of New Zealand. However, thanks to the Internet, almost any book ever published, even if out of print, can now be found.

With the above in mind, and having a publisher in the United States decidedly interested in my project to tell the story of New Zealand's participation in the war in the Pacific, I thought for the first time the story of this small nation's contribution and sacrifice would have an audience beyond its borders. Not only is this book about New Zealand's contribution to the war effort, it is also about how two nations came to know each other for the first time, and how that relationship, in spite of disagreements and controversy over the years, has remained strong.

When the United States entered the war following the Japanese bombing of Pearl Harbor, the war in the Pacific became a U.S. theater of war. All forces in that theater came under U.S. command. The Pacific Theater of Operations was divided between Gen. Douglas MacArthur of the U.S. Army in the Southwest Pacific Command, and Adm. Chester Nimitz of the U.S. Navy took charge of the rest of the Pacific area, which included New Zealand.

Both Australia and New Zealand felt especially vulnerable after Japan entered the war because so many of their young fighting men were off helping the British in their struggle against Nazi Germany. As stated above, the population of New Zealand at this time was only around 1.6 million. It had more than 60,000 men serving overseas, the majority of them in the army. A number of other New Zealand troops were still in New Zealand, along with 100,000 underage and overage Kiwis serving in the Home Guard. However, like Australia and the U.S. during the early days of the war, New Zealand forces had little in the way of armaments with which to defend themselves, and most of what they had was in the form of antiquated arms left over from the First World War and before.

New Zealand sent troops to Fiji, Tonga, and other islands that they saw as a buffer to a possible Japanese invasion. The U.S., likewise fearing a Japanese invasion of Fiji, Tonga and Samoa, started sending U.S. forces to these islands, knowing that if they were taken and held by Japan, then the supply route between the U.S. and Australia and New Zealand would be jeopardized.

Similarly, U.S. military personnel were being sent to Australia and New Zealand in an effort to assuage their fears of a Japanese invasion, while at the same time making it possible to allow New Zealand and Australian forces to continue fighting alongside the British in the Middle East. Within four months of the Japanese bombing of Pearl Harbor, there were well over 100,000 American military personnel serving south of the equator. The U.S. Thirty-seventh Division was sent to Fiji (and later to Auckland), and U.S. Marines were sent to Samoa. In turn, these two nations in the Southern Hemisphere would serve as supply bases and launching pads for the sea and land counteroffensive that would take place against Imperial Japan in mid–1942.

Following the naval battles in the Coral Sea in May 1942, and Midway shortly thereafter in June, New Zealand and Australia both had reason to relax as far as fear of any possible Japanese invasion was concerned. The First Marine Division, under Maj. Gen. Alexander Vandegrift, was eventually sent to New Zealand to combat-load their ships and prepare for the first ground counteroffensive of the war in the Pacific by American forces — Guadalcanal. Elements of the Second Marine Division, most of which went directly to Guadalcanal from California, also joined in the fight that was to last the better part of six months.

While U.S. Marines were landing at Guadalcanal in August 1942, Australian forces were engaging Japanese troops who were pushing from north to south over the Owen Stanley Range in Papua New Guinea, towards Port Moresby, eventually stopping them and pushing them back with terrible losses on both sides.

By mid–1943, elements of the Third New Zealand Division (3rd NZ), minus one brigade, were serving alongside U.S. Army troops on Guadalcanal, and thousands of RNZAF personnel were likewise serving with American forces in the same theater, and had been since early in the campaign. Almost all of their aircraft were U.S. built, such as Corsairs, Venturas, and PBY Catalinas. At the same time, there were thousands of Americans serving in New Zealand. This included two Marine Corps divisions, several U.S. Army divisions, and U.S. Navy and Army Air Force personnel. However, by October/November 1943, the number of Americans in New Zealand began a rapid decline, as the Second Marine Division — including survivors of Guadalcanal — moved out for the invasion of Tarawa, and the war in general moved north.

In April 1944, Silverstream Hospital in Wellington, built by and for

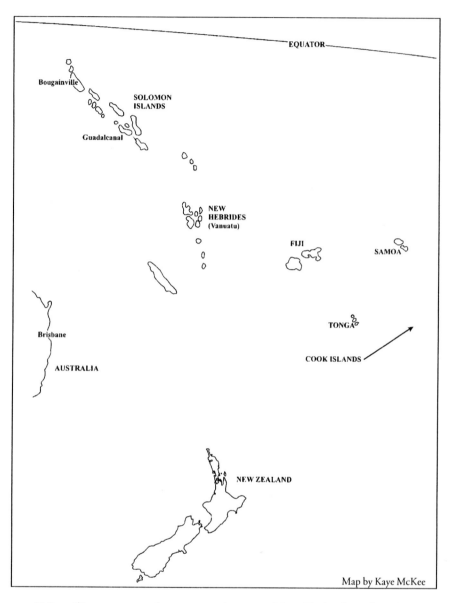

EQUATOR

Bougainville

SOLOMON
ISLANDS

Guadalcanal

NEW
HEBRIDES
(Vanuatu)

FIJI

SAMOA

Brisbane

TONGA

COOK ISLANDS

AUSTRALIA

NEW ZEALAND

Map by Kaye McKee

U.S. military personnel, was turned over to New Zealand, and in October of that year the U.S. Naval base in Auckland was closed. That same month, the 3rd NZ Division was officially disbanded, with some of the men sent to Italy to reinforce the 2nd NZ Division that had been fighting alongside their British counterparts since the early days of the war. The remaining veterans of the 3rd NZ Division filled gaps in "essential industries," such as agriculture. New Zealand was a primary breadbasket for the armies and navies fighting in the Pacific, providing mostly meat and dairy products.

What has been described as "The Friendly Invasion" of New Zealand by American forces was in fact just that. Very few New Zealanders had ever met an American before they landed suddenly on their doorstep in 1942, and most of the Americans who came here had never even heard of New Zealand. Most New Zealanders I interviewed for this book said that before the marines arrived, about all they knew about the U.S. came from Hollywood — cowboys and gangsters.

By 1942, most of New Zealand's young men had been overseas for almost three years, and most New Zealanders of all age groups and of both genders felt protected once U.S. forces, with all of their equipment, arrived. Before that, with most of New Zealand's fighting men in the Middle East, they were fearful of a Japanese invasion.

Young — and not so young — New Zealand girls found new excitement with the arrival of so many young and seemingly exotic Americans on their shores — polite young men with dollars to spend who courted New Zealand girls with flowers, chocolates and hard-to-obtain nylon stockings. Mothers and fathers, who worried about sons they had not seen for so long, took in U.S. Marines, sailors and soldiers, and gave them a home away from home. Most of these young Americans were teenagers. Some had lied about their age in order to get into the fight, and an America desperate for men to fill the ranks in a war of national survival turned a blind eye in too many cases. Some of these American fighting men were as young as thirteen and fourteen, and would die before they were old enough to shave. They were away from home for the first time, many of them; and they were frightened and homesick. Young or not, they found a second home in New Zealand. Families signed up to take in American servicemen for an evening, a weekend, or even several weeks. Those who wanted to work on a farm in the New Zealand outback when they were on leave could do so. In some cases, American servicemen simply latched onto a local family and an unofficial adoption took place, especially if eligible young girls were part of the family make-up. No matter how you look at it, Kiwis and Yanks fell in love with each other. It was a new and exciting adventure for all involved.

However, it was not all sweetness and light. Many New Zealand parents were not happy with the more carefree dalliances going on between

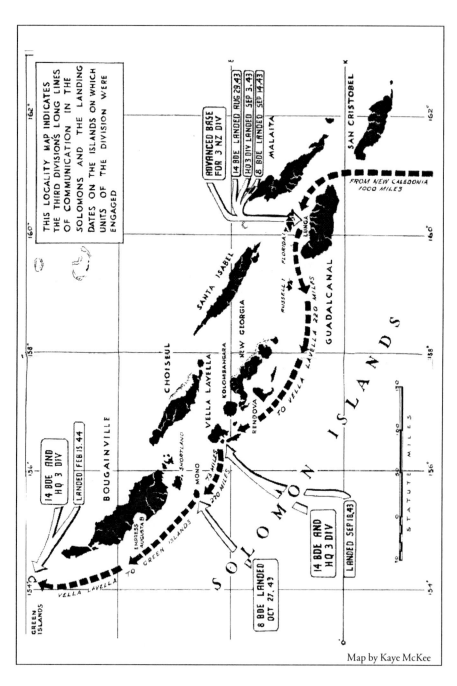

Map by Kaye McKee

American servicemen and New Zealand women. There were unplanned pregnancies and hushed-up abortions. There were children born out of wedlock with promises of marriage that too often never came about, sometimes because the fathers were killed in combat. In other scenarios the fathers simply failed to return to New Zealand after the war to take responsibility, and instead started second families in the States.

Years later, when New Zealand women for whatever reason tried to track down boyfriends from the war years, or when New Zealand children of U.S. servicemen attempted the same, their efforts often came to a dead end. One of the reasons was that the men being sought had given false names. One of the favorites with some men was "Nosmo King." Another reason, however, was — and still is — New Zealand's privacy laws. For American veterans who did try to find children they fathered, these privacy laws made their efforts difficult. Those who did succeed in finding those they were looking for did so through the efforts of individuals, newspaper ads, contacts with military association newsletters, or a combination of all of the above. Still, for many the search took years, and for many others, the search continues.

After Guadalcanal had been declared secure, except for mopping up, U.S. Marines of the Second Marine Division arrived in New Zealand to hook up with the rest of the division that had not yet been bloodied. Most of them were sick with malaria and other tropical diseases. Some went to Silverstream Hospital in Wellington, and others were taken in by families from all parts of New Zealand and nursed back to health by loving families. As a result, friendships were made that have lasted to this day, and in some cases involve several generations, as families have stayed in touch and exchanged visits.

In February 1943, New Plymouth — where we now live — saw the arrival of the first American servicemen. They were the sick and wounded — mostly U.S. Marines and sailors — freshly back from Guadalcanal. There was an official reception by the mayor of New Plymouth and other dignitaries. Local families took in these American veterans in ones and twos, parties and dances were held almost every night, and no American in New Plymouth during this time ever had to buy a ticket to go to the local movie theater.

Opposite: **Solomon Islands map (3rd NZ Div.) (This map is the collective product of the Third New Zealand Division Committee, now defunct).**

By the war's end, over 1,400 New Zealand girls had married American servicemen. Some of these marriages lasted a lifetime, while others ended in divorce. Some New Zealand girls went off to the U.S. to start new lives and never returned. And in other cases, American servicemen elected to stay in New Zealand. And those Americans who did not marry New Zealand girls started coming back to New Zealand in the 1960s for reunions, to reconnect with friends and families they had not seen since the war; and in some cases to look up old girlfriends. War may have been hell, but time spent in New Zealand before and after island battles was heaven.

As pointed out above, although the story of these two nations coming together and discovering each other for the first time might be viewed as a love fest, there were problems. The main problem was women. Most of New Zealand's eligible men had been gone for three years or longer when the first U.S. servicemen arrived on New Zealand shores. The women were doing most of the farm work, as well as taking care of families and working in other industries. There wasn't much excitement for them, certainly little or no romance. When the Americans arrived all of that changed. There were dances, parties, weekend barbecues, romance and even sex. Of course, all of this filtered back to the New Zealand troops serving overseas in the form of letters from friends and family, and even Dear John letters from girlfriends, and in some cases wives.

Some of the longer-serving veterans of New Zealand's Second Division started coming home in 1943 on furloughs, and they were not happy to be greeted by walls of sailors, soldiers and green-uniformed U.S. Marines, who seemed to have a monopoly on New Zealand girls. A combination of alcohol and jealousy resulted in any number of fights and near riots.

Racism on the part of American forces added to the conflagration. The U.S. military was segregated at this time, and when members of the Maori Battalion came home on leave they were not about to put up with racist remarks from white U.S. Marines and sailors. A potentially explosive situation that could have become even more serious was calmed by the intervention of Maori elders, especially the likes of Princess Te Puea, who helped soften American attitudes by organizing Marae visits, where Americans came to learn and understand Maori culture, and know Maori as individuals.

It didn't take long before Maori girls, like their Pakeha (non–Maori) counterparts, took an interest in all the young American men suddenly made available to them. Like other New Zealanders, men of the Maori Battalion had been overseas for almost three years.

There were other problems besides women and racism, but they were minor in comparison. For example, the dockworkers, known as "Wharfies," were a powerful unionized group in New Zealand before, during and for some time after World War II. When Maj. Gen. Vandergrift was preparing to land U.S. forces in the Solomon Islands from their jump-off point in New Zealand, the Wharfies refused to combat-load his ships because their union agreement stipulated that they didn't have to work in the rain. And even after U.S. military officials had come to a wartime agreement with the union regarding some of the finer points of their union contract there were still instances when the Wharfies refused to work in the rain or during holidays. On one occasion in 1943, 180 of them were arrested for refusing to load or unload ships.

Also, throughout the war years, both U.S. military and New Zealand civilian police were kept busy rounding up American deserters, who preferred life in New Zealand to combat in the Pacific. The official count was 190 at one time, and in the process of rounding these men up they were surprised to find an American sailor who had jumped ship in New Zealand twenty years earlier.

Prior to the coming of the war with Japan, New Zealand had been a nation living in isolation, both geographically and culturally. Most of the population was made up of immigrants from the British Isles, or their descendants. There was a smattering of other nationalities going back to the early nineteenth century, when Europeans first started to settle in this island nation. Even a few French immigrated to South Island and established the town of Akaroa in the 1840s.

Even before organized settlement started, whaling and other ships pulled into New Zealand ports, where inevitably disgruntled seamen jumped ship and took to the bush, eventually being adopted by local Maori, who valued new ideas and technologies.

Polynesians — today's Maori — came to Aotearoa (New Zealand) centuries before the first Europeans even thought of crossing the Atlantic, and were well established here when the first European explorers arrived. Abel Tasman was the first in the seventeenth century, followed by Capt. Cook more than 150 years later.

Since the end of World War II, New Zealand has opened up even further. Tourism, once almost an unknown quantity in New Zealand economics, started taking off in the 1960s and 1970s, and is now a major economic indicator. Likewise, immigration continues to be a major contributor to the essence of New Zealand life to the extent that twenty percent of today's New Zealanders were born overseas. My wife and I and our three children are among them. Like a Kiwi told me not too long after we moved here, "If you live here, mate, you are a Kiwi," and that is how we feel. We have never been made to feel like outsiders.

Having said that, before you launch yourself into the individual stories that make up this book, a few words need to be said about the joys and frustrations, as well as the insights and limitations of oral history research and gathering. First of all, I think it needs to be pointed out that when a total stranger is interviewing people, certain processes take place in the minds of those being interviewed. Most people do not want to offend, and this can affect what they say in an oral history interview. Geoffrey M. White and Lamont Lindstrom made this observation while interviewing Pacific Islanders for their book *The Pacific Theater: Island Representations of World War II.*

As an example given by White and Lamont, if an American was interviewing an islander, then the islander's story might lean towards how brutal the Japanese were, and how grateful the islanders were when U.S. Marines came and saved them. That same islander, if interviewed by a Japanese, might not put his story in those terms, and possibly add something to the effect that before the war Japanese and Pacific Islanders had friendly relations, and that Japan brought industry and prosperity to the islands that they had not known at any other time in their history. Both presentations of the same story are basically true, but skewed.

I came across the same problem when interviewing Micronesians, and as a result tried to find ways of getting around that dilemma when interviewing New Zealanders for this book. Before each interview, I would tell people to forget about my nationality, that I am not out to write a feel-good book about Americans and New Zealanders during the war. "If there were problems, I want to hear about them. If you had any bad experiences, tell me what they were."

This may have had the desired affect to some degree, but I doubt that it was 100 percent effective. An example is when one veteran of the 3rd NZ Division talks about men in his outfit — including himself — getting Dear John letters, and finding out those letters were directly the result of the presence of large numbers of American servicemen in New Zealand. He says that he felt pretty low at the time, but more than sixty years later could brush it off as just one of those things. He went on to point out, however, that for two men in his outfit it was more than just one of those things. They killed themselves after receiving Dear John letters.

On the other hand, I felt my nationality proved beneficial when interviewing Maori. With words such as, "Since you are not from here, I'm going to tell you..." and they would tell me what it is like to be strangers in their own land, what it was like to be Maori before and during the war, and what it is like to be Maori today. Through words, facial expressions, and body language I knew that if I was a native New Zealander I probably would not have gotten the stories I did from Maori. A native oral historian would probably have gotten the basic story line, but with certain omissions.

I think it also important to include archival research when doing oral history interviews. At the very least an oral historian needs to have strong background information on the subject related to the people being interviewed. At the same time, it is almost a cliché to say that writing can be a lonely experience. With oral history, the bonus comes with not only discovering little treasures in the form of documents, but also linking those archival nuggets with real people who lived a part of history up close.

My subjects in this book deal less with the killing and suffering that mark so heavily a war that took tens of millions of lives. The war in many of these personal narratives is almost a backdrop. For parents in New Zealand, the war was the same as for parents in the United States and other parts of the world. It was a time of anxiety and waiting, hoping sons would survive and come home. For some young men and women, however, it was a time of adventure and romance.

For those who survived, returning home was a time of deafening quiet, to pick up where they had left off, get married, raise families, and make a living. The killing and suffering were behind them, but so was the thrill of an adventure few of them would ever have again.

I think if I had tried to interview these same people when they were in their thirties or forties, they would have had little to say. There were so many from that generation still around. World War II was still a part of their recent past. They still had lives to live and goals to meet. It has only been in the past few decades that men and women in their seventies and eighties, and sometimes nineties, have come to a time in their lives when they are willing to sit back and reflect on the century that was theirs.

PART I

Voices of
New Zealand Veterans
of the Pacific War

1. Thirty-Six Battalion, Third New Zealand Division: Robert Gordon Dunlop

Dunlop was born in the small farming community of Hawera, Taranaki, North Island. Hawera is south of New Plymouth, on the west coast of New Zealand, with the majestic Mt. Taranaki, a.k.a. Mt. Egmont, in the background—so named by Capt. Cook when he first sailed this coast. Dunlop's ancestry is Scottish on his father's side, and English on his mother's side. Most of his family before him made their living from farming, as does Dunlop to this very day. The fact that he lives just up the road from us made it easy for me to drive over and interview him. One of his sons took over stock control for the morning so that we could sit down and record his story.

The Dunlop family, like so many others, suffered during the Depression. His grandfather, who had a large dairy farm near Hawera, built a four-room cottage on the farm so that Dunlop's family would at least have a home of their own during those lean times. One room was where all six Dunlop boys slept, including Bob.

When World War II came, young Dunlop wanted to enlist right away. However, his father, having fought in World War I, refused to let him. Dunlop, as a result, had to wait two years until he was twenty-one before he could enlist without parental permission. As a result—or one might say by chance—this delay in entering the military resulted in Dunlop's being made a part of the New Zealand Third Division, which was the one New Zealand division that served in the Pacific Theater of war, and consisted of only two brigades instead of the usual three. The New Zealand Second Division was formed up earlier in the war, and was sent to the Middle East, as was the Maori Battalion.

My father was the oldest in the family, and he worked with my grandfather on his farm. Eventually, my father took over the place. When we

Bob Dunlop on the left, with fellow 3rd NZ Division mate Ken Butchard. The photograph was taken in 1941 at Trentham Military Base on North Island, New Zealand. The 3rd NZ Division was the only New Zealand Army division to fight in the Pacific. It was disbanded in 1944.

were young kids we were privileged to see all of the early aviators that came
to the Hawera Aerodrome, which was on leased land of my grandfather's
farm. There was Kingsford Smith, Guy Menzies, Ulm, Amy [Johnson]
Mollison, Jean Batten (Jean Batten died of natural causes]; these were early
aviators who flew the Tasman. Jean Batten went missing later on a
trans–Pacific flight.

Right in the middle of the Depression, my father leased fifty acres
and milked thirty cows on it. I often said that my father had a small number of cows and a large number of kids; it was really hard going.

When war came, it was a shock. The British Prime Minister, Cham-
berlain, had made some agreement with Adolf Hitler, and came back and
claimed that it was peace in our time. And I think a lot of people felt that
the threat of war was past. But it wasn't long after that that Germany
entered Poland.

I was a young agent — a stock agent — at the time. I worked for a firm
and we would buy and sell cattle on behalf of farmers, and charge a commission. I was at a person's place at about 11 o'clock in the morning when he
came over to me and told me we were at war. He had been in the First World
War, and he was emotional and had tears in his eyes, and he said, "People
like you, Bob, thousands of you are going to die — all you young people."

He was quite upset about it, but I thought it would be a great world
adventure. I was only nineteen at that time and wanted to go, but my father
had been in the First World War and he didn't like the idea of me going.
I was the second oldest and wasn't involved as far as the farm was concerned, and felt I was available to go. I was disappointed at the time, but
now I'm pleased that he stopped me. But as soon as I turned twenty-one,
I asked to be put in the next draft, or ballot I think they were called.

In August of 1941, I went to Trentham Military Camp. We were being
prepared to go to the Middle East. I was on final leave before going. We
had all been issued with kit — uniforms and all that was required for the
Middle East. That was in December, and [then] Japan bombed Pearl Harbor. When that happened, I had one day final leave and we were all recalled
to Trentham, just out of Wellington, and sent up to Papakura, which is
south of Auckland; and there the Third Division was formed [29 Dec.
1941].

New Zealand had made a commitment to join the Allied forces —
America — in the Pacific. That was a big commitment really for such a small
country like New Zealand. We already had a division in operation in the

Middle East. It was normal to have three brigades to a division, and there were three brigades in the Middle East, but we didn't have enough personnel to make another complete division. We had less than 2 million people in New Zealand at that time.

On the first of January, or shortly thereafter, we embarked on a boat called the *Wahine* to go to Fiji. I was a bit surprised, because there were already some [NZ] troops in Fiji. They must have been on garrison duty in Fiji before Japan entered the war. We were there for about eight or nine months, I suppose. We never saw any action; what we did most of the time — we were digging an underground hospital and defensive positions around the coast. We also built a concrete seawall.

We were in a camp called Samambula, and went out each day from there to do work on various weapons pits and things like that. There were no Americans there when we arrived. They must have arrived about six months later. They arrived on a boat called the *President Coolidge*, and it wasn't long before they started building camps, and we became outnumbered.

The Americans were bloody great! We saw quite a lot of the Americans. There were a few punch-ups; they were mostly alcohol stimulated. Then some Americans stopped at Fiji, and then went on to New Zealand right away. That gave a lot of grief to some of our fellows, because they had girlfriends back home. But the Americans improved our rations. Their rations were far more superior than our bully beef and biscuits.

We used to ask the new Americans that arrived where they came from, and I can remember one of our chaps asking a Yank where he came from, and he said, "Ohio." And our chap said, "Oh, O-H-10."

This Yank said, "Yeah, yeah, you know that place!" This Yank was quite pleased, and the New Zealander said, "Yeah, who's got the store there now?"

Our camp was right close to Suva, so we were where all the new recruits [the Americans] were coming in — patronizing the hotels and all that. These Americans would ask us where Auckland was, and our chaps would tell them about all the cannibals that lived in Auckland, and other stories. These Americans didn't know anything about New Zealand. Some didn't even know if they had to get on a truck and drive to the other side of Fiji from Suva to get there, or get back on the boat. They were good fellows, but gave the impression of being born in a city, and wouldn't know a cabbage in the raw.

We had these trucks with a Kiwi [bird] stenciled on the door panels, and it was frequent that a Yank would ask, "Say, guy, what's that chicken on your truck?"

Eventually, the Americans outnumbered us, and we more or less became redundant and returned back to Auckland sometime in '42. Our battalion — the Thirty-sixth Battalion — was sent to Norfolk Island. We were there about nine months and did point duty — coast-watching. I don't think we would have done much bloody good if the Japs had come. We were only about a thousand men, or 1,200 — something like that.

Norfolk Island was absolute paradise, except that we slept under old houses, and every morning we would get up and shake out our blankets and catch about 150 fleas. And when the inhabitants of Norfolk Island heard they were going to have an infantry battalion come to protect them they dispatched all of the females over five and under ninety to Australia. They weren't going to have an infantry battalion establish a new lineage on the island.

There were at least two suicides that I know of, where some fellows received letters from fiancées, saying the engagements were over. That was the American influence that had something to do with that, I'm sure. It was almost to be expected. I knew two girls who married American servicemen. And I know another Hawera girl who went over to America on holiday after the war. She had the address of a friend who had married an American, and when she was there she rang her up. Her friend said, "Well, I'll have to have a look at my diary to see if I can fit you in or not." She became a great socialite, apparently.

I had my first girlfriend when I was nineteen. She was a real blonde — an attractive girl. I started dating her, but I was in competition with a lot of other guys. But I was working for a firm called Newton King as a stock agent, and had a motorcar that I could use for my own private use. This allowed me to take her to all sorts of social events, which were all at her suggestion but my expense, but all the petrol was supplied by Newton King.

When I was on final leave, she suggested that we get engaged. I didn't think that was a good idea because I didn't know how long I would be overseas, and I didn't know if I was going to survive the war. Besides, she was very popular and I didn't think she was going to stay at home while I was overseas, so I told her I didn't think it would be such a good idea but that I would like to stay in touch with her.

She wrote regularly. I got a letter a week, and they all ended with how much she loved me, but after about eighteen months I got a Dear John letter. I was disappointed, no doubt about that, but there was a guy in my outfit — Archie Cursey, from Dunedin — who got one of these letters too; and his attitude was a bit of a comfort to me, because he said, "Don't worry if you breakup with a Shirley; they're like tram cars; if you miss one, another will come along shortly."

Later, I heard from a friend that Elsie was having a pretty good time with the Americans.

I enjoyed Norfolk Island; the inhabitants were good to us. I had come off a dairy farm, and there was a man [on Norfolk Is.] called "Cobby" Robinson who used to operate the lighters [boats] that unloaded the ships that came in. But he also had a herd of about five or six cows, and I used to go and milk his cows for him, and then his wife would give us meals. She would make lemon tarts and things like that for us, and looked after us well. On the island, she was known as Aunt Jemima, and she lived to over 100 years. And I don't think "Cobby" Robinson really liked milking his cows, because he got later and later coming home to make sure the cows were already milked by the time he got home.

Later, we went to New Caledonia, but we were later than the rest of the division arriving there because whereas we had gone to Norfolk Island, the rest of the division had gone straight to New Caledonia. They did mostly garrison duty.

I had learnt French in high school, and I thought this was a great opportunity to polish up my French. Almost the very first day, there were two kids about ten or twelve years old; they were playing down under a bridge, and I said in my New Zealand French, "Qu'est-ce que tu fait la?" — What are you doing there? And these two fellows looked at me like I was mental, so I never tried it on anyone else again. I never had the courage.

I never had much close contact with the French after that. We used to buy the odd bottle of wine, but we weren't too accustomed to the niceties of drinking wine. The first few bottles we drank like beer.

There was a brothel in Nouméa; it was called the Pink House, but I can't give you any details about it because my son's sitting here. I don't know that too many of the fellows.... I don't know that any of them from our unit that patronized the place. Well, I think there were some that did, but it wasn't generally known. There was a line-up — a queue — there, and you could make money if you were in the front of the queue and sold your position to somebody at the end of the queue. The value of the position depended on the length of the queue.

There were a lot of Americans there. We were at a place called Ouenghi that was near an airstrip — an American drome [airstrip]. We often did guard duty there — I don't know why. DC-3s were most of the planes they had there. One time, one of the fellows and I went to one of the air force fellows and asked if we could go up in one of the planes. He said, "We're taking this plane up for a test. There's no seats in the back, but you're welcome to go up." So this other fellow and I went up, and oh for God's sakes we dived down at these bloody boats that were in the harbor, and I'm sure to this day that I saw the bloody sun coming through the bloody floorboards.

We went upside down, and tossed around in the bloody back of the DC-3. I resigned myself to crashing, and then suddenly he would pull out. I didn't know those planes had that maneuverability.

This bugger told us they were taking this plane up for a test, and I thought there must be something the matter with it, and I was quite sure I would never get down [alive] again. And when we finally got down, I crawled to the edge of the tarmac and lay in the long grass there for about an hour before I came right. I never asked to fly again with an American aircrew. If they had offered, I would have turned it down.

From New Caledonia we went to Guadalcanal, but I can't give you the dates [14 September 1943]. We went up there on destroyers as far as I can remember — to Lungu Beach. What impressed me were the number of sunken vessels, and the destruction, and the defoliation. The whole foreshore was stripped.

We had a camp that was almost backed on to an American rations store, and a couple of our fellows set up a still. We would go over [to the American camp] and get a lot of grapefruit tins and put it through the still — the distiller — and then sell it back to the Yanks. They gave us $30 a bottle for it. It was their own ingredients they gave to us, and then bought it back at $30 a bottle. You could put a match to it and get an almost colorless flame — pretty pure spirits, really.

My memory is not good on a lot of these things, but I would say we were on Guadalcanal for maybe a month. I know it wasn't very long before we went to Mono Island, just below Bougainville. We embarked on destroyers [APA — destroyer transport] at night and arrived off Mono just before daylight [27 October 1943].

The destroyers opened up and softened up the foreshore of Mono Island. We disembarked down nets into LCIs [possibly LCPs], and they had wooden sides. Our company — A Company of the Thirty-sixth Battalion — was the company chosen to be in the first wave. We were under fire as we came in, and I can remember looking around and thinking it was quite interesting until I looked at the side of the LCI, and like a sewing machine, splinters started flying off the side of the LCI. I got down and was almost at the same level as the keel after that.

When we got ashore, we had to clamber over rocks under mortar fire. Nobody was killed on the boats, but some were on the beach. And our captain didn't follow the practice that had been adopted by the Americans. The American practice was to land and form a beachhead. Our captain — our company commander — didn't form a beachhead; he just went straight ahead. In a way, that was a benefit because the Japs had mortars and mountain guns trained on the beach.

The American destroyers softened what they thought was ahead of us, but instead they softened us up. Several of our fellows were killed by the American destroyers. And I saw the fellow next to me — in front of me — with a whole lot of bullets run up his back. They were machine gun bullets, so it must have been Japanese firing from behind us. That night when I took my clothes out of my haversack I found a shirt with one of the sleeves in tatters.

We had to dig a perimeter around what was the Japanese headquarter, which was pretty empty by that time except for the ones that had been killed. There was a big marquee — a big tent. After I dug my foxhole, I thought I would have a look around inside the marquee for a few souvenirs, because the Americans were good at buying souvenirs, and they always had more money than we did. I ended up with a big clock, a Japanese flag, a Japanese rifle, a bottle of sake, and a Japanese water bottle with Japanese writing on it.

When I came out through the tent flap, a Japanese ran out beside me. He fired a shot into the air, all our fellows dropped to the ground, and the Jap ran straight through them and into the jungle. I would like to think he is alive today.

I was grateful to him, really. He must have had a bead on me [in the tent], and he could have shot me so easily, but if he had he would have alerted all the rest of the men — the rest of our company — and he wouldn't have got away.

You know, as far as the Third Division in the Pacific was concerned, we were hopelessly ill equipped. Our rifles were left over from 1914 to 1918, bolt action, with a bloody magazine that would only hold five bullets. Each platoon had a big, heavy antitank gun. It speaks badly for the intelligence of the New Zealand Army when they supply antitank guns to a unit in a jungle on an island and no tracks where tanks could ... Ah!

My God, we had antitank but no antiaircraft, and the rations they gave us.... We would get four-gallon tins of butter — butter in the tropics. To get into this butter tin you had to do it with your bayonet and stand back because it would spray everywhere.

We didn't stay too long on Mono Island, maybe a month or three weeks. We had a perimeter to defend. Our foxholes were pretty close together but it didn't seem to make any difference to the Japanese. They penetrated our lines, and several of our fellows were killed at night. And the nights were the most frightening for me, and I think a lot of our fellows were trigger-happy. There would be grenades going off all the time. They would hear a noise and throw a grenade at it. A couple of our fellows actually got killed doing that. They dug a fairly deep foxhole and put coconut logs across the top. They went to throw a grenade, and their hand hit the log. The grenade fell back into the foxhole, and they were both killed.

What I was going to say about the nighttime — we would go out on patrol in the daytime, and come back and hold this perimeter at night. Sometimes I would see faces in the gaps of the trees. I don't know, I guess I was over tired, or something. I even found myself talking to some of those faces.

It seemed like the Japanese had these land crabs as allies. You would be in this foxhole and it would rain at night, and these foxholes were in coral, so the rain didn't soak away. They would be half full of water, and then these land crabs that were pretty big, would fall into the water and there would be a big splash, and you were pretty bloody sure that a Jap had jumped in on top of you.

And there were these fireflies that would fly around at night, and they seemed to circle your head. They seemed like they were illuminating your head to give a good shot for the Japs.

We had a general called Barrowclough, who was in charge of the Third Division, and I think that he had gone to MacArthur, the American general, and begged him to give our fellows a bit of action. Anyway,

I think that's what happened to make New Zealand boys look like bloody heroes.

After Mono, we came back to New Caledonia for about a fortnight, and then it was decided that the war had gone on to a sufficient level by that time that there was no longer any use for the New Zealand infantry in the Pacific. I thought there was no bloody use for them right from the beginning. Anyway, from there we went back to Auckland. Some of the fellows were recruited to the Middle East. I got into an "essential industry," and went farming for a fellow called Corrigan. Farming was considered essential. My father got me the job; I don't think he wanted me to go back to the war.

It seemed a bit lonely afterwards. You miss your mates and all that. I joined the RSA — Returned Servicemen's Association — in Hawera. I didn't go there too often because people would come along and ask, "Where did you serve?" — and it would be somebody who had served in the Middle East, and they would look down their bloody haughty noses, and say, "Oh, you were a bloody coconut bomber, or a banana picker," or something like that. Over in the Middle East, they were men of steel by contrast. We never boasted about our Pacific experiences too much.

2. Medical Doctor with the Third New Zealand Division: Arthur N. Talbot

Dr. Talbot was born in September 1917 in Timaru, South Island, New Zealand. Talbot's father was an eye, ear, and nose specialist at the Timaru Hospital, and must have had some influence on young Arthur, because he grew up to become not only a doctor like his father, but also an eye, ear, and nose specialist, as they were called in those days. He went to medical school at the university medical school in Dunedin, South Island, and Christchurch Hospital, also on South Island, where he qualified as a medical doctor in 1940. He then worked at the Timaru Hospital for a year before getting an appointment at Wellington Hospital in 1941. After the war, in 1947, Talbot moved to New Plymouth, New Zealand, when the population was around 20,000. Today, as I write this almost sixty years later, it is just over 70,000.

Talbot's father, who was one of twelve boys, lost two brothers in the First World War, one at Gallipoli and another at Passchendaele. As a result, he was protective of his own sons. Talbot senior was made a major in the Third New Zealand Division during the war, and was serving in that capacity at the age of sixty-four, when ill health forced him to return to New Zealand shortly after young Talbot joined him in New Caledonia.

While at Wellington Hospital, it was a very grim time. I remember the hospital windows were all sandbagged. Most of the eligible New Zealand men were overseas in the army, and then these large numbers of Americans arrived. These were the marines who were preparing to go to Guadalcanal. This was 1943 — the early part of 1943 [the marines landed on Guadalcanal in Aug. 1942]. These young men were the pride of American manhood — handsome, generous — wonderful young men. And of course they took the New Zealand girls by storm. There was a story going around at the time that the New Zealand girls were wearing a special kind of panties — one Yank and they were off.

I remember we were all impressed with what fine men these marines were, and of course with the terrible casualties that they incurred. They were the pride of American manhood, really.

There were Jap prisoners in New Zealand and they rioted. I wasn't there, but I remember my friends showing me bullets that they had fished out of these Japs. Of course, it was all hushed-up because there were New Zealand prisoners of war, and we were fearful of reprisals.

Towards the end of 1941, I learned that my father was not very well. I went down to army headquarters and was greeted by the Assistant Director of Medical Services, Brig. Blinham Bull, who said, "What-ho, Talbot rattling the saber?" and promptly enrolled me into the army.

Now, before this [going into the army], all medical students had gone

into an annual [military training] camp, the Otago University Medical Corps, where we did army drills and parades. We were very irreverent as medical students, and took no notice of army discipline. Anyway, I was then commissioned as an officer and spent one day at Trentham Military Camp. I was then put on a Dakota transport — that's a C-47 — and we flew non-stop to New Caledonia.

As we flew at fairly high altitude, people got colder and colder, and bluer and bluer. We finally descended into the airport at Tontouta Airport, and stepped out into the tropical heat still in our serge battle dresses. I was then sent to the #4 New Zealand Hospital, which was at Bourail [New Caledonia]. This was in 1943 — the end of 1943. My father was back in New Zealand by this time [but not before Arthur arrived]. He was sixty-four years old.

Dr. Arthur Talbot, like his father, was an eye, ear, and nose specialist; and like his father served in the 3rd NZ Division in the Solomon Islands during the war. After the 3rd NZ Division was disbanded in 1943, he was sent to Europe to serve with New Zealand forces in that theater until war's end.

At this time my father, my older brother, and myself were all in the army, and we were known as "the father, son, and Holy Ghost." We had a tented hospital at Bourail, about 120 miles north of Nouméa. Our chief problem there was the mosquitoes, which were as big as dive-bombers.

Later — in '43 — I was shipped up to the Solomons — up to Guadalcanal. I went up on an American troop ship. It might have been the *President Coolidge* — I can't remember. However, I can remember being woken up before dawn every day. "All hands, all hands...." We all had to get up and put on our lifejackets, because dawn was the time when the Jap submarines would attack.

On Guadalcanal, I was sent to the New Zealand Casualty Clearing Station, which was at Lunga Point. It was well established at that time in tents and Quonset huts. After a while, a group of New Zealand nurses arrived, and that caused great excitement among the randy Americans.

There were some battle casualties. I think there were about fifty from Velle Lavella, and we dealt with some civilian casualties. We had native laborers, and of course there were always traffic accidents. I remember one day there was a truckload of frizzy-haired natives that rolled over near the hospital. Several of them were brought in, including a little boy. He was lying on the operating table, and we had a nurse with us who had been up on one of the other islands early in the war and had come out by submarine. She knew Pidgin English.

As this little boy lay on the operating table and the anesthesiologist approached, he looked up at the nurse and said, "Missy, me die finish?" And she said, "No, you no altogether bugger up dead finish. You eat kai tomorrow." Kai is food. And apparently "altogether bugger up dead finish," means to die, but to just die is to go to sleep. Anyway, the boy survived.

This particular nurse was Merle Farland, and she had been behind Japanese lines — a missionary nurse up there — and when this blonde girl got off the submarine, an American sailor said, "Ah ha, Amelia Earhart has been found!" Anyway, she was great because she knew a lot about tropical medicine and could speak Pidgin English.

After a while, I was sent on a cruise, as you might say, on various ambulance units, carrying some optical equipment, and some ears, nose and throat equipment. I called in at Velle Lavella. There was a tented field ambulance unit there, and [on] Mono Island, which was just near Stirling Island. The thing I remember about Mono Island was the noise in the jungle at night. There were these toads that kicked up a terrible racket at night.

You hear this croaking and squeaking, and you would look down and there would be this little thing the size of a [small] leaf. Now, the moment the noise stopped you knew someone was creeping around in the jungle.

One of the other things I remember about Mono Island was looking over at Stirling Island, where the Seabees had constructed a magnificent coral runway that went the whole length of the island, about a mile long. And that was the first time I had seen a Mitchell bomber [B-25]. There were also some Catalinas [PBYs] in the bay.

During the night, we were often disturbed by one Jap [airplane] who came around with engines desynchronized, kicking up a lot of noise. We called him "Washing Machine Charlie." One night I was lying in my little coral foxhole, and another doctor was lying about twenty feet away. I was lying there with my tin hat over my face, and when I looked over at him he was lying there with his hands over his face and his tin hat over his crown jewels. He had his priorities right. He subsequently became a psychiatrist.

My next trip was up to Empress Augusta Bay on Bougainville. We were in a perimeter and the Jap guns were firing in at us, and outside of the Officers' Mess was a sign that read, "A Jap shell landed here. It destroyed three crates of fresh eggs."

From Empress Augusta Bay, I was flown up to Nissan Island, where there was a field ambulance unit. There was a big round lagoon there, and our boys were fishing with grenades and getting a lot of fish. There was an airstrip there, where occasionally a Japanese plane would come and shoot up the airstrip. And one time about 200 Liberator bombers flew overhead. We thought they might be on their way to bomb Truk. About four hours later they came back, and a few of them had their undercarriages dangling, and some of them were on three engines. That was the biggest raid I had ever seen.

The Pacific [War] was won by the conquest of malaria. We had very strict malaria control — long sleeves, no washing after sunset. We were given this malaria suppressant, Atabrine, which stained our skin yellow. The [American] Marines were at first reluctant to take this because they said that atabrine makes you sterile. But the American doctors were too clever for them and said, "Well, if you don't take the atabrine you will get malaria and become impotent."

We didn't work directly with the Americans, but the Americans did provide us very generously with all the medical equipment wanted. However, we felt poorly paid compared to the Americans. The Americans wore collars and ties, you see — at least back in New Zealand. The other thing was the very generous treatment we got from the American PX stores. We could buy almost anything we wanted there. Spam, however — we came to hate Spam. We were on mostly American rations, but in New Caledonia our messing officer managed to get a lot of food from the French, but it was all army food from Guadalcanal northwards.

I do remember being on one of the president boats [troop transports] on Thanksgiving Day. We were taken down to the air-conditioned salon, where we had white tablecloths, silver, and the usual Thanksgiving dinner. We just thought that was wonderful after living in tents.

The Americans had lots of equipment that we didn't have, but they were very generous towards us. There was this American saying that "it takes twenty minutes to make a machine; it takes twenty years to make a man, so we will fight our war with machines." The overwhelming impression, of course, was the huge industrial might of the Americans.

A lot of the men used to look for souvenirs [in the jungle]; they would get a Japanese tooth, put it on the handle of a knife, and flog it off to the Americans for $10.

One of the problems we had was the boredom and the heat. We [the Third NZ Div.] felt like we were doing nothing, that we were rather worthless. We felt like we received poor treatment from the New Zealand Government. We felt like everything important was going on in the Second Division [the NZ division that fought in the Middle East]. So there were a lot of problems with depression, and the feeling that we weren't doing anything worthwhile. We felt like the poorer relation, because everything glamorous and exciting was going on in the Middle East. Also, the intense boredom of military service in the tropics — there was just nothing to do.

Also, I wasn't involved with this, but there were natives on Pinipel Island [near Nissan I. in the Treasury group] infected with yaws [a skin disease], and we treated it quite effectively with injections of arsenic.

Following all that, it was all collapse for the Third New Zealand Division in the Pacific. We were brought back to New Caledonia, and subsequently back to New Zealand, where we were given leave, and then sent as reinforcements to the Second Division in the Middle East. I think that was September 1944. I had been married two weeks.

3. From Wellington Hospital to Fiji: Dr. Alan Hayton

Dr. Hayton was born in Hawera, North Island, New Zealand in 1919. He was the youngest of three boys. He also had two sisters, one of whom was younger than he. His father was a plumber, who emigrated from Yorkshire, England, to New Zealand in 1901, and worked in several parts of New Zealand before finally settling in the Taranaki. His mother was one of three girls born to a tailor in Wanganui, just south of New Plymouth.

Dr. Hayton graduated from Boys High in New Plymouth, and then went to medical school in Dunedin, one of the oldest cities in New Zealand.

During the war years, Hayton did much of his medical training at Wellington Hospital, before being posted to the army. He worked as a doctor at various military bases around New Zealand before being sent to Fiji in 1945. In Fiji, he was part of the medical staff serving Fijian and New Zealand forces, some of which gained fame from serving as commandos behind enemy lines on Bougainville in the Solomon Islands.

After the war, Dr. Hayton continued his medical training both in New Zealand and in England. He is a Fellow of the Royal Australasian College of Physicians and a Fellow of the Royal College of Physicians (London). He eventually settled in New Plymouth, where he is now retired.

My life seemed to be around being a student at school at the New Plymouth Boys High School, where I was from 1933 to 1936. It was what they called in those days "swatting," studying for exams. My aim was, in the fourth form, to pass an examination called "the matric — matriculation," and then at the end of the sixth form sit for an exam called the "Bursary."

If you did reasonably well, you acquired what was called a "Taranaki Scholarship," which provided so many pounds a year [towards university]. You see, it was early while I was in school that my sister was a nurse at the public hospital, and a very good nurse she was too, and I became enam-

Dr. Alan Hayton, in the back row, far left, spent most of the war years serving as a doctor at the Wellington Hospital. He later worked as a doctor at various military bases around New Zealand before being sent to Fiji in 1945.

ored with doctoring. So I was fortunate enough to win a Taranaki Scholarship, and my father put a little bit of money in the Dunedin Savings Bank for me, so off to Dunedin I went where I lived in humble digs.

Let's put it this way, I went there in 1937, and as soon as I got there I joined the Otago University Medical Corps, and went to every one of the annual camps all through my years as a medical student. As a fifth-year medical student, I was commissioned as a second lieutenant, and stood a bit of service over one of the long vacations in a field ambulance in camps in the Wairarapa.

The Medical Corps was a *Dad's Army* sort of thing [a reference to a BBC-TV comedy series about the Home Guard], where we went to annual camps in bell tents and had a bit of training. At one point, we had to do a course called "T.I.T." — Territorial Infantry Training. We learned how to use a rifle and a bayonet. And I remember going on maneuvers out in the back of Canterbury somewhere, and one of the other medical students took me prisoner and jabbed me in the backside with a bayonet a bit too hard. And I still think of Peter Jenkins with some annoyance.

One other vivid memory I have — it was a sunny day in a corner of a paddock at Burnham Military Camp, and we were in a little group there. There was an army officer giving us instructions on the Thomas Splint. The Thomas Splint was a lifesaver in World War I, and prior to the introduction of the Thomas Splint people with injuries of the legs often died. It was a big iron thing with padded leather around the groin, and a clip in the boot that added a little bit of tension that would immobilize the leg.

We were getting instructions on how to put on a Thomas Splint, and I must have been a little sleepy. When I opened my eyes, there was Maj. Iverach looking down at me, and he said, "Good God, Hayton, before this war is finished for all we know you might have to put a Thomas Splint on a patient in the dark and wearing your gas mask!"

Doug Iverach, a good chap — he was one of the doctors at Dunedin Public Hospital, and he got the M.C. — Military Cross — in World War I. People who got the M.C., I always thought they must have been good soldiers.

I was a sixth-year medical student at Wellington Hospital as a house surgeon — a junior doctor. I got through that, and then spent another year at Wellington Hospital, and another six months after that. And at that time we had what they called "Manpower Regulations." The superintendent of the hospital had the power either to retain you as a doctor or release you.

While I was at Wellington Hospital, it was either the First or the Second Marine Division [came to New Zealand]; there were Yanks everywhere! They were well dressed and well provisioned, and I guess one could say they engendered a little bit of jealousy on the part of people in Wellington. They used to come to the hospital and wander through the corridors of the nurses' home looking for girls. They were not backward in coming forward. I think there were a few terminations of pregnancies done discreetly by some of the senior doctors at the hospital.

The house surgeons' quarters at the hospital were directly above the main entrance to the hospital, and we could look out the window and see American Marines in their beautiful uniforms, with badges here and badges there. They all seemed to be covered with badges.

Dr. Alan Hayton

And then there was the Japanese prisoner of war camp out at Feather-ston, and one afternoon there was a riot there. I remember the shooting and them being brought into the hospital, but I can't remember anything about the wounds. I looked after a ward full of the wounded from that riot, and they were like a lot of happy children. One night after tea, I went in and I had a postcard with Mt. Egmont on it. I showed it to some of those Japs and said, "Mt. Fujiama," and they said, "No, no — Mt. Egmont!"

Another interesting memory I have of the Japs there; one night I hap-pened to go to the ward in my gray slacks and a sports coat, and they all crowded around me, feeling the material of the sports coat. They were a happy crowd.

Occasionally one of them would die in the ward, and when the body was trundled out one of the officers or NCOs — I don't know which — would give the order, and the others would sort of stand at attention in bed, if you can imagine that.

Also while I was there, the American Navy erected a hospital at Sil-verstream; and while in the process of being erected one or two Ameri-cans would be patients in our hospital. American naval officers would come in with their beautiful, clean-looking uniforms. One of them in particular, the head of the American hospital, a Dr. Gardner, is so vivid in my memory because he was a neurosurgeon from Cleveland, Ohio.

He got to talking to the surgeons in our hospital and did a few oper-ations. One in particular I remember; he was operating on the cerebellum of a child. I admired his technique and admired his skill.

The other doctor I remember from out at Silverstream was a young doctor from San Francisco by the name of Ralph Scovel, and he met and married my cousin. After the war, he practiced in San Francisco, and then retired to Walking Horse Farm, out of Sacramento. He's been dead for years, but my cousin, Isabel, lived for many years near Mt. Shasta, but is now living with family in a place with the unusual name of Weed [Cali-fornia].

There were these two cooks in the U.S. Marines. And there was a young lady; she was an entertainer, I suppose we will call her. She had been entertaining a South African seaman, who must have gotten a little deranged emotionally, because on this occasion he barged into the young lady's place of residence where she was entertaining the two U.S. Marines. He had a gun and shot them both dead, and one of the bullets went through the lady's voice box, for which she had to have a tracheotomy.

37

There were two dead bodies in the ambulance, and Sir Randle Elliot, now a retired eyes, ears and nose specialist who lives in Wellington, was on duty and the story he told was how he went to the ambulance to pronounce these two men dead: "They were in the full-dress uniform of a couple of U.S. Marines on rest and recreation. They were stark naked except for a contraceptive *en situ*."

At the end of the six months into my second year [at Wellington Hospital], I was released and went into the army at Trentham Military Camp, waiting to be posted somewhere — marking time. I was eventually posted to Papakura military camp, and then one morning at about 0400 they put me in a truck and took me out to Whenuapai, where I found myself sitting by myself in a Liberator bomber. Off we went to Fiji.

After we landed, I walked out of the cold interior of the Liberator in my battle dress, and it was like walking into an oven. It was so blazing hot! Later, they put me in a lovely little biplane with cane seats in it, and flew me over to Nausori, and from there over to Samabulai military camp. This was 1945, and nine months of not very much to do, and it was very hot.

This was a time when I learned quite a lot about tropical diseases. One was filariasis, a mosquito-borne disease that the Fijians were subject to, due to a little worm that got into the lymphatics down in the pelvis. It caused a condition called elephantiasis, where the legs become very swollen — like an elephant's legs. Sometimes it affected the testicles. There was a chap in Fiji — in Suva — whose testicles were so big that he had to carry them around in a wheelbarrow.

The other condition that intrigued me was a tropical eye disease called trachoma, and I was right in the middle of a great trachoma epidemic on Fiji. Trachoma was endemic among the Fijians. Trachoma affects the eyelids. It roughens up the eyelids, which roughens up the cornea of the eye causing the cornea to go opaque. It is a cause of blindness all over the world.

A specialist in the civil hospital in Suva diagnosed trachoma among the Fijian soldiers. It caused such a panic because it was feared that some of the New Zealand officers and NCOs would get it. As a result, they flew a lot of specialists up from New Zealand to examine these cases of trachoma, and decided it was not trachoma; it was just a form of conjunctivitis. So the trachoma epidemic was a nonevent.

That was 1945, and halfway through the year the atom bomb went off and that was the end of the war. Then I was involved with medically boarding Fijian soldiers back to their villages, and I had a lovely trip going around to all the little islands in Fiji in a small ship called the *Viti*.

My great friend, Bill Geddes, was a New Zealand soldier with the [Fiji] Commandos on Bougainville. Bill Geddes and I were friends over many years, and he ended up a professor of anthropology at Sydney University. He married a very nice Maori girl by the name of Ngaire Te Punga, and she is still alive and living in Sydney. She is from a well-known family. Her father was a Lutheran minister down near Fielding, and her brother was an officer in the Maori Battalion. [Actually two brothers were officers: Maj. Paul Te Punga, K.I.A., and Capt. Roy Te Punga, who lives in Wellington. Two other brothers, Martin and Walter, became physicians.]

I came home around Christmas, 1945, and got married. Then I was made a senior medical officer, and my job was to look after the medical requirements at a little hospital at Fort Dorset, at the entrance to Wellington Harbor, where we had coastal artillery. I was there for a year or two. Eventually I got out and went back to Wellington Hospital.

I spent two years back at Wellington Hospital, and then a year in Napier. With the little money I made there and a "Rehab Bursary," I went to London to study. I then came back looking for a job anywhere in New Zealand, and in the end settled in New Plymouth, because my mother and father lived here.

My brother Stewart was in Italy and got wounded south of Florence. My brother Gilbert was in the Royal Air Force. He was lost when the *Laconia* was sunk.

4. Kiwi Sailor
in the British Navy:
Stanley B. Martin

Stan Martin was born in 1922, in Palmerston North, North Island, New Zealand, but grew up in New Plymouth, where his father worked at the Taranaki Herald newspaper. When World War II came along, Martin was in the Territorial Army, and after Japan bombed Pearl Harbor many felt sure New Zealand would be invaded. As a result, it wasn't long after that the Americans began helping New Zealand in preparation for that possibility. However, New Zealand began to relax — if only a little — after the Japanese had been defeated at the Battle of Midway in June 1942.

Although New Zealand had her own navy, most of her larger ships were built in England, and given to New Zealand to man and maintain. They were still part of the British Empire, and were thus designated Her/His Majesty's New Zealand Ships — HMNZS. At the same time, many New Zealanders were on loan to the British Navy, both officers and enlisted men. Many of the aircrews serving on British aircraft carriers were made up of men from New Zealand, South Africa, and Canada, as well as England.

Martin was among those on loan to the British Navy, and first served on HMS Glenearn, a British troop ship, and was later transferred to HMS Indefatigable, a British aircraft carrier.

After the war, Martin went to work for Newton King as a stock agent, and is now retired and living in Palmerston North with his wife, June.

Some years after the war was over, a lot of marines returned to New Zealand for visits, and to look up old friends who had taken them in and befriended them. Some came back looking for old girlfriends. Somewhere along the line, Martin got involved in helping them, and had remarkable success. As a result, he and his wife were made lifetime honorary members of the Second Marine Division Association and have been to many of their reunions in the U.S. and one in New Zealand.

Before, and for a time after, Pearl Harbor, Stanley B. Martin served in New Zealand's Territorial Army. However, as was common in British Commonwealth countries, Martin later transferred to the New Zealand Navy, and served on loan aboard British ships until the end of the war, first on HMS *Glenearn*, and then HMS *Indefatigable*.

The Australians put great stress on the Coral Sea battle [May 1942], because if the Japanese had taken Port Moresby, then they would have gone on to Darwin, but for New Zealand, it was Midway [that mattered]. Midway destroyed their [Japanese] power of any further southward expansion. Before Midway, our government stopped reinforcing our division in the Middle East, but after Midway our government knew that we could continue to reinforce it.

A friend of mine who still lives here in Palmerston North and myself, we got disillusioned with the army. The army deals with big numbers. There is no individualism as there is in the air force and the navy. With those two services, you can volunteer for a specific part of the force, but with the army when you go in with 100 men—fifty go to the artillery and fifty go to the infantry. So we went into the navy.

In New Zealand, the navy was considered the "senior service," just as it is in Britain, and as such it had the veto over the air force and army. In early '43, we went up to the navy base in Auckland to present our case. They said there was a long waiting list, but that they were short of men for RDF — radio direction finding. That was what radar was known as then. We were required to do a minimum of three months of training on shore stations before we were allowed to go to sea.

We had four radar posts around the Port of Auckland, and four around Wellington. One of them just happened to be up on a hill behind Paekakariki, behind the camp where all the marines were. We would go in and out of Wellington on the same trains as them. They were just marines to me. I never envisioned that I would become a life member of their association in subsequent years and go to their reunions all over America.

They were great guys; I never had any problems with them. June had problems, you might say, because she worked in Wellington. About the time she was getting off work at 5 o'clock, the marines were coming in on leave from Paekakariki, but she was engaged [to Martin] and wasn't going to get involved.

Subsequently, we were sent to the British Navy. About 4,000 New Zealand naval men were sent to the British Navy. Even though we were colonials, you might say, of Britain, we never got along with the British. We were more akin to the Australians and Americans. I think both being colonial nations founded from Britain, we had sort of— not a revulsion.... They thought they were the kingpins of the world, and they weren't. Later, when we served alongside of Halsey's Third Fleet, I think most of us wished we were on his ships. We had to do 30 knots to 35 knots to keep up with the American carriers, and the whole ship [HMS *Indefatigable*] would vibrate at that speed.

The first British ship I was on was HMS *Glenearn*. She was a troop ship. The Americans had a very big base at Manus in the Admiralty Islands. We used to go in and out of there quite a lot. After we had left Manus one day, and were heading for Leyte, we had a violent explosion. We carried about 348,000 liters of fuel oil for our landing craft, and it went up. We had some blokes killed, and I was right in the epicenter of that but survived. I was blind and deaf for a few days, and they thought I might stay that way, but I didn't. Anyway, there was a big fire and the ship was down at the bow, and we thought we had had it, so we headed down to Hollandia in Papua New Guinea. There was no smoking and no hot food because the whole ship was reeking of fumes. We buried a lot of the dead guys at sea. We had to flood the mess decks and we didn't get a lot of those guys out until we got to the Philippines. The Americans had a big base there [in Hollandia] with a hospital. We put our wounded ashore there, and some of them died there.

When it was obvious on the fifteenth of August [1945] that the war was over, well, the night before Halsey came on the intercom to the fleet and said, "The armistice [surrender] is supposed to be signed tomorrow at 9 o'clock." And we thought, "Are these Japs that have been trained as suicide pilots going to give in without another fight?"

This was communicated to Halsey: What happens if the Japanese, after peace breaks out after 9 tomorrow, don't stop fighting? And Halsey, being a bit of a humorist, said, "Should the Japanese attack after peace has broken out, you will shoot them down in a friendly and peaceful manner."

Anyway, the next morning our kites [planes] took off and were over their target when the Japanese finally surrendered, and they came back without dropping their bombs. But six suicide planes followed them back, and all of our gunnery crews were off celebrating. Our gunnery officer was off in the wardroom drinking his grog.

I said to our boys, "What about these suiciders we have on the radar?" And they said, "They won't touch us; the peace has been signed. The *King George V*," which was our flagship, "...she's flying the cease fire [flag]," someone said. And the next thing you know these two suiciders come screaming down at us. Well, as it turned out, one of them was not a suicider. The back one was an American Corsair. We had pulled our air cover down. The Americans had more sense. They kept their gunnery crews in place and some planes in the air. Well, this Corsair hit the Jap, and he disintegrated. Bits of it fell on one of the New Zealand cruisers, the *Gambia*, that was behind us.

We were the only British carrier to go into Tokyo Bay for the surrender, plus the battleship, [HMS] *King George V*. Most of the ships went in on the fifteenth, but we stayed out because our airplanes were out looking for POW camps, so we stayed out until the morning that the peace was signed. That was a Monday, and we only stayed until the following Thursday, and then headed down to Sydney.

Immediately after the surrender, two of our carriers were detached, one to Singapore —*Formidable*— and the other —*Indomitable*— to Hong Kong. Both had large hangar deck capacity, and were used to take on prisoners of war, but first they had to fly their squadrons ashore to make room.

Yes, the British are a haughty race, and they looked down upon us, what they called colonials. We didn't take it; we stood up to them. We didn't get along with them on their ships. It wasn't a period I would want to duplicate. And the British didn't know what a decent meal was. The Americans, they lived well. Just to tell you an example, we in the New Zealand Navy victualled on what would be the equivocal of $.35 American money per day. We got to the British Navy, and they were victualling on what would be the equivalent of $.15 American per day, and I don't think we even got that much spent on us.

When I first went on board [*Indefatigable*], I was put in Mess 66, right on the water line. If we were going to hit a mine, that's where we would have got it, and with the system of all hatches being locked down [dogged down] as soon as we went to action stations.... The navy reckoned it was better to lose a few men rather than the ship, but that wasn't the sort of death I favored.

The air down there was putrid, and I had a mate who was in Mess 13, which is not a good omen, but it was just one step down from the flight deck. He was from New Plymouth also, so we were cobbers — grew up in the same town together. So I went to the skipper, and the Pommies [British] said, "You won't get it, Kiwi, you won't get it." I was going to ask permission to shift from Mess 66 to 13. I said to the captain, "I'm not integrating down there. If I get up to Mess 13, I've got at least one other New Zealander to be with, and I will be a much better crewman."

He [the captain] turned to the master-at-arms and said, "Any problems with that, master?" And the master said, "No."

"Permission granted." So I moved up to Mess 13.

Look, half of the men I served with couldn't read or write; they weren't educated. I got the shock of my life one day; one of them turned to me and says, "Hey, Kiwi, I got a ledder from me mudder; would you read it to me?" And one said, "I haven't written to my mother; would you write it for me?"

What did I have in common with that? You see, in our navy we had to pass an educational test for acceptance, and I thought the same would have applied to the Poms [British]. In the batch that went in the same day as me, some missed out on [failed] that test, [and were] sent into the army.

A lot of the aircrew — about twenty-five percent of the aircrew — were Kiwis. A lot of them had been men I had gone to school with.

Now, particularly during the Okinawa campaign, at the end of the day — after dark, about 8 o'clock at night — mostly Halsey would come on the blower and let us know the results of the day's activities. Each ship had a code name. On our ship we had a big F on the flight deck; it stood for "Flounder." That was our code name for recognition by our aircraft, but for radio recognition our code name was "Pussycat." They couldn't use "Flounder," because that would have been giving it away to the enemy; they would know which ship was which.

This day I think was one of the biggest attacks we had had from suiciders; the sky was just thick with them all day. By then, we had been equipped with Bofors [40mm antiaircraft guns], and I had to admire the gunners who would sit down there on those open decks with these suiciders screaming down at them.

We had had a tough day all day that day, and after we broke down from action stations [general quarters in the U.S. Navy], Halsey would come on and tell you how many planes had been shot down during the day. He would say, good effort by this ship, and good effort by that ship. On this day he said, "A special saucer of cream for Pussycat." He maintained that we shot down thirty-two planes that day, but I am skeptical that we could have shot down thirty-two planes in one day.

Now getting back to the Bofors — your Admiral King — Ernie King — in charge of the American Navy — he didn't like the British. He didn't even want them there [in the Pacific], and I don't blame him. But we found early on that the Japs wanted to get at the carriers, and we didn't have enough antiaircraft. We had Oerlikon [20mm], but they couldn't stop a plane in full dive.

It was obvious we had to get Bofors, but Ernie King wouldn't give them to the British. Different men had been sent across to get King to alter his mind, but he wouldn't. Then there was an Admiral Somerville [Admiral Sir James Somerville]; he was a very personable, likable man. Admiral Somerville went to Washington. His sole purpose was to try and talk King around into supplying our fleet with Bofors. There had been several highranking British officers go across, and they all failed. He finally got an appointment with King, and his staff told the story afterwards about tables being thumped and voices raised, and everybody thought, "Oh, oh, another one down the drain. He's not getting anywhere with King!"

But as the story came out later, Somerville said, "Adm. King, we are fighting alongside your fleet. We are losing men we shouldn't be losing, because we don't have adequate antiaircraft fire. We are losing ships that we can't afford to lose just because there is one man in your naval department who refuses to give us Bofors."

King stood up and said, "Tell me that man's name and I will rectify it immediately!"

And Somerville said, "It is a grizzly old bastard by the name of King."

There was a silence, and then King stood up and said, "Okay, Admiral, you'll get them."

That was in June [1945?], we went down to Sydney for repairs and replenishment, and when we pulled into the wharf in Sydney we could see all of these cases stacked up. They were Bofors, and the minute we tied up, all these Aussie workers besieged the ship, and mounted them all around the island and different parts of the ship, and boy, did it make a difference. But that is how we got Bofors out of Ernie King.

Most of our carriers had American planes, Hellcats [F6FS], and Corsairs [F4Us]. They were both stable planes, but the English Seafire was no good for carriers. They were too light and the undercarriage was too narrow. And once a carrier plane hits the deck it has to stay there, but we were the only British carrier out there most of the time that still had Seafires, and they were too light. They would bounce [when they hit the deck] and miss the tripwires [arresting wires in the U.S. Navy].

Another fault with the Seafires were [sic] their range; they could manage a two-hour spell as fighter cover over the fleet, but without extra fuel tanks they usually didn't have the range to be used as fighter escorts. And the extra fuel tanks slowed the plane down and had to be ditched before they could land.

Our one great advantage was that we had armored flight decks [U.S. carriers didn't, and suffered for it]. I can still see a huge dent right outside of our radar office where a suicider hit us. If we did not have that armored flight deck we would have been gone! But that extra four inches of steel slowed us down.

I saw the *Bunker Hill* get hit one day; oh, boy, it just went right through the flight deck to the hangar deck, where all the planes were with ammunitions and all fueled up.

And I'll tell you something that is a pertinent point, or significant. At the end of the war, we were in Tokyo Bay for the signing of the peace, just adjacent to the *Missouri*. I was on HMS *Indefatigable*, and afterwards we came down to Sydney, and went into dry dock. Then she came over to New Zealand to show the flag. That was in December [1945], and there was a big civic ball in the Wellington town hall one night. June and I went onboard the *Indefatigable* one morning and said, "Can we get tickets for the ball tonight?"

The ship's padre was there, and he said, "No! No! You're not getting any; you're New Zealanders!" The sub lieutenant that was there never said a word.

I said, "Hey, hang on; I've been serving on your ships." But it didn't matter, and that was the typical attitude of the British towards us. So we gave up, and we were walking along when the sub lieutenant came running after us and he said, "I heard all that. That wasn't very nice; here's two tickets."

We got into the ball, and our New Zealand Prime Minister at the time was a Mr. Peter Fraser, a Scotsman. There was a crew of 2,300 on our ship, so there was a fair crowd there. Anyway, Peter Fraser is going around and he sees my New Zealand shoulder patch and he says, "Oh, you were on the ship?"

I says, "Yeah, Mr. Fraser."

He says, "Did you enjoy it?"

I just screwed up my face at him, as if to say, "Oh, come on; be sensible. Did I enjoy it?" And he was a Scotsman, of course, which is significant, and he said, "No, we are different, aren't we?" And he said something else to me that I found difficult to understand a prime minister telling a naval rating. He said, "If we'd had our way, none of you boys would have gone to the British Navy."

5. From the Cavalry to Corsairs: Des H. Turnbull

Des Turnbull was born in Stratford, North Island, New Zealand, in 1921. His father was a World War I veteran and fought at Gallipoli, where he was wounded and then sent home as a result. After the war, Turnbull worked as a tailor. He has two older brothers, one of whom fought with New Zealand forces in Italy during the war. The other brother was a pilot in the Fleet Air Arm.

Turnbull was in the New Zealand Army for almost three years before being posted to the Air Force. He started off the war in the Manawatu Mounted Rifles, and ended the war flying Corsairs in the Solomon Islands. After the war, Turnbull tried his hand at a number of different trades before answering a call to the ministry. Although now a retired Presbyterian minister, he continues to officiate at weddings and funerals, and lives in New Plymouth, New Zealand.

The war started, and along with some cobbers [friends], I joined up. That would be about 1940, I think. I did my army training just out of Stratford, and the sergeant there recommended that I go to an NCO course in Wellington. I went to Wellington on this course, and then was training with the Manawatu Mounted Rifles, who were then going from horses to motorized. These were utility vehicles with machine guns in the back. I think they were Brenn guns.

I got corporal's stripes down there, and came back to teach the chaps about transferring from horses to a more mechanized cavalry. We didn't have much in those days. We were caught with our pants down. But when I got back I was told, "We are staying with horses. The army has changed its mind."

I had never ridden a horse, and here I was in charge of seven blokes. They had all ridden horses since they were kids. Some of them were farm kids and brought along their own horses, and that suited the army because they didn't have to go out and commandeer them from farmers. We were

Des H. Turnbull: He flew F4U Corsairs, an American-built fighter plane. And like most New Zealand squadrons that flew this fast, rugged fighter, they entered the fray in the Solomon Islands late in the fight, and saw little or no air-to-air combat. Turnbull is among the men in flying gear, fifth from the left.

sent to Foxton, a horse camp down there on the racecourse, and I had a horse that hated being conscripted and put on a train to Foxton. She was a fat old mare, really fat, and my short legs stuck straight out when I sat on her. She did everything she could to destroy me. The first time I went out on this horse, we had to get up early in the morning to go out on a maneuver. I put the saddle on, cinched it up, hopped on, and finished up under her stomach, simply because she had extended her stomach as I pulled up on the girth straps. And when she relaxed, I ended up below.

Norman Taylor, an ex-farmer, said "Leave it to me, Des."

I thought he was doing the same thing I did, but when he had the strap pulled up, he brought his knee up into her belly. She gave a big cough, and he brought the strap up a couple of more inches. Then he said, "She'll never do that again," and she never did. But she caught up on me in another way. We were on parade as a brigade with two regiments at Foxton. We were on parade and at attention on our horses, and Col. Foley from the First World War, and Col. "Cocky" Davis, another First World

War man, were riding down between our rows inspecting us. My horse literally sat on her bottom, and I sprawled onto the ground. It was hilarious and all the chaps started laughing even though we were on inspection.

But after that we graduated on to Brenn carriers and light tanks, and then to heavy tanks — Valentine tanks, they were, and then Matildas. At that stage, I was a sergeant and a tank commander. A number of chaps got killed on one of our maneuvers. It was a sad thing; some of the infantry were riding on one of the tanks when it rolled over. Jack Transome was a junior officer, and when it rolled over it pretty much cut him into two. It was a terrible sad thing, because he would have been an outstanding officer.

They moved us from Wanganui Racecourse down to Fielding, and were starting to break the regiment up. I was then sent on final leave before being sent overseas. When I got back to camp, Derek Bridgwood, our orderly room corporal, said, "Des, you are going into the air force."

I said, "What?" After two and three-quarters years in the army, and after doing what I was doing....

He said, "Yes, the Japs having already bombed Darwin twice...."

We realized we had to go meet them. We couldn't wait for them to come to us. Anyway, I had to start all over again. I started at Harewood, near Christchurch, taking courses in navigation, meteorology, pyrotechnics, theory of flight, etc., at designated camps in the Delta area near Blenheim. I was then sent to Ashburton. That was an Elementary Flight Training School — EFTS — that's what they called it, where I soloed in DeHavilland Tiger Moths. Then at Woodbourne — again near Blenheim — we went through the various stages there on the Harvard aircraft, and lost a few chaps there; and not in ordinary crashes, either. Two of the chaps, Gerry Friel and Peter Brown, were out doing under-the-cover — blind flying. They must have finished in the sea; we don't know what happened to them. They just disappeared.

We got our wings there at Woodbourne. That would be in early 1944, and from there I was posted to Ohakea, on North Island, and trained on American Kittyhawks. We lost some chaps there too. One chap, Bill Alexander — a part Maori — was so concentrated on the ground target [he was shooting at] that he ended up going into the ground.

Then I was posted to Ardmore, in Auckland. I went from Kittyhawks to Corsairs there. That was March 1945. I did my first solo on 7 March. The Corsairs were a much better aircraft. They had a wider undercarriage than the Kittyhawks. They were a lovely aircraft, and I still think they were one of the best aircraft in World War II. However, I did smash one up completely during my conversion period before we were sent overseas.

I was sent up with four others in different directions to get experience at night flying. I had done two landings and was coming in to do my third and final one. You feel with your wheels for the ground, then throttle back, and bring your stick back. Everything seemed good as gold, and then the flare path lights went out, or I thought they had. When I looked out, about fifty feet below they were still there. I guess I didn't throttle back enough and staggered back into the air. I grabbed the throttle to go around again, but it was too late. She just fell out of the sky on her left wing. She catapulted onto the grass, but landed right side up and didn't catch fire. I walked away without a scratch except for a cut finger on my way out.

I went up in a Harvard after that with a friend, Bernie Hoskin, who was a flight lieutenant. He said, "A pity about this; you probably would have been recommended for a commission. But the main thing is to get you going again so you can go overseas."

I was a noncommissioned officer pilot for the rest of the war — a flight sergeant. Anyway, I carried on and got posted overseas. We were transported in various stages in C-47s to Los Negros, near Manus Island — in the Admiralty Islands. We had a narrow neck of land there with two landing strips on it. There was a big American base there, which had increased to 120,000 service personnel by the end of the war. I think there was just a causeway between Los Negros and Manus. The Americans were mainly on the Manus part. The Americans had floating dry docks there, and one of them had been bombed by the Japanese a fortnight before I got there.

We didn't spend a lot of time with the Americans, but we put concerts on together, and I was in one where I was in charge of an orderly room in an act we were putting on. I marched these chaps onto the stage and said, "Attention!" And when I said that, air got behind my top false plate and it shot out into the air. I grabbed it as it went out, and put it back in.

Wing Commander Wilks, in charge of the New Zealand base there, said to me afterwards, "Turnbull, did you mean to do that with your teeth?"

I said, "Did it look convincing, sir?"

He said, "It certainly did, but I'd like to see you do it again."

We got along extremely well with the Americans throughout the war. The only unpleasant situation I had with Americans was when, up in the islands, one or two unsavory chaps brought around some very bad photos of naked women, trying to sell them. I told them where to go.

No, we got along so well with the Americans, and I tell people so often that we've got to stick with Uncle Sam, because we wouldn't be here without him in the last war.

However, women were a challenge. I knew a girl who had moved up to Auckland — moved up there with her family — and I was in the army at Waiouru at the time, and I went up to Auckland, hoping to see her there. But when I got off the train, there she was with a junior American officer. She said, "Hello." It was a bit of an awkward situation. Uncle Sam won out on that occasion.

6. Corsair Pilot,
No. 16 Squadron: E.T. Lang

Lang was born in 1924, in Featherston, a small town in the Wairarapa Valley just north of Wellington. He was one of 8,000 New Zealanders trained as pilots during World War II to fly a variety of aircraft for the RAF, the RNZAF, and the Fleet Air Arm. He trained in Tiger Moths, a biplane not all that different from the Stearmans my mother trained in during the war in Sweetwater, Texas, when she was in the WASPs (Women's Air Service Patrol). Lang then graduated to Harvard trainers, and the P-40 Kittyhawks. Before entering combat in the Solomon Islands, his squadron — No. 16 Squadron — was issued the newer, more powerful and rugged Corsairs (F4U), a plane much favored by the U.S. Marine Corps in the Pacific at that time.

The RNZAF had 424 Corsairs in more than a dozen squadrons during the war. They operated exclusively in the Pacific Theater of war, including New Zealand. No. 16 Squadron had between twenty-four and twenty-eight pilots, several of whom were noncommissioned officers. However, the number of pilots at any given time varied depending on operational and combat losses.

By the time Lang arrived in the Solomon Islands in 1944, RNZAF pilots saw little in the way of air-to-air combat, confining themselves mostly to bombing and strafing assignment against Rabaul on New Britain Island, and in support of Australian troops mopping up on Bougainville after U.S. Marines had secured part of the island. By the end of the war, of the 15,000 RNZAF personnel serving in the Pacific, 407 became casualties, 345 of whom were killed.

After the war, Lang finished his studies at university, eventually going into dentistry and a career in orthodontics. He settled in New Plymouth, New Zealand, where he still lives.

I went to boarding school in Wellington — Scott's College. I got university entrance pretty early in life; I was about sixteen with a view of a career in law. Then the war started, of course, and with the Japs coming into the war the end of 1941, I applied to enter the air force as soon as I

RNZAF pilots flew in over 400 American-built Corsair fighters in the Pacific during the war. E.T. Lang was one of them. It was also the mainstay of U.S. Marine Corps fighter pilots in the Pacific.

turned eighteen. I was posted to the Forth Battalion, Wellington Regiment, and put into camp in Johnsonville, which is up the rail from Wellington. Most of the officers were our ex–school teachers; it was pretty cozy stuff.

We spent about four or five months down on the Wellington wharves, loading ships. It was pretty heavy work. We went down in buses in the morning and worked twenty-four-hour shifts, which seemed pretty ridiculous, and then had twenty-four off. The "Wharfies" [dockworkers] were pretty helpful; they showed us how to handle the stuff.

I was down there for about four months, and then luckily my posting to the air force had come through. The air force just took what they wanted. What they were after were people with a little bit of education, because it saved an awful lot of instruction. I had had a year of university by then. I did sixty hours in Tiger Moths — little two-wing things — in

54

Ashburton, South Canterbury, and then did another sixty hours at Blenheim — Woodbourne — flying Harvards. I think we might have done two sets of sixty hours. We won our wings after that second set in Harvards.

Having done that, we were then posted to an OTU — Operational Training Unit — at Ohakea, where we converted to P-40s. I flew P-40s right up until the squadron went operational. We must have had about eighty hours in P-40s — fairly intensive stuff, and then we were posted to squadrons. I was posted to No. 16 Squadron. A lot of the pilots that came to our squadron had come from training in Canada, and I think our average age was around nineteen.

Ardmore was the fighter base near Auckland. We trained in groups of four, and we trained quite hard. Then we were sent off to Espiritu Santo, New Hebrides, where, to our surprise, we converted to Corsairs. We had never heard of them, so it was a bit of a shock. A New Zealander by the name of "Grata" Greig trained us. I think a squadron just before us had converted on Espiritu Santo, then us. I think we were the last, and then they set up a conversion unit in New Zealand.

First of three tours in the Solomon Islands, 12 June 1944 to 22 Sept. 1944: During the conversion course in the New Hebrides, we were told that with the Corsairs, if you stalled them then you would get a left-wing drop and go down, so I was very, very careful. And on my first run I hear from the tower, "Kiwi chicken in the groove, take a wave-off; there is bruiser behind," and I wondered what the hell that was about, but kept on stooging along; I was going to get that plane onto the ground. Then over the top of me — fairly low — flew a Liberator, and he had to go around again.

When I landed all hell was breaking loose, because unfortunately this Liberator had been bombing Truk, and I think they even had wounded on board. My C.O. said I had better go over and see the Americans and explain what had happened. I told the Americans I didn't quite understand the language, and that perhaps next time you could say, "New Zealand fighter," or something we are used to.

They said, "Oh, no, that's okay." They were very nice about it, but I was a bit mortified that this well beat-up bomber had flown God knows how many thousands of kilometers, coming back to land and here I was concentrating on getting this plane onto the deck. But their C.O. said they were fine.

From then on, knowing that the American vernacular was different than ours I got on fine. And frankly, I preferred the American controllers to the Kiwis and/or Australians, because they spoke clearly, especially through aircraft noise. I guess they were just more incisive speakers.

We got on very well with the Marine Corps, but of course they were flying Corsairs too, and we lived more or less in the same camps. They were great pilots — tops! And they were very good about equipment. I remember there was a shortage of belly tanks, and if we wanted belly tanks the marines just gave them to us. The converse, too, was that we had a reasonable supply of liquor and they didn't. A bottle of whiskey taken across to the American mess would work wonders.

They were great guys, really; that's why it makes me so cross when I hear this undercurrent of anti–Americanism here in New Zealand. These longhaired liberals we have out here; I would like to see them stuck on a coral island.

We had tremendous respect for the Seabees. The ones I saw were largely black. They were fantastic! They were building airstrips, these great big black guys on their bulldozers, and they could build them quick.

We had a few Maori pilots out there too, but not in my squadron. I knew several of them. One was named Tirikatene. He came from a big family, and his father was an MP — a member of parliament. They were a well-known Maori family.

The conversion training was pretty fast, and then we were sent up to Guadalcanal — to Kukum Field — a short little field, and some distance from Henderson Field. They didn't bother cutting the palm trees at either end, which made takeoffs and landings interesting. We did about three weeks of training there — a lot of dogfighting, often with American Army Air Force Lightnings — P-38s. Then we moved up to Bougainville — Torokina airstrip — a fighter strip on the beach. It was beautiful.

In September '44, two Corsairs collided in midair. One of them was from our squadron, and he was killed. He was a short, dark chap; that is all I remember about him. I remember that, because we hadn't been up there very long. I remember the funeral too — first time I had been involved in anything like that. Most of the midair collisions were in bad weather when planes tried to stay in formation.

We were doing a lot of attacks on Rabaul on that tour, and it was very active there. Our role was dive-bombing and strafing, and there was a lot of flak! We had no air-to-air combat. We saw the odd Jap plane from time to time, but [their air force] had virtually been knocked out.

On that first tour, when we were on Bougainville, we lost three out of a formation of four planes to bad weather. There was a garbled message from one of the pilots, and we felt they had come down in the water up the coast a bit. Our squadron leader, Merv Jones, said, in view of the appalling weather, "There's no way I'm putting more guys in the air. I'm not going to risk any more pilots." Then a Marine Corps colonel called up and said, "You guys got a bit of trouble up there?"

Our C.O. said, "Yeah, but I'm not putting any more men in the air."

The colonel said, "Ah, that's nothin', we'll go and have a look."

They took off and didn't find anything, but I thought that was a pretty noble gesture.

After our first tour, the squadron went back to Ardmore, and got chopped up a bit. That was in October '44. Some were sent to new squadrons that were being formed, and once you had done three tours you were pensioned off. I stayed in No. 16.

When we got back to Ardmore, we had leave. I lived way at the bottom of North Island, and at Port Depot we were told that if we grabbed our gear there were seats for us on the Night Limited, which was the night express train going to Wellington. And being officers, we traveled first class. So my mate and I got on this thing, and we were thin — you lose a lot of weight in the tropics — and I suppose we were yellow from the Atabrine. All we had on were our shorts and shirts, and it was pretty cold, but we were exhausted.

We woke up during the early hours of the morning, and I found a greatcoat over me, and my mate had a greatcoat too, and they had major general's stars on them. We said to them [the two generals], "We appreciate this very much indeed, but...."

One of them says, "Oh, you poor little buggers, you're damn cold, and we have proper uniforms on." I will always remember that. That was the first time and the only time I ever wore a general's greatcoat.

Second tour to the Solomon Islands, 22 Nov. 1944 to 8 March 1945: On our next tour, we ranged further up the chain to Green Island [also known as Nissan I.], which was pretty active then. From my point of view, we did one hell of a lot of flying, and we lost a few guys in bad weather, three from 16 Squadron and four from 14 Squadron. I was a bit lucky; I had done my stint in the morning. The ones who were lost were in the afternoon strike, and for some reason we were never sent replacements.

I also remember Christmas Day [1944]. I had done a dawn patrol, and had come back thinking, "That's my day." I was looking forward to Christmas dinner. I knew they had brought up lots of beer, and we continued to draw the rations of the guys we had lost.

There were two squadrons on the island, and I got a call from our squadron leader saying the squadron leader from the other squadron, Vanderpump, had been shot down over Rabaul Harbor, and they want us to go as escort for the "Dumbo"—Catalina, and to keep the Jap gun positions quiet. I was surprised they just sent two of us. So that is how I spent Christmas Day, strafing the shore guns, which we did successfully, and Vanderpump was picked up by the Dumbo.

We came back somewhat tired and disheveled. We arrived back about 3 in the afternoon, and we figured the boys would have kept us dinner, but they hadn't kept us a damn thing! No food, nothing! Then a call came from No. 14 Squadron — the other squadron — and it was Vanderpump who had asked to see us.

I thought, "Oh, God, what did we do wrong over there?"

We went over there, and Vanderpump produced a bottle of whiskey and said, "Well, I haven't had any Christmas dinner either, so we'll have a few drinks."

Third tour, 1 April 1945 to 22 June 1945: That last tour, we were back up on Bougainville — a new airstrip called Piva. I think we only lost one plane on that tour. He lost power and went into the jungle. That tour we were pretty much confined to Australian Army support on Bougainville. The marines were there when we first went up, but had gone on to other battles.

We got on well with the Aussies, and they were brave. They would mark targets for us, and we would drop bombs fairly close to them, but they seemed to trust us.

It was on that tour that the Aussies made a landing up near Buka — the Porton Plantation. Their barges ran aground off the beach and they had to swim ashore, and there were sharks in the water. I saw them from the air, and Jap guns were hitting the water. We were strafing them and trying to knock them out.

I came home after my Green Island tour, and I didn't weigh very much. That was from flying hard, not getting enough food, and perspiration. You were only expected to do three tours. Some were discharged, but two of us from our squadron were posted to instructor school at Wood-bourne to learn to be flight instructors. We didn't think much of this idea at all, but we had no option. We flew down together in a Harvard, a two-seater, one behind the other. We did a particular hairy landing one day, and I said to Butch, "Christ, Butch, what the hell you doing? That was a hairy landing!"

He said, "I wasn't flying the damn thing; you were!"

I said, "I wasn't flying it!" So here comes a staff car racing across the runway with some irate wing commander. He said, "You two go pack your gear. We don't want your sort as instructors!"

We packed our bags and went back to Wellington, and I was posted to rocket school—firing rockets from fighters. I had just gotten started at rocket school when the war ended, and I was out in a fortnight. However, I was given the option of going with the squadron that was going to Japan for the occupation, but I had had enough and thought I should start thinking about the rest of my life.

7. Kiwi Ace in the Pacific: Geoffrey Bryson Fisken

Geoffrey Bryson Fisken was born in 1915, in Gisborne, which is on the east coast of North Island, New Zealand. His family was prosperous in that they owned several sheep stations of several thousands of acres, as well as a number of smaller stock and dairy farms.

Fisken lived at a time when most children either walked or rode a horse to school, and sheep and cattle were herded to market along existing roads, and not transported in trucks as they are today. He seems to have liked the farming life, because that is what his main occupation was both before and after the war. However, he did have a passion for aviation at an early age, and soloed in a Tiger Moth biplane by the time he was fourteen. "Tiny" White, George Bolt, and "Mad" Max McGregor, all early New Zealand flyers, were his mentors and instructors in flying during his youth. And although he had an interest in flying that went back to his early days, after he soloed at the age of fourteen, he didn't fly much after that until after New Zealand had been at war for almost a year. He tried to enlist early in the war, but because he was a farmer and farming was considered an "essential industry," he was rejected. However, in 1940, he tried again and this time was accepted. He trained at Bell Block, just outside of New Plymouth, and at Ohakea, just north of Palmerston North, and graduated as a sergeant pilot in 1941. Soon after that he was sent to Singapore to serve in RAF Squadron No. 205. He started off in multiengine flying boats— old Short Singapore Three flying boats and later PBY Catalinas— both of which he hated. After much pestering of his superiors, he was finally able to transfer to a fighter squadron, which was what he wanted.

Fisken started off flying Royal Australian Air Force Wirraways, and then Brewster Buffaloes, two obsolete and underpowered fighters that would soon be replaced by new fighters with more power and survivability in combat against the more nimble Japanese fighters of the day.

After his conversion to Buffaloes, Fisken returned to Singapore in RNZAF

Geoffrey Bryson Fisken, New Zealand's #1 fighter ace in the Pacific during World War II. Because of wounds received in air-to-air combat, his war was over in 1943.

Squadron No. 67. It was during these early days of the war that Fisken first drew blood in air-to-air combat with the Japanese. By this time, however, he was with No. 243. Within a month after the Japanese had bombed Pearl Harbor, Fisken was an ace. However, most of the other New Zealand pilots in his squadron had been lost along with most of their aircraft. As a result, he and the remaining New Zealand pilots from 243 were amalgamated into Royal Australian Air Force Squadron No. 453 in Singapore.

It was during the final days of combat in the skies over Singapore that Fisken was wounded in aerial combat. He eventually escaped from Singapore and made his way back to New Zealand via Australia. After recovering from his wounds, he trained in P-40s, a much more powerful aircraft than the old Buffaloes, and returned to combat in the Solomon Islands, where he scored more victories. However, because of problems from his earlier wound, he was invalided home and discharged in December 1943.

After surgery to repair his injured hip, he returned to farming. Today, he is a retired widower and father of six, living in Rotorua, in the center of North Island, New Zealand.

After school, if Tiny White wasn't doing anything he would take me flying. One day he put his hands in the air and said, "Take off." He still had his hands in the air when he told me to land. I landed okay, and Tiny said, "You got your license, but you can't get it because you're too young." I was fourteen.

My father, Robert, used to fly everywhere with Tiny. Every chance he got he flew; he enjoyed it quite well too. And my sister was one of the first women to get a license in New Zealand. Her name was Una.

Tiny boarded at our place, and later on he was C.O. of all Commonwealth pilots in Canada. He went over there to run the show, and he used to write to my mother a lot and tell her how things were going, and what I should do to get into the war. My mother, Grace, never flew; she was a staunch stay-on-the-ground person. She wasn't very big; she was only about five foot tall, but she did rule the roost. She had five children, and I was the youngest.

I didn't fly after that for a long while. After I left school, I went out on to one of the [sheep] stations and worked on the station for a while — quite a while. We had two big stations of about 10,000 acres, and we had at least three farms. One of my brothers went on one, and a cousin was on another one. My dad did all the buying and selling, and things like that. I can remember several times as a kid we had sheep going for sale in Morrinsville, which is in the Waikato. One time we had 55,000 sheep on the road in 5,000 mobs, with two drovers driving each mob — from Gisborne to Morrinsville. It took them ten weeks. There were no trucks in those days; sheep were driven everywhere, and sheep only went about eight miles a day.

There were paddocks all over for you to stay every night, and a lot of wool sheds on the road. You could camp in them; you didn't have to put up a tent every night. I liked sheep farming, and since the war I have run several big stations.

Tiny was in Canada and wrote and told my mother that the war was about to start soon, and if I wanted to get into it early I better get into it now. That was 1938. I never met up with him again. I went to join up with the air force, but it took two days to get to the camp from the station I was running. I only lasted a day. They told me to go back because farming was considered an essential service. But eventually I did get in and finish my training. Then they said you're going overseas. We got on a boat and went over to Australia, and collected up with a Dutch boat over there, and had a leisurely trip through all the islands. The one that took my eye was Bali, because the women had sarongs, but only as high as their waists. They had nothing above their waists, and after a week on that island my eyes were so sore I could hardly see out of them.

There were no passengers on that boat. There were four air force pilots and two Jap internees that were being deported. They had been living in Australia, and were not allowed off the boat at any time. But we spent about a week at every island we stopped at.

When we arrived in Singapore, we were marched into a shed — their air headquarters — and we were posted to 205 Squadron, which was a flying boat squadron. They only had three or four at that time; they were Singapore Threes, they called them. Eventually, they got four Catalinas, and they were just about as bad. I hated them, being that I had been brought up on single engine aircraft. They would cruise along at about ninety knots, but I didn't last long on them.

I think I drove the air force orderly room mad. I had been pestering the orderly officer there, putting in for a transfer almost every day. Then I heard that the Brewster Buffaloes were coming along, and I was transferred to one of the fighter squadrons that were going to be formed. They were [No.] 67 and [No.] 243, and they were RAF.

There was another fellow and myself that went to [No.] 21 Squadron — an Australian squadron flying Wirraways. They were a glorified Harvard, with retractable undercarriages. There were about four English pilots there, and the two of us. We only stayed with the Wirraways for about two weeks — two and a half weeks — then we started training in the Buffaloes. This was still in Singapore. The Australians had two squadrons there, [No.] 21 and [No.] 453.

RAF Squadrons No. 67 and No. 243 are formed up in Kallang, Malaya:
We got at least four pilots a month, or every three weeks, from New Zealand. So they formed [No.] 67 Squadron first, and then [No.] 243. These were RAF; there were no New Zealand squadrons there.

Just before the war started [before Japan entered the war], we used to fly to Kota Bharu, on the border of Siam, or Thailand, as it is called now. They had given in without a fight to the Japs, and there were 4,500 Jap aircraft up there at Singora. And at that stage, [No.] 67 was moved to Burma, but I only flew up with them for the night and flew back again to Malaya.

We used to have some fun before the war started; we used to go over Singora, and the Zeros would get all around us and escort us back over the border, but no combat at that time; the war hadn't started [pre-Pearl Harbor].

The Buffalo was a beautiful aircraft to fly; I enjoyed flying them. The only thing wrong was they didn't have any horsepower to get anywhere fast; their rate of climb was slow. My friend that was with me in [No.] 67 Squadron — a fellow called Vic Bargh — I was talking to him the other day and he really liked the old Buffalo, and he flew Spitfires after that.

We were back in Singapore when the Japs bombed Pearl Harbor, and the next night they came over us, but didn't drop anything. There must have been fifty or a hundred planes just to show us how good they were, I suppose. Then the next day, it started in earnest. They came over the next day, and we sent our squadrons out. [Fisken was in No. 243 by this time.] A lot of our pilots didn't come back. They outnumbered us sixteen to one.

About the only thing the Buffaloes could do better than the Jap planes was to dive; they would get in a high speed when in a dive, and the Japs would never follow you in a dive. The first plane I got, that might have been a Ki-27; I'm trying to think now. We came out of a cloud — the bloody cloud formations over there were marvelous — and I think we were only a couple of hundred feet above the Japs. One of them turned in towards me and started firing straight away, and I always armed my own guns and set my own sights the way I wanted. Yeah, he turned and started firing at me and I fired at him. He passed underneath me, but I must have hit him, because he was only about ten feet underneath me and blew up and put me into a spin. I spun down about 4,000 feet or 5,000 feet before I could get the devil out of it. I don't have my logbook here so I'm not sure if that was the first plane or the second.

The clouds would go anywhere from 2,000 feet to 30,000 feet, and one day we were about 4,000 feet above these Jap bombers. There was a fellow, "Blondie" Holder, with me, and we put our Buffaloes down in a dive and went straight through the formation, and I got one on the way down. Then I came up underneath them and got another one, and "Blondie" got one. It was only the two of us, and we had a good day.

Blondie didn't survive the war; he died. I'm not quite sure, but I think he was test flying a plane and crashed. But after the first fortnight, out of fourteen pilots, we had lost about ten. A lot of them tried to dogfight; that was suicide. I didn't dogfight; I dove at them and got out.

Eventually, we ran out of pilots, and they sent us to join No. 453, and that was a waste of time. They were an Australian squadron, but they wouldn't fly. They preferred to be safe, and they got in a lot of trouble. They lived as they wanted, the Australians at that time. They had about three or four planes in the revetments, and another fellow and I, Rex Webber, test flew the planes for them, but they never took them up. Rex was a professor at Massey University [after the war], and he kept a diary about the Aussie pilots. In the book, *Bloody Shambles*, it tells you the same thing.

I have to think now; I can tell you I was injured. There was only two of us that took off [this was in February 1942]. Rex Webber was the other pilot; the rest of the squadron wasn't interested. There were only four New Zealand pilots left by this time, and two of them were transferred out — Charlie Cronk and Bert Wipiti. He [Wipiti] was a Maori pilot, and he could fly; he could fly all right, but the New Zealand government transferred him away from us — he and Cronk — to India. Cronk killed himself landing there one day, and they sent Bert Wipiti on to England, where he joined a Spitfire squadron. And from what I can make out, he met some 109s [Messerschmitts]. He and his C.O. attacked them and neither of them came back. He would have been better off staying with us. But anyway, that day I shot one down first, and then another plane hit me with a cannon shell in the back on my armor plating. The cannon shell evidently split up and bounced into my hip. When I landed and got out of the plane my mechanic fainted because he saw all the blood down my leg. He was pointing at my leg before he fainted. When I looked down, there was about a four-inch piece of steel sticking out of my hip. We couldn't get it out with a pair of pliers, so I had to go over to the hospital to get it cut out. And every morning after that the doctor would come over and inject something into my leg that deadened the pain so I could fly.

Shortly before Singapore fell: The rest of squadron 453 turned up when it was time to go home. We said we wanted to go too, but they were going to leave us there because we were New Zealanders; we weren't Australians, Rex and I. But a revolver is a persuasive item, you know, so we got out. We got out with the clothes we were standing in when we got on the boat. We went onto Ceylon to pick up the remnants of the 8th Army before going back to Perth. After several days we got to Melbourne and saw the New Zealand High Commissioner and was told to get back to Perth to catch another ship leaving for New Zealand in a few days.

Back in New Zealand: At Lyttleton, they took everybody off the ship. They assembled all the air force personnel and took them out to Wigram, but I was left on the ship because they were going to send an ambulance for me. But the wharfies had other ideas, and put me on a trolley. They wheeled me up to a pub and we had a few drinks, which I wasn't used to at the time. The ambulance girl, I remember, was very mad when she found me.

After that, they told me I could come home for a holiday. I got to Wellington from Wigram to get on the train to go home and thought I better call home and tell my mom. So I rang her, but she couldn't speak to me. My sister came on the phone and managed to talk, and said the other two had fainted, that they had got a message the day before from the Minister of Defense to say I was missing and believed killed. So when my mother heard my voice she fainted.

I only had about two weeks' holiday when I got a message to report to Ohakea. I was still on crutches, so I didn't understand why I was taken so early. I couldn't fly; I couldn't do a damn thing. But it was only about a week or two before they got my leg right and I didn't have to have injections to fly.

No. 14 Squadron is formed: There were about five 488 fellows [No. 488 Squadron — RNZAF] in Malaya, and there were three of us from [No.] 243. The rest were all ex-instructors. I was a Flight Sergeant up till this time, and then they made me an officer. And by this time, we had P-40Es — I think they were. I think we trained on them for about nine months. They were quite a good plane — quite a bit faster than a Brewster by a long way. Then we were sent over to Guadalcanal; we flew our own planes from Waipapakauri in the Northland to Norfork Island, which was about 500 miles over the sea. I had to turn back because I kept dropping out of the sky [engine problems], and I had to come back on my own. When I landed back at Waipapakauri, my motor cut out.

The others went on and got into a tropical storm and landed in the sea off Tontouta in New Caledonia. They all got out, though, and were sent back to New Zealand to get new planes. About a month later we all flew back up and had no trouble at all. We landed at Tontouta, and then on to Espiritu Santo. We stayed there for quite sometime, because No. 15 Squadron came in and took our aircraft, and flew on to Guadalcanal. That would have been around May 1943.

Eventually, No. 15 Squadron finished their tour and went back to New Zealand, and we had new aircraft by this time; they were P-40Ms — a bit faster than the others. We moved into Guadalcanal, with the Yanks. They were quite good to us. They built the fighter strip at Kukum Field, and we moved there. It is now a golf course the last time I was over there. The Yanks were on one side of that drome, and we were on the other. They were flying Lightnings and a few Tomahawks, I think.

When we first went up there, there was this P-40 with a black cat on it. It was one they pulled out of the sea and put back together, and as soon as my C.O. saw it, he yelled out, "That's yours!"

I got a couple on American Independence Day, I think it was. One of them flew straight up in front of me; well, I mean he was dead as soon as he pulled his stick back. It didn't take much to sight in on him. And then his number-two pilot stayed out alongside of me for a while, and then he came in at me and I turned in towards him. I shot him down as well.

Before we got into this fight — before the Japs dived in on us, we were escorting these boats [ships] down the channel. They had been hit by torpedoes, and a New Zealand boat was one of them — the *Leander*. Then I got up to about 16,000 feet and I saw this squadron of Mitsubishis heading for the boats, so I took the outside one and gave him a five-second burst. He blew up, and then I got covered by about six Zeros; they were coming down at me, so I got the hell out of there as fast as I could.

I was credited with eleven victories, seven probables, and two damaged; but where they got the two damaged, I don't know. Some of the probables may have been victories, but you don't see everything because you are too busy trying to save your own life.

My leg was starting to give way every now and again, so they put me in the hospital and invalided me out of the air force. That was in December 1943. I've got an artificial hip there now. I was quite happy to get out of it.

It's a funny thing; it was on Guadalcanal, and I had shot a plane down one day. I was a great fellow to go and lie down afterwards and have a sleep, and I could sleep quite easily. But this day I thought, "If I had been shot down, my mother would have been terribly upset," and there I am shooting bloody Jap planes down, and they had mothers too. Maybe they were upset, but I didn't like the Japs because my number-two pilot went up in my place because I had malaria. He got shot down and the Japs cut his throat with a pocketknife. He bailed out, and the Japs got him. His name was Jack Burton. The Coast Watchers saw it happen, so I didn't have much time for the Japs. But anyway, I started thinking they had mothers too.

I went straight back to farming once I got my leg operated on, and stayed on the station. I was quite happy there. They weren't doing anything in the islands after that anyway. The New Zealand squadrons weren't doing any good. The Corsairs never shot any planes down. They never saw any to shoot down; the Japs were moving out.

When I was there, the Japs were in their prime. They had Munda, and it was nothing to see forty or fifty [Japanese] planes in the sky.

Our relations with the Americans were pretty good, and when they [PBYs] went to rescue a pilot they always asked for New Zealand [fighter] pilots to cover them. I remember flying out one night to help pick up a Yank pilot that had been shot down. He was about forty miles away from Munda. The PBY flew out just above the water, and we flew at 500 feet. They landed, and they were twenty minutes on the water getting this fellow; I timed them. He was saying goodbye to all the natives on this island. I know what I would have done with the bloody pilot; I would have kicked his ass as high as I could. Anyway, they got him and when we got back as far as Guadalcanal, I called them up and said, "Hey, you've got four pilots here, and they all have dirty underpants, staying so low waiting for you on that pilot."

The next day, a fellow in a jeep drove up and asked for Warrant Officer Fisken, and he said, "I've got a parcel for you, sir." I opened it up, and there were four pairs of underpants. So I thought, "Well, the Yanks do have a sense of humor."

I asked them later why they always wanted New Zealand pilots to escort them and they said, "Because our pilots leave us if it gets too tough. New Zealanders won't."

We normally have a fighter pilots' reunion every year, but they are getting fewer and far between. They're dying off. Out of the original No. 14 Squadron, there is only another fellow and myself left, and I don't expect to be long now.

8. No. 1 Squadron, PV-1 Venturas: William John (Bill) Edhouse

Edhouse was born in 1922, in Ohakune, North Island. His paternal grandfather immigrated to Australia from the Isle of Man, and his father and his father's three brothers later immigrated to New Zealand, where they became involved in the timber industry. His mother was born in New Zealand and is of English ancestry.

Edhouse enlisted in the Royal New Zealand Air Force, and flew as aircrew on Lockeed Venturas, a small twin-engine bomber provided to New Zealand and other Commonwealth countries through a Lend-Lease agreement with the United States. The Ventura was an improvement over an earlier plane built by Lockheed called the Hudson. The first New Zealand Ventura squadrons left for Guadalcanal in October 1943, nine of which were lost by war's end.

Edhouse flew with No. 1 Squadron throughout most of his time in the military, later transferring to a PBY Catalina squadron, another U.S. designed and built aircraft.

Edhouse finished off the war as an air traffic controller at an air force base near Auckland, and after the war trained in carpentry. He had a long career as a builder, and is now retired and living in New Plymouth, New Zealand.

I had two sisters and six brothers. That was normal to have large families in those days. Two of my older brothers served in the army, and one of my younger brothers and I went into the air force. My oldest brother served in the Pacific, and the other one who was also in the army served in New Zealand, and we all survived the war. My brother who was in the air force was ground staff in the Pacific, and I was aircrew.

I was still in school when the war started [1939], but I didn't think

Jock Leaf (on the left) was Maori from the Auckland area. Bill Edhouse and Jock met while serving together in the Pacific, and remained friends throughout their lives.

it would affect New Zealand. After I graduated from high school and we went home, everybody was talking about the Home Guard, but New Zealand wasn't ready for war. My older brother was called up, and I could see it was going to be my turn shortly; and from what I heard about the army I knew I didn't want to be a foot-slogger. I didn't know enough about the sea to join the navy, so I thought I would join the air force. I can't remember how I went about it, but I think I must have done it through the Post Office. Everything in those days was done through the

70

Post Office.

I got this telegram from Wellington to "report forthwith." That was a funny word in those days — "forthwith." It said I had to go to Te Kuiti for the selection committee at 0915 hours. I thought "0915 hours" was some kind of a code, so I asked my dad what it meant. He said, "You have to ask the Post Office."

It may sound silly now, but in a small village that was only sixty-seven miles away from Te Kuiti — I think it was — I had to catch a train from Taumarunui, a small town off the Central Plateau, about fifty miles from Ohakune, that left in the middle of the night. Transport was different in those days; it was all by railway.

Now, I have only told this to a few people in my family, but when they ask, "How did you go to war, Dad?" I tell them, "I went to war in a night cart."

We didn't have a sewage system in those days, and the town contracted out to have all the night soil picked up from homes. I was trying to get to the train station in the middle of the night on my bicycle. There was fog around and I heard the train blow its whistle, and it sounded as if it was only a mile away; so I stood on my pedals and the chain came off the sprocket. Then I saw lights coming towards me, and I flagged this thing down, and it was the night cart — night soil cart. He took me to the station to catch the train, so that is how I went to war. I was in the dung before I even got started.

I got to Te Kuiti all right, and lo and behold, I was the only one to arrive. There was one member of the committee of three who was supposed to interview me, and he didn't have the keys to the hall where the meeting was supposed to be. Anyway, I answered all their questions, and they thought I was proper materiel for the air force, but I had to take a correspondence course first. It was the equivalent of a university entrance course. That took about three or four months, I suppose.

What happened next? I think I spent about six weeks in the army. There were a lot in my age group waiting to be taken into the navy, or whatever, and so they put us in the army temporarily to give us an introduction to military service — marching and camp living, and that sort of thing.

We were sent to a place in Auckland, a place called One Tree Hill — Cornwall Park is where we were camped. I think I might have finished my correspondence course by then. They took us out on what they called army maneuvers. They took us way out in these trucks with all of our gear, and dumped us on some farm and told us we had to live off the land, but it was only for twenty-four hours. To me that was child's play, because in Ohakune — growing up — we lived off the land. We knew how to stalk a rabbit and a stag. We had done all that as kids. That was the very thing I was trying to avoid, and we had to walk back. But then we came to a tram stop, and I nudged the guy next to me and said, "You on?"

We disappeared onto the tram, and the column marched on. I told the tram conductor, "See, we got to get back to camp to get the tea on." He said to put our gear in the corner and away we went. At the gate to the camp, we told the guards the same thing, that we had been sent off ahead to get the tea on.

But that was the army side of it — I got out of it pretty quickly.

When I finally got into the air force we had to take classes in learning Morse code, and what else did we learn — mechanics, navigation, and theory of flight. It was a different world — different from what we were used to. Looking back, it was well worth it; I don't regret it.

I finished up at Rotorua, what they called "ITW," Initial Training Wing. From there, we were earmarked to go to Canada to train, but just as we were getting ready to go — about three days before — I get a telegram from the Air Department to report forthwith — this word "forthwith" again — to Ohakea.

There were fourteen of us out of that bunch that was supposed to go to Canada, that were retained to do a special course. Putting two and two together, they wanted us to stay behind and help the Americans. Admiral Halsey was the commander, and I think he wanted New Zealand to do more. The Japs were on their way down; there is no doubt about it.

At Ohakea, we trained in Hawker Hinds. A Hawker Hind is an upgraded Tiger Moth. We trained in those planes for the next twelve months, and were posted up to the north of Auckland — patrolling up there. Then we were posted to a base near Whangarei, a base called Onerahi. This was all in 1942, into '43. They closed us down in Onerahi, and shanghaied us over to Gisborne to take over some Grumman Avengers. They were going to train us in torpedoes and send us to Papua New Guinea, because the Japs were coming down through Papua New Guinea for Ozzie [Australia].

What happened next was the Venturas arrived before the Avengers, so they sent us up to Whenuapai, in Auckland. They [the Venturas] were

72

to replace the Hudsons, and they needed aircrew. As it turned out, we were the very first [New Zealand] crews to take Venturas. Even the mechanics didn't have a handle on them. The pilots had to do a conversion, and it was [a minimum of] ten hours before they could qualify, but there was nobody around to train us. There were no American aircrews. We had to find out everything by ourselves.

The pilots had to learn how to fly the damn things, and I was on the gunnery side of it. The Ventura was a good plane in the right hands, but in the wrong hands ... *kaput*!

My understanding was that they were to replace the Lockheed Hudson, and they were an improvement. They had double the power, double the range, and double the [bomb] load. The ones we had were the PV-1s, which was the navy model. There was another Ventura, the B-34; that was the army model. The power was there, but they needed bigger wings [for better stability].

I can remember when we took one on its first test flight. We got 354 mph out of it. That was colossal speed. It could fly on one motor, but in good hands; you know what I mean? But as far as my part in it, I had to learn all about the turret, and the guns and things like that. I was sitting in the seat up in the turret, and said, "What's this for?" I pulled it, and the next thing I know I'm sitting on the floor [in the fuselage of the plane]. It was a quick release system. Yeah, I was on the ground when I did that.

The turret had high speed. It was a Glenn Martin turret, and everything was electric. We had to do an extra month of training because they found problems with the fuel tanks and something with the undercarriage. Yeah, I think we were expected to have a month there, and I think we were there for a bit more than that. We didn't get away until the 19th of October 1943. We took the first lot away.

I flew with Tom Mounsey. He was my skipper, the best skipper I ever had. He became a director of Air New Zealand eventually. Now, to get to Henderson Field [Guadalcanal], we left Whenuapai. The first hop was from there to Norfolk Island, about 400 miles north of New Zealand. There were six of us — six planes. We stopped there that night, and when I woke up the next morning I could smell oranges. It was a beautiful place; I had never been there before. I was fruit hungry. In the middle of North Island, you don't get much fruit there in those days.

The next day, we took off for New Caledonia. We got there and didn't like the smell of the place — the dust and the food didn't taste very good, or let's say it was strange. Grapefruit juice, for instance — it had a horrible taste. I'd never had that before. Everything was strange — dehydrated food. Our New Zealand cooks didn't know how to cook dehydrated foods, but they should have learned. The best spuds I ever tasted were made by the American black fellows — darkies — I don't know what you call them. I don't think you are allowed to call them Negroes anymore. I spent a lot of time with them, and I give them full marks; they knew how to cook a decent meal out of dehydrated spuds. They fluffed them up. Our blokes made them like large grains of rice — coarse stuff. Add water; that's all they did.

From New Caledonia we flew to Espirtu Santo. It's called Vanuatu, now. We called it Santo. That was the first time I saw fireflies. I don't remember much about Santo other than that; we only stayed the night, and were off again the next morning.

The Ventura was a fast plane. We could keep up with the Corsairs [F4U] and the Lightnings [P-38]. We did a lot of patrolling in the Pacific, and if the fighters needed [help with navigation] getting back to base, we could escort them. We could keep up with each other. Yeah, the Americans did welcome the New Zealanders with their Venturas; there is no doubt about it.

Today's Henderson Field is a modern international airport. In 1943, it was a big runway, but it wasn't tar-sealed. It was crushed coral, bound by oil, I think it was. Our job was mainly reconnaissance work. We were called "BR," Bomber Reconnaissance Squadron, so we could do both bombing and reconnaissance.

Each day, we did dawn patrols in segments, looking for ships and movement of any kind, which was then reported to headquarters. We flew all the way up to St. George Channel [between New Britain Is. and New Ireland Is.] and Rabaul [New Britain Island]. That's what they called "Maximum Effort," and we had to use drop tanks [extra fuel tanks].

We did a lot of bombing, but we didn't get too much into the plane to plane [action]. The nearest I got to getting shot down was by two P-38s. I think we were on Munda by then, but at any rate, we were approaching Cape Saint George, and as we were stooging along — my job was to keep a 360-degree lookout — and I spotted these two planes way the bloody hell up above us — two P-38s coming up behind us. They were about 3,000 or 4,000 feet above us. I kept an eye on them, and they were looking to come at us out of the sun; that's what they were aiming to do. I warned Tom, the pilot, and he said to keep a close eye on them, and that's what I did. And sure enough, they peeled off at us, and if I hadn't had my American sunglasses on I wouldn't have seen them.

It was incredible the speed; it was the first time we had been attacked like that. I could hardly keep track of them, and as they shot past, Tom rocked the wings a bit to wave them away. I was waiting for the first puff of smoke from them, and I would have given them both barrels [.50-caliber machine gun he had in the turret], but I don't know if I could have even hit them, they were going so fast. Luckily, they didn't shoot us, and we didn't shoot them.

Now, how we got to Munda is an interesting story. We got diverted there from Henderson Field. The Americans had Venturas there [on Munda], and they were all lined up on the runway, and they had been shot up the night before. The Japs had come over and strafed the hell out of them. When we landed on Munda we were taken over by the American command in what we stood up in, but we were under American command wherever we were anyway. All of our personal effects were still at Henderson Field. We must have been up there for a week, ten days, or more. From there we went off and did a mission, and when we came back to land they had a camp already set up for us.

There on Munda — when we first got there — I can recall going down to what they called the "chow line." It was raining, and we had these flimsy, waterproof capes to keep the rain off; and they gave us these big tin dishes, or trays. We were six planes and another thirty mouths to feed, and they didn't have enough food for us. The chef— cook — a big black fellow, was very apologetic. All he had to give us was a scoop of beans.

The Japs were still on the island, and there was talk of the Japs joining the chow line, but I think that was just talk; I don't know. Scuttlebutt, I think they called it, but there was talk that the Japs could join the chow line, and who would know the difference?

But getting back to Munda — some of the jobs we did — one that comes to mind is when we knocked out a Japanese lookout post — a radio post — that relayed to Rabaul when there was a raid coming. The Coast Watchers were given the task of locating it, and they did. I think it was on Choiseul Island, and we were given the task of going in to knock it out. This [native] coast watcher — his name was Martin — was trying to describe where to go and how to hit it, and when was the best time to get there. I think he said that the best time would be around 6 in the morning to catch the Japs while they were doing their morning ablutions.

When he was finished telling us, we bundled him into the plane and took off, and we found it. It was about a two-hour trip, maybe a little longer, and this chap — this native — looked bored. He didn't have anything to do. I don't think he had ever been in an airplane before, so we tuned on to a Sydney radio station and put headphones on him. His mouth fell open and his eyes popped out. He'd never heard music coming out of headphones before. And I thought he had bitten his tongue, because it looked like he had blood in his mouth, but it wasn't; it was betel nut. He was chewing that, and his teeth were red, and his tongue was red. Yeah, I thought he had bitten his tongue.

Our headquarters was at Henderson, but we eventually moved up to Munda. It was closer to where the frontline missions were. Our bombs were delayed action because we did low-level bombing. We came in under 500 feet.

The first raid we did was against Kieta Airfield on Bougainville, and it was my first experience of dropping live bombs. Our job was to make it unusable — hit the runway — and that is what we did. We dropped the bombs, and we were on our way out to sea. We were about a mile out when we got hit by a terrific shockwave from the delayed action bombs. I'd never experienced that before.

We did most of our jobs on our own, but we did some combined jobs. The best one I can refer to was when we operated from Munda, and dropped mines — magnetic mines — in the Buka Passage. The Buka Passage is the little strip of water between Buka Island and Bougainville. There was an [Japanese] airfield on both sides. That mission was the longest ten seconds of my life; let's put it that way.

I think it was in November; it was a night operation, and we were flying up the coast of Bougainville. There were eighty-five aircraft in the air that night, and they were all heading for the same point in the dark — no lights. Halfway up there, we get a recall because of rough weather, but there was no rough weather where we were.

Now, with that mine in a Ventura, we couldn't close the [bomb bay] doors. It was that big. We took off with the bomb [bay] doors open, and we had to come back like that. We couldn't drop them in the ocean because they would have been a menace to our own shipping. One of the pilots dropped his in a mangrove swamp on Munda, and we landed with ours, and that takes some skill, because there was only about ten inches between the mine and the runway.

Anyway, we took off again the next night and did the job properly. The Mitchells strafed the searchlights and guns, and things like that; and our job was to get in there unseen and drop our mines. I guess the rest was a diversion so we could get in there, and we were down, oh, I think it must have been between fifty and a hundred feet. But like I said, it was the longest ten seconds of my life. Tracers [bullets] were going over the top of us, and after we dropped our mine, tracers starting coming at us from up front. There was a pear-shaped island dead ahead as we came from east to west [actually, north to south].

On the way back, near Empress Augusta Bay [on Bougainville], there was a big battle going on down there, and there was a ship on fire. We diverted a wee bit to go and have a look, and as we got closer all hell broke lose down below. It looked like a dirty big hosepipe. An American destroyer was having a go at us, so we got the bloody hell out of there.

I did two tours in Venturas — I think they were three to four months — but by the end of my second tour the fighting war was virtually at an end [in the Solomon Islands]. That is when I went into PBYs — No. Six Squadron over at Halavo Bay, Florida Island. That was mostly humanitarian work, delivering mail and medical supplies to mission hospitals; and the natives would give us sacks and sacks of fruit. Sometimes we would pick up somebody needing medical attention. War wasn't all bombing and killing.

I think it was the middle of 1944, and I had the opportunity to go with a new Ventura squadron, but the fighting war was finished [in the Solomons], and I couldn't see the sense of it.

Our relations with the Americans were good. The Americans are just like the New Zealanders individually, but as a group.... What I mean is there are two occasions on the American calendar, Independence Day and New Year's Day, when the Americans let their hair down. Things could get out of hand.

There were two Maori in our squadron. One died just this past Christmas time. Him and I knocked around for sixty-three years. His name was Jock Leaf. His father was a captain in the Maori Battalion. They are a well-known family in North Auckland. Jock and I joined up together, did our training together, and went away together. Jock was sent home after his father got killed overseas. I was on control tower duty at Whenuapai the end of 1945 when I got out.

I had done three operational tours when I was offered the job of gunnery leader in No. Eight Squadron — Venturas again. I didn't fancy going back to the fighting side of the war, but they were short of air [traffic] controllers, so I jumped at the chance. I could have gone to Ohakea or Whenuapai. I took Whenuapai.

I was on shift when the war finished, and the prisoners of war had to be brought home, and that was one of the first things that happened after V-J Day. I was on the night shift again, and there was a new fellow — "Bluie" Orr was his name. He rang up and said there was an RY-3 coming in. An RY-3 was a converted Liberator [B-24]. It had seats for passengers — it was no longer a bomber — and they were bringing back these prisoners of war from Singapore.

We had about twelve or fourteen blokes scattered along the length of the runway, lighting these flares right down the length of this short runway. We had everything going, and I looked up and here come two landing lights. He hit the end of the runway, spot-on.

When he hit that runway, there was a shower of water [from all the rain]. That plane bowled right past me. He couldn't stop; his brakes weren't working, and he went right off the end of the runway. It was just farmland off the end of the runway.

I followed this plane, and it had disappeared off into nowhere. I took off in my van and found it at the bottom of a farm. It had ploughed its way right through fences and trees, and the smell of petrol was everywhere.

I left the lights on on my van so I could see. Nobody was hurt. The front cockpit chaps were climbing out through the windows. The pilot was a Captain McLean — an RAF chap.

Yeah, I did my six months up there, and I enjoyed it. The war was over and I survived it, and I was thankful; and to have a job like that, I wouldn't have minded staying on. But I was a realist; the war made me a realist. The war gave me a different attitude on life. I didn't take things for granted any more. I got married and had a family; I had my priorities.

9. The Dumbos at Tulagi, Six FB Squadron: Charles Lawrence (Joe) Laird

Joe Laird was born in 1923 in Wellington, New Zealand. His ancestry is Scottish and English. His family moved to Wanganui, on the West Coast of North Island, in 1925, and that is where Laird grew up and spent most of his life until he entered the military. His father was an engineering salesman who traveled a lot, but at least he had a job during the Depression, and the family did not suffer the way many families did during those prewar years. Tourism was unknown in New Zealand in those days, and Laird remembers a Dutch girl in one of his classes as the only foreigner he ever met before the war.

The U.S. Navy designed the PBY Catalina as a long-range patrol bomber in the early 1930s. However, in World War II it was used for a variety of jobs, such as antisubmarine patrols and search and rescue. New Zealand had two Catalina squadrons in the Pacific, and continued to use them for some years after the war.

As a teenager before the war, I remember there was a big row about Japanese ships coming into the port at Wanganui to pick up scrap metal. And there was also a feeling that Japanese fishermen — allegedly fishing — were measuring their lines — taking soundings. Realizing that my age at that time was five to maybe thirteen, and involved in my own doings — making canoes to going eeling, and that kind of thing.

In 1939, when we went to war with Germany, I was sixteen. I wasn't concerned about England being at war; I was concerned about New Zealand being at war. I heard discussions on the trams by the elders on how long they thought the war would be — their concern about it. There was no war in the Pacific at that time; it was all about Europe, and the feeling then was that it would be a long one.

I was drafted on October 28, 1941, into the Territorial Army — the

Charles Lawrence Laird: He flew as aircrew on PBY Catalinas in the Solomon Islands. He is second from the left on the bottom row.

Queen Alexandra's Mounted Rifles. That was in Foxton, and Foxton was a big camp in those days. I don't recall how many horses were there, but it was in the hundreds.

After Guadalcanal, there was a feeling in New Zealand that the danger of invasion [by the Japanese] had passed. But of course, at that time, you know, we had no idea; there was nothing in the newspapers. We had no idea what a thrashing the north of Australia was getting — Darwin and all around there. The Japs wiped out an Australian Catalina squadron in the Gulf of Carpenteria — wiped it out. We didn't know about any of these things at the time, but we were aware of the Japanese threat.

One day a brigadier — I think his name was Paron — came to see what armaments we had. It was rumored that a Jap invasion would land at Mokau Beach [north of New Plymouth] to seal off North Island, and then use Auckland as a base against Australia. In other words, he wanted to see what we had in order to defend against a Jap landing. We didn't even have three rounds of ammunition for every rifle, and not a rifle for every man. We had two Hotchkiss machine guns, and the bore in them was smooth, and I don't think we had much ammunition for them, as I recall.

At this point, I applied for the air force. In U.K.— in British forces —
they have a [system] called "Senior Service." In other words, if the navy
wants you, they have first pick, and the air force was senior to the army.
Col. Stewart was our O.C.— Officer Commanding — and he refused my
request. However, the concept of "Senior Service" was not a theory, but
a fact. My transfer to the RNZAF was confirmed. That was in '42; I can't
remember the month.

I transferred to the air force because I couldn't see any future in the
New Zealand Territorial Army. The ones who stayed all went overseas, and
they all finished up in Italy in the armored brigades.

I became a member of the ground staff in the air force. Tom Mania-
poto, a big Maori, was in our group. He was a chief in one of the Waikato
tribes, but he was just another aircraftsman in the air force.

The first Americans I ran across were based at Paekakariki. A marine
by the name of Kirkpatrick is a guy I sat next to at a combined get-together
between the New Zealand Air Force in Wellington and the American
forces. Around Lampton Quay, or thereabout, were [U.S.] Navy on leave
and thousands of U.S. Marines. There were more marines in Wellington
than I think Kiwis. My impression of the [U.S.] Navy — by God, I was
gobsmacked [astonished]! We got on very well, but as a New Zealander I
could not understand the way they treated their Negro mates. I can recall
being in Wellington — there was a Negro, and his white mates were calling him "Chicken shit," and whapping him with a rolled-up newspaper.
It just didn't seem to me that the treatment — the camaraderie — between
them was quite what it should have been when they were all on the same
job. He [the Negro] was good-natured about it and just walked off, which
was the logical thing to do, because he was outnumbered about four to
one.

In Nelson [South Island], we did our basic engineering training, in
my case as a mechanic. The training was absolutely tops. It was like going
to university. I re-mustered into aircrew as a flight engineer/air gunner.
From there I finished up in the Catalinas. I could have been on Venturas
or anything, but I figure I was lucky to end up on Catalinas. They were
a great kite [airplane].

We did all of our training and gunnery in New Zealand, and then
we went to Fiji. In Fiji, it was to do our air-to-air gunnery and training
with depth charges as preparation for antisubmarine action. We also trained
in night flying — all that kind of thing — to prepare us for when we went

up top [the Solomon Is.]. That was December 1944 — after a year of training in New Zealand, and six weeks in Fiji.

We were issued our kites in Fiji, and from Fiji, we went to New Caledonia — landed in the harbor at New Caledonia — refueled and took off for Tulagi in the Solomons. It was a big supply base then. Off Tulagi was Gavutu, which is where the Americans had their net and boom base. Their job was to put the nets and booms out at night so that the Japs couldn't sneak in and make a mess of things. Our base was perfect for the flying boats.

Our base was twenty minutes by water from the American base, and that was Gavutu Island; and like I said that was strictly for net and boom. Our job was to patrol — to look out for submarines — and we patrolled a hell of a long way out, as far up as the Marshall Islands. We carried depth charges if we should sight a sub. We were [also] on air/sea rescue, looking for downed planes or men overboard. Our job was to search for them. And I think the worst job of the lot was searching for men overboard, because that meant that you sat for hours on end with binoculars, looking. You were dead scared to let go, because if you did — if you blinked — some poor bugger below might get missed.

It was an enervating experience to fly over an American convoy and have every gun in the convoy follow you, especially when you had read the reports from Europe about "friendly fire." The Americans were known for their friendly fire. So when we were flying around an American convoy, reporting success or failure, we had those bloody guns down there following us around all the time.

On occasion we found oil slicks that gave us indication where kites had gone down. Once we found that, we almost knew we had something. Then we would do a circle around to see if any men had gotten into a dinghy. We saw where they had gone in but never found any men. Men overboard — we never recovered any of them either. That was our job, but our degree of success wasn't very high.

About once a fortnight we would take a doctor out, and we used to drop in at all these outlying islands. We would take the doctor, and he would do whatever he could for the islanders, and as a result of that we saw most of the islands. We actually had physical contact with them, and the one thing that impressed me about the islanders was that if you happened to be part of the landing party that went in with the doctor, invariably they would take you to their church. The church on their island was their focal point, and they were all very religious.

When we landed, we always landed in lagoons, and landing in lagoons was a sight, because depending on how many canoes they had, every canoe was manned; and as soon as we landed we would have a line of canoes all going hell-bent for leather, escorting us to where we were supposed to go.

The closest we got to the Japanese was when we went up to the Marshall Islands, and the night before we got there, the last Japanese bombing of the port there happened.

The 505 Seabees were the Americans that did the net and boom, and they used to come to our base. As you know, the American Navy is dry, but every week the Seabees used to bring a barge-load of booze over to us, and then on Wednesday and Saturday nights the American servicemen would come over to our base and help us drink it. The incongruity of it occurred to me only after the war.

The Americans we associated with on Tulagi were all workingmen. Take away his accent, and take away our accents and you couldn't tell the difference, one from the other, except the Americans all had a pair of gloves hanging out their hip pockets. We didn't. As a Kiwi, that was something that always amused me. They always had gloves, and they always wore them for work.

One time, I went over to the American camp; I was invited over there for something, and I was watching them dumping truckloads of rifles and other equipment — truckloads. They backed them up to the edge of the wharf and tipped them in. I think when the American forces moved forward, they didn't take what they brought in. It's written off—finished. They just dumped it. My jaw dropped open; I couldn't believe it.

I spent a day at the American base — had dinner with them in their mess, and there must have been eighty to a hundred men in that tent. And the difference, as I noticed there, was when they ate their meal the fork was the sole implement. We would use a knife and fork; they just used a fork.

I noticed that after dinner, when we left the mess, the sergeant-of-the-day, or whatever you call him — a big guy — watched everybody. I learnt afterwards that you can take what you like but if you don't eat what you take you gotta make an explanation.

There was no comparison between American food and ours. What I mean is, the American cooks were the best in the world, and the New Zealanders the worst.

There was no comparison between our pay and the Americans'. What did I make back then? I think it was seven bob a day; that is seventy cents at the conversion rate at that time. I don't know what the Americans were getting at that time, but I would think it was ten times that amount. So obviously they could treat the women a lot better than the Kiwi could. I think that caused a certain amount of dissention.

One thing I can tell you, the Maori Battalion was back on leave in Wellington when we were beginning our ground staff training, and they had been in the Middle East from 1939, right through. That would have been early '42, I think. They had been overseas three years, and some of the marines treated them like they would treat a Negro; and the Maoris wouldn't take it. The Maoris were three years blooded soldiers, and the marines had yet to be, so there was a big street brawl over that one.

The heads must have gotten together over that, because I met a guy — Biern was his name — a marine. What they did after that street brawl — we all went to a concert. The Kiwis were there, and the Americans were there, and they sat us one Kiwi, one American — one Kiwi, one American. They were all evenly spaced — full integration.

In terms of getting things done, the Americans and Kiwis had a hell of a different system. As far as the Americans were concerned, they had complete autonomy — I think that might cover it. They could make their own decisions, and they could do it because they had the gear to do it with. So, you know, it was like we've got a problem; here is the background we have to solve that problem; let's do it. So they could do it on the spot. Therefore, their decision making was much, much quicker than ours could ever be.

We [Kiwis] had all the equipment for repairing our own planes, but we didn't have the resources backing it up. Once that [the resources] was expended we couldn't replace them immediately. We could borrow small stuff from the Americans, but if the Americans lost a kite, they could call up San Diego, I think it was, and say, "We lost a PBY; we want a replacement." We, on the other hand — the New Zealand forces — couldn't ring up San Diego and say, "Hey, we lost a kite; we want another one tomorrow." The replacement time for us had to go around and around a few circles. So where they [the Americans] could be completely spontaneous, we couldn't. Now, I was only just a little sergeant, so I wasn't that high enough to know how things worked, but that is my presumption.

Gail Nielsen, who I got to know very well, and his mate, Staggs, were of Norwegian extraction. The U.S. Navy was 40 percent illiterate. That's not me saying that; that's Gail Nielsen from Salt Lake City. He and his mates would come over to our canteen on a Saturday night, and we would talk. And to my amazement, and to Nielson's, that is where I heard that 40 percent of the U.S. Navy was illiterate. They were scraping the bottom of the barrel. And, boy, when they played cards on a Saturday night, the eyes and the knives used to flash. It made me aghast; I couldn't imagine anybody ever getting so serious over a card game.

Most of the American camps had built little amphitheaters, and every now and again there would be a USO show, and if we were close enough we could go and see them. Sometimes it was live, and sometimes it was just movies.

Everything about America was interesting. It was a different culture to us, and therefore it was interesting. As I said, they [Americans] used to come over to our base on a Saturday night, and a Wednesday night; and all that sort of information was talked about. What we did was probably different to what they did in this respect; most of the fun we had we made ourselves. On the weekends, you could go down to the beach, go fishing, eeling or whitebaiting, or whatever in the rivers. If you had a rifle, you could go out after deer, pig, and goat.... That was largely our entertainment. But most of the Americans I met were from big cities, and therefore their entertainment was, in my opinion, in a can; you paid for it — theater, baseball parks and that kind of thing. I met Americans who never even heard of New Zealand —"Where's that?"

I can remember when victory in Europe was declared. Generally speaking, I think there was some mild celebration, but we knew that our war wasn't finished. We didn't know about the atomic bomb, and the expectation was that as far as Japan was concerned there could have been a couple of million more casualties. That was the feeling, and that is probably the way it would have been if it hadn't been for the A-bomb.

My skipper, Ken Smith — once Japan had thrown in the towel — called us all in and asked us what we wanted to do. Ken asked me, "Joe, what do you want to do? You want to stay in or do you want to go?"

I said, "Well, Ken, I'm twenty-three; I've got a man's body and a boy's knowledge, so I'll go."

As it turned out, I went in on the 28th of October, and five years later I came out on the 28th of October. Adjusting to civilian life was pretty tough. I didn't miss the discipline, but it took quite some years before I got to the stage where I could change from being a boy in a man's environment. That was tough for a lot of the younger men who had only known military service. You go in at eighteen, and when you come out you're not equipped economically for the world.

10. A Stranger in Her Own Land: Tracy Tapuke Magon

Tracy Tapuke Magon was born in 1924, in New Plymouth, North Island, New Zealand. She was the fourth of thirteen children born to Reti Mana Tapuke and Jane Skipper. Magon doesn't know the entire story of how her mother came by the name of Skipper, because her mother wouldn't talk about it. However, as far as she knows, her grandfather on her mother's side was off a whaling ship, but didn't stay in New Zealand.

Her father was a farmer in Bell Block, now a suburb of New Plymouth, but in those days little more than a village. He was of the Iwi [tribe] Te Ati-awa, and his Marae [tribal meeting area] was Murupautu.

Magon says that although she started off life speaking Maori at home, she soon forgot it because when she went to school it was forbidden. As a result, today she only speaks English.

Magon enlisted in the New Zealand Women's Army Auxiliary Corps in 1942, and soon left home for the first time and headed for the big city of Wellington. She stayed in the army until 1947 before returning home. However, she got itchy feet and joined up with a girlfriend and went on a "working tour" of New Zealand, eventually settling in Christchurch, South Island, where she worked in a garment factory for fifteen years. She eventually married and raised four adopted children of mixed ancestry. She moved to Waitara, just north of New Plymouth, in 1997, where she still lives.

In New Zealand, the WAACS were formed in January 1942. By June 1942, there were around 3,000 New Zealand women in uniform, and by July 1943 the WAACS reached their peak strength of 4,600. By March 1944, those numbers were reduced to fewer than 2,000.

I never knew English until I went to school. That's when we had to change over or we would get the strap. Even though we were black as..., we had to be Pakehas [Europeans, or non–Maori]. There was a Maori in Parliament — he decided that we would get nowhere being Maori. His name was Sir Apirina Ngata. He felt Maoris had to speak English if they wanted to get anywhere, and we got a lot of straps at school if we forgot and started talking in Maori. But that was my generation; it's different now. We're getting back to it. They have classes in Maori. Maoris are all going back to being Maoris.

My father was a farmer, but it wasn't a big farm. We had a big house; it had one, two, three, four bedrooms; but it was still a bit tight with thirteen kids.

We all got enough to eat, but it was a bit scarce at times. But we managed because we were able to go to the beach and get seafood, and we had a big garden. And we killed a cow or pig when we needed to.

I only just remember the Depression. I remember my father worrying about [how he] couldn't afford to get flour from the store. I remember him being quite worried about that, and thinking he might have to sell a pig to buy groceries. But apart from that, we had the basics — potatoes, kumara, corn, and a pig and a cow, you know.

We all milked cows before we went to school, and when the war came my older brother went away and I had to take over the milking. His name was Donald Puke. He dropped the "Ta" from his last name when he went in. He went into the Maori Battalion, and was killed at Cassino [in Italy]. I was in the army by then and got a week's leave to come home. When my mother got the news — I was in Wellington at the time, so I only heard — she collapsed. He was the oldest boy, and there were eight girls before the next boy was born. Yeah, so that was quite a big shock to her. She was only fifty-six when she died. My father wasn't much older than that when he died of a heart

Tracy Tapuke Magon knew only the Maori language until she came of school age. Today, she speaks only English, and feels like a stranger in her own land. During the war, and for several years after, she served in the New Zealand Women's Army Auxiliary Corps.

attack. My mother must have been around sixteen when they got married, so she lived long enough to raise all her children.

I had three cousins who fought in the war, and they came back but died soon after from wounds. They were all in the Maori Battalion.

I got fed up with milking the cows one day, and I joined up too in 1942, when I got eighteen. When my brother left, I had to take the milk to the factory, and that was by horse and cart, you know. There were four other women in our area that had to take milk to the factory after their men went to the war. Anyway, I came home one day and said to myself, "There's gotta be something better than this." So I went to town and joined up. My parents didn't know until it came time for me to leave. My father just looked at me; he didn't say anything. My mother never said nothing either, so....

I left New Plymouth by train, and when I got to Wellington it was raining, and when I got off the train it was scary. There were lots of people and lights. I came from a little country town to a big one like that. Anyway, from there we were taken to Miramar [in Wellington], the base camp there. That was a bit scary too; I remember crying all night for about two or three nights, but I got over it.

I had three months of training there; you know, route marches, and I tried to use a gun and gas masks, and all the other things like cleaning your hut. After three months there, they shifted me to Signals, and I was there for a long time, but I wasn't very good at it. I don't know what you would call it; it was flags and things going up. I was at it for quite awhile but they finally realized that I wasn't very good at it; so then they sent me out to Trentham, which was another camp. When I got out there, I was put in mess work. It was in 1947 when I got out, and I spent the whole time there, not cooking but washing the dishes.

The first three months I was in the army I gave up my weekend leave to save it up so that I could come home. I was homesick, very homesick. I would leave Wellington on a Saturday morning, get to New Plymouth at night, and leave on Monday morning to get back. For three months I did that. After that, I didn't come home so often. I had got a bit used to it by then.

When I had time off I didn't do much; just go into town to the services clubs, and go to the movies and dances. That's about all. I met a lot of American Marines. Yeah, they were very nice. I met them mostly in services clubs, and they used to invite us to their camps. We played games with them. We called it "rounders," but they called it softball. They were teaching us to play. It was marines against all the women, so it was more or less a get-together.

I had a few friends who married Americans. I had one friend who wasn't in the army who married an American. Actually, I don't think she married him; he got killed, but she had three children by him — lovely children. Two of them were twins.

I never got involved with them [the U.S. Marines], never got any chocolates or stockings, or chewing gum or anything. No, but I met a lot of these fellows in the canteens, and they were all homesick, and their families were worried about them; and worried they might get married over here.

I only remember one name, and he was Jimmy Aldaz, from New Mexico. I remember him because we went to the pictures three times, and it wasn't together; we just happened to run into each other at the movies. He wrote to me when he left here; they were in Hawaii. I didn't hear any more, so I just assumed he was killed.

The black Americans were very nice too. They were very quiet, you know. They sat by themselves a lot. I used to feel sorry for them actually, because that's how Maoris feel, like they don't fit in. It's still that way. If I go to a function and it isn't a Maori function, then I just sit there in a group [with other Maoris]. Maoris still feel apart. Some say it isn't that way any more, but it is. That's how I feel, and that is why I understood how black Americans felt.

Mostly, I met them [black Americans] at dances, but I couldn't dance with them because they did the jitterbug. I couldn't do it. Yeah, the white Americans, they were a bit noisy, but the black Americans would sit there and get up and have a dance, and then go back and sit; and they were always together.

In the army I didn't feel different because there were a lot of us; we were one. There were a lot of Maori women in the army, and I had Pakeha friends too. There were some that didn't quite like getting involved with us, but it didn't bother us really.

My auntie lived in New Plymouth, and she used to have them [American servicemen] in for meals. Her name was Ivy Papakura. She only had a little wee flat, and she used to have them over for meals. My mother told me about that when I was home on leave once. Mum said to me, "Did you meet any Americans?"

I said, "Oh yeah, I met a lot."

Then she said, "Well, your auntie has them over for meals." And then she said, "She asked them up for tea, and they were quite surprised when they got there that it was a meal."

After I got out of the army I came home. There were no cows. My father sold the cows because the younger ones weren't into milking cows. I stayed home for a long time, and then rang a girlfriend, Sybil Mason; she lived in Gisborne, and her and I did a working tour around New Zealand. We worked anywhere — went down south and worked the South Island. Then I got a job in Christchurch and stayed there fifteen years — the same job, in a clothing factory.

I was thirty-one when I got married — no children, but we adopted four. Two of them are now in Australia, and the other two are still down in Christchurch. They were illegitimate children from single mothers. We had our problems with them, but they were worth it.

It's funny, because all of them are white as..., but they are into their Maori side, except for one; she couldn't care less. She works her butt off, that one, and doesn't have time for those things. The others all class themselves as Maori. I never pushed it on them; they just did it themselves. I found out when I asked them what election roll they were on. They put themselves down as Maori. That's how I found out.

My husband wasn't a Maori, but when I went to one of his functions I felt left out; and he felt the same when he came to one of mine. He would just sit there, and if nobody talked to him he would just sit there. But we had a good marriage. He had retired, and we came up here to live, and he just dropped dead. That was about nine years ago.

I don't have much else to say. I don't live a very exciting life, I'm afraid to say.

PART II

Voices from the
New Zealand Home Front

11. A Marine from Georgia: Joan Hay Cudby

Joan Hay Cudby was born in 1923, in Wellington, New Zealand. She was the third of five children. Her father got the family through the Depression thanks to government "relief work," which might best be compared to the CCC (Civilian Conservation Corps) established by the Roosevelt administration in the U.S.

In 1915, at the age of seventeen, Joan's father, Caryll James Hay, was in the New Zealand Army, and was severely wounded at Gallipoli, where so many New Zealand and Australian men lost their lives. It is remembered in both countries today on ANZAC Day. He was the youngest in a large family, and Cudby's mother, Gwendoline Harrison Hay, was the oldest in a large family. Harrison's mother died when she was only twelve, and when her father remarried a few years later, she was sent off to live with and work for another family. At age eighteen, when she was free to set out on her own, she met and married Joan's father and they were two people who started off life on the rough side. Although Hay's father had suffered a groin wound at Gallipoli, and was told he would never father children, he sired five. During World War II, Joan had two brothers in the military service, one in the air force, and one serving in the army in the Middle East.

I think my father was invalided home, not only with this wound, but also with a neurosis to a large degree. My mother said that not long after they were married and they had their first child, he was working on a demolition site in Wellington, and a wall collapsed beside him. He went to hospital and my mother was told that he should never live in the city again because his nerves were shot to pieces. She took him into the country, to Masterton, and stayed with him in a boarding house for the best part of a year, having to feed her baby and him because he was so out of it.

He eventually recovered and returned to Wellington, and that is when he got involved in all sorts of organizations, whether it was the Labor Party or the local rugby club. My father became a big man in politics; I think you would call him a Socialist in those days — the Labor Party, which was one step away. He was the campaign manager for one of the ministers who was elected in 1936, when the Labor Party got in and a lot of changes took place, lifting New Zealand out of the Depression. Because he was connected with the Labor Party, he was appointed to various jobs in the government. He used to always say to my brothers, "Oh, if there is another war, you don't want to go; it's terrible!"

At the beginning of the war, he was the organizer of the Home Guard in New Zealand. In fact, when the American Marines arrived in 1942, he was still traveling around New Zealand, organizing the Home Guard, and he became quite concerned about all the marines who were coming over to the house while he was away. But like my mother used to say, "These boys are like our sons. If I can do for them what I would like for somebody to do for my sons, I'll do what I can." And that is why she got involved with the American Hospitality Club in Wellington. It was on Manners Street, and it was where New Zealand families could sign up to take in invalided Americans. They would call up Mum and say, "We have a couple of young men who need a little bit of home comfort," and she would say, "Certainly," and she would fuss over them; and they all called her "Mom." Most of them had malaria.

Erastus Winn Roberts was a young U.S. Marine from Monroe, Georgia, when he met and fell in love with Joan Hay Cudby, a young New Zealand girl. Their story is typical of that time in New Zealand during the war, when so many New Zealand men were serving in the Middle East.

They would come and stay for a week or perhaps two weeks. We had one young fellow who took very ill while he was staying with us, and Mum had to get in touch with American authorities. I don't know what it was called, but it was an American hospital in Anderson's Park. He was only seventeen. Mum used to go up and visit him and would take him a chocolate cake, and of course all the other poor boys would say, "Ah, Mom, bring me a chocolate cake too."

She used to visit them regularly, and always bring them cookies and cakes, and lemon pies, and everything she could think of. She was a wonderful cook, my mother.

I had an old aunt, who was very, very wealthy, and she complained about the war years because she had to cut her golfing days down to two a week. She was on the Red Cross committee, and at the end of the war, she got a citation in 1952-53, from Queen Elizabeth for all the good work she had done during the war. Even to this day I get so angry when I think about all the work my mother did for all those boys, and she didn't get a thank-you from anybody. And it was my first husband who said that it was not everybody who got the citations that earned them.

When war started in 1939, the first thing my father did was go and offer his services. This after he said, "Don't ever go to war," to his boys. He was only forty-one, but of course they wouldn't take him. He wasn't well enough to go anyway.

My older brother went into the army right away, but my younger brother didn't go in until later; he was a year younger than I was. He trained as a pilot, but never actually served, because the war ended before he finished his training. My father was over his neurosis by then, and was very proud of his sons for enlisting.

I had just started working in 1940; I was eighteen then — around about that. I went to work for a lawyer after I finished business college, but only worked for him for a couple of months when he was called up. The government was looking for staff, and I went to work in a government office and worked there for the whole of the war years, because it was considered essential work. I did shorthand and typing — a lot of work for Ministers of the Crown, and that sort of thing.

I was seventeen when the war started, and my first boyfriend joined up and went overseas, and he was killed. He hadn't been long in the Middle East, when he was killed. He was on a lorry, and it was hit by a shell. I don't know exactly what happened. The awful part about that was that they never found a single thing that they could identify as him.

One of the things we did was type out ration cards, and we worked overtime when we did that. Someone came in with some tea for us [one night] and said, "Oh, the town is full of American soldiers!" I came out of the office about 7 o'clock that night with a girlfriend, and she eventually married a marine and went to live in America after the war. His name was George, and she had a child by the time she went over there. Her last name was Clark. I heard years later that she had a very bad marriage, but she never came back to New Zealand.

Anyway, when we left the building that night we were accosted by these three young men in uniform. "Excuse me, ma'am," and we grabbed each other because the only knowledge we had of Americans was about gangsters and cowboys in the movies. We didn't know if we were going to be raped or lassoed. And then, one of them said, "There are going to be thousands of us marines here and we want to get our bids in." And then we really thought we were going to be assaulted.

One of them could see that we were upset, and he said, "Don't misunderstand him. What he means is that we would like to get to know some girls."

I told them that I would go out with them, but not before they had met my parents. That was a Friday, and I arranged for them to come to the house on Sunday. All that Friday night and Saturday, I wondered, "How am I going to tell my father?" Anyway, I plucked up enough courage and told him, and he was quite pleased. He said, "You have done the right thing."

Those ones that came that first day, the Sunday — well, we always had a big roast dinner on Sundays. But at 4 o'clock we would have what was called a "high tea." A trolley was brought out — what we called a "tea trolley." It would have scones and pikelets [small pancakes], and always a sponge cake and some cookies. Well, those boys ate everything on that trolley. At 7 o'clock the table is set, and they couldn't believe it. They thought that the high tea was — I guess you would call it supper. They were horrified to think that they had cleaned off all the plates.

Whenever the marines came to our house after that, they always brought chocolate and peanuts for my father, and nothing for my mother, but when they left to go [overseas] there was one boy who gave my mother a docket [receipt] for an [clothes] iron. He said, "Our iron has packed-up [stopped working] and we had to take it in to get repaired, but it's not ready yet. So if you want it, Mom, you can go and get it."

For years and years, Mum used this iron, and she would say, "Well, I got something from the Americans." She had to pay for it, though.

One marine I got friendly with was Lou Pescatore, and he was from New Jersey, a town called Parsippany. He was here for about two months, I suppose, and they [the marines] had lots of leave, so every night after work he would be waiting for me. But I was still carrying a torch for my boyfriend who was killed in the Middle East, and he [Lou] was engaged to a girl in Parsippany.

We were just like kids in those days; that's all we were — seventeen, eighteen, nineteen — not like nineteen-year-olds today. We were like brother and sister with one another.

I'm jumping a bit now, but in 1973 I went to America, and stayed with his [Lou's] fiancée, Lillian Sheriff, who I wrote to when I first met Lou. We kept correspondence all those years. They didn't get married. He met somebody in Australia, and broke his engagement off with Lillian, but she married a soldier after the war, and on the same day as I did. She had her first son on the same day as I did. She had a second son when I had a second son — same year. She had a daughter the same year I had one, and then another daughter, so she beat me by one. And we both married accountants. Our lives paralleled each other like that.

When I went to America, we had our photos taken together. We could have been sisters; we looked so much alike. She actually served in the American Navy during the war. She died last year, but I had two lovely weeks with her in Parsippany, and I would have loved to see Lou Pescatore, because he had come back from the war, and was the recruiting officer in a nearby town, but she [Lillian] wouldn't let me go see him, and I didn't press it.

I think the New Zealand servicemen were becoming a little touchy because marines had all the girls, and the New Zealand boys were finding it hard to find a date. But there was also a story about a marine on a tram who tried to throw a Maori soldier off. He must have been a Southern-states boy. Whatever it was, it didn't do much good for public relations.

I was in a dance hall with a group of friends when the announcer came on and said, "Any marines who have girlfriends with them leave quietly." When we got outside, the street was lined with New Zealand servicemen and [U.S.] Marines. I said, "I'm not going to walk down there!" They were catcalling, and they were throwing things. It was terrible!

We walked behind them and got down to the taxi station, and we got home all right; but that was a very bad time. I don't know what it was like in other cities, but in Wellington, it was bad.

This other boy.... I was at the pictures, and he came and sat beside me, and we became very friendly. That would have been late in 1942, and his name was Erastus Winn Roberts, and I called him Pat. He was a really nice, fine young man, and we really did fall in love. He was from Monroe, Georgia — 217 Highland Ave.

I had had a thyroid operation, and only worked half days the entire time he was there [in New Zealand]. I used to get off work at 1 o'clock, and he would be waiting for me outside. We spent all our days walking and talking, and just enjoying each other's company. He had his photo taken and I had my photo taken at the same time, and then he was transferred to Australia. We were both heartbroken. We had been together every day for two months. He used to come out to the house all the time, and the whole family really liked him. It was quite a serious affair. I used to write to his mother and his sister, and they were looking forward to me being apart of their family.

But one day we were walking down the footpath, and coming toward us was an American sailor — a black man, which didn't mean anything to me — and he [Roberts] pulled me to the side. I said, "That wasn't very nice, Pat; you didn't give me a chance to say I was sorry."

He was absolutely livid! "Sorry?" he said, "You apologize to him?" he said.

He was furious! He said, "He shouldn't be walking on the same side of the street as you. His place is in the gutter!"

I was really upset about that. We hadn't had a lot to do with Maori in those days because there weren't a lot around in our area, but they were the only dark people we knew, and nobody I knew ever spoke about them like that. Of course, I realized later in life that I never could have lived in Georgia because of that.

After he had gone, I didn't go out with anybody for a long time. I stayed at home moping — all sad and sorry. Then one day my mother said to me, "You are too young to stay inside. Go out and enjoy yourself with your friends."

I said, "No, I don't want to go out and enjoy myself." In fact, when I was engaged to Pat, and thought I was going to America to live after the war, I would go to a place called the Young Eagles Club in Wellington, which was a club organized for girls who were engaged to American servicemen. Sometimes, we would have guests come and tell us about the various states we were going to go and live in, the cooking and way of life, and everything. Mrs. Roosevelt came out to New Zealand at one time, and said we would be very welcome, and made us feel like we were going to be a part of the American community. I can remember that quite plainly, but we had to prove that we were actually engaged to American servicemen to belong to this club.

I would write to him [Roberts] every night, and then one night a friend rang me up and said, "Look, I'm in an awful pickle." A chap she had been going out with had brought a friend along, and she said, "I'm stuck with two men. Do come and help me."

Mum said, "Go on, go out; go to the pictures with them."

So I went out with them and that boy used to come to our house a lot after that, and that photo I had taken the same time that Pat had his taken — well, he took it out of my album and put it on his locker. Then somebody from his outfit went to Australia, and of all the thousands of marines, this fellow is stationed with Pat, and he sees my photo on his locker, and he tells Pat there is another marine back in Wellington with a photo of this same girl [Joan] on his locker. So that was the end of a beautiful romance. Pat wrote to me, explained to me what had happened, and said he wouldn't accept any explanation. I never heard from him, his sister, or his mother ever again.

Again, when I went to America in 1973, I stayed with another marine I had met in Wellington. I wrote to his mother during the war, and when he got married after the war, I continued and wrote to his wife, and she was always writing and saying, "Come and have a holiday with us, Joan." His name was James Dean and he lived in Los Angeles. And while I was there, I tried to ring across to Georgia, and the telephone exchange said, "That party disconnected that phone two weeks ago."

When all the marines finally left [New Zealand], we were devastated in a sense. The New Zealanders were still away, and the Americans had gone, and we had to come down to reality. We just had to get on with it without any escorts to here, there and everywhere. But the Americans made us feel special. They were always very polite and caring. We were used to walking behind the boys, and if you fell into the gutter, well, too bad. The Americans would take your arm and help you across the road, and they always said "Ma'am" and "Sir" when referring to your parents.

The New Zealand boys started coming home after that, some of them on leave. That was 1944, I suppose. They had been overseas for three or four years, and some of them refused to go back. There were some men in New Zealand who had been stopped from going to war because they were in essential industries. So when those boys from the Middle East came back and saw these guys in their cushy jobs they got quite upset and said they weren't going back. A lot of them stuck to their guns, and didn't go back. My brother-in-law was one of them. He refused to go back.

One of my brothers was gone for five years, and didn't come back to New Zealand until 1947. He came back with an English wife and twin daughters.

My first husband, Fred Alistair Leith, was in the artillery, and he was actually born in India, and came to New Zealand in 1939. His father was a tea planter in Assam, and his mother was an Indian lady. He was called an "Anglo-Indian," and they were [treated like] nothing, really. He was sent to school in Kalimpong, to Dr. Graham's Homes — an orphanage. He worked in my office for a while before he was called up, but I didn't have any romance with him until he came back from the war. But when he came back he rang up the house. I said to him, "Where are you?" And of course he didn't have any family in New Zealand, and said that he had been booked into the YMCA.

My mother said, "Oh, that poor boy! He has been fighting for this country for five years and he has to stay at the YMCA? Ask him if he would like to come and stay with us for a couple of weeks." So he came out to our house for two weeks, and he never left. He and I got involved, and we got married in 1945.

12. Taking in the Sick and Wounded: Darcy and Dallas Knuckey

Dallas Clifford Jones Knuckey was born in 1910, in Wellington, New Zealand. Her ancestry is part English and part Maori. Her grandmother on her mother's side was Ngapuhi—Bay of Islands, North Island. Her father worked for the postal service and as a result the family moved often. Young Dallas attended seven different schools while growing up, and remembers World War I, and the flu pandemic that followed. She met her husband at a dance at Rawhitiroa Hall, outside of Eltham, where the Knuckey family had a 180-acre dairy farm. They met in December 1932, and were married less than a month later. During World War II, she worked as a volunteer with the Women's War Service Auxiliary and other volunteer groups.

Darcy was born in 1908. His grandfather was one of the first Europeans to settle in the Taranaki region of New Zealand in the 1840s. Darcy farmed until 1958, when he gave it up after suffering a stroke. Fifty-eight years later, he is still going strong. The Knuckeys moved to Mt. Maunganui after giving up the farm, returning to live in New Plymouth, at the suggestion of their daughter, just two years prior to this interview.

DALLAS: The Depression was difficult, but we were fortunate in that we were dairy farmers. I remember when the war started. I was keen on netball — basketball in those days — and I was attending a big tournament in a place called Invercargill, in the South Island. On the way back — it was 1939 — on the radio it came over that war was imminent. My brother Bruce was in the air force. He trained in New Zealand, and then went to England to complete his training, etc., etc. It was a shock to us, because five days after war was declared, he was killed. He was flying fighters, and was shot down by friendly fire. It was a dreadful shock to all of us, but especially for my mother and father. They never really recovered from it. My mother died in 1963, and my father a year later.

DARCY: I tried to enlist, but my father put in an objection. He said somebody had to work the farm.

DALLAS: Eltham was a great little town, because everybody wanted to help. We felt so sorry for those boys [American sick and wounded], and we felt that they would enjoy farm life. I was on the Comforts Committee, and the word came through asking for volunteers. We volunteered, and I know of three other families that volunteered, but I know there were more than that. We were allocated with two. Jack Place was one of them, and the other died soon after he went back to the islands. His name was Joe, but I can't remember his surname. They were both marines.

Jack was really sick — suffering from malaria — and all he wanted to do was go to bed, and to keep warm. There wasn't much I could do to keep him warm, but we had a big open fireplace, and he spent most of his time on the couch by the fire. It was just a matter of looking after him. He was only with us for about a week or ten days that first time. He went

Darcy Knuckey on the left, and his wife of 74 years, Dallas, on the right: Like many other families in New Zealand during the war, they took in sick and wounded servicemen and helped nurse them back to health. The Knuckeys and Jack Place remained friends until Jack's death in the 1980s.

back to Silverstream, which was the hospital [in Wellington], and then back to the islands.

He made other visits after that and our horse was his attraction. He would get on that horse and ride the five miles to Eltham flat-out. He liked being on a farm where he could be free and easy and away from military life.

Eventually, he was given the job of rounding up deserters, which I don't think he really liked. He spoke often about his wife, who was in Palo Alto [California], and we told him that we hoped we could come and visit him there some day — to meet his wife and son [there is some confusion as to whether he was married at this time]. He never talked about his time on Guadalcanal — not much, no.

The women found Jack very attractive. I had a friend in Wellington, who liked Jack a lot. I think she met him at our place. If anything, he didn't chase the girls; it was the other way around. He was aloof from romance, but whether it was because he was married, I don't know.

One thing I can remember was when we went to Palo Alto, after we had been out on a cruise ship. We flew from Honolulu to San Francisco. I can recall so well when Anne [Jack's wife] was getting our breakfast that first morning. She came out with a little teapot. She said, "I bought this especially for you, but would you please tell me how to make a cup of tea?"

I'll never forget that; it seemed so strange. I thought that was just great! Ann took me out shopping, and Jack took Darcy out to play golf.

DARCY: I played golf with a couple of colonels and a General Binns [sp?] at a golf course at the Presidio [San Francisco]. He was a very nice chap, but he died later on in a car accident. Jack was still in the marines [a later photo shows him in an army uniform]. He had become a lieutenant colonel.

DALLAS: When Jack was with us [in NZ] he never talked about the islands. He talked about what he wanted to do when the war was over. He came back to visit us [in NZ] after the war, but I don't remember what year. It might have been 1947.

DARCY: I think the only time we saw him was during the war. I don't think he came back after the war. He developed emphysema, and the last time we saw him at his home he was dragging an oxygen bottle around behind him.

DALLAS: He was a very sick boy at the end of his life. We never heard when he died.

13. The Names in the Hat: Ngaire Baker Duncan

Ngaire Baker was born in 1924 in Blenheim, South Island, New Zealand. Her father, Walter Eric Baker, was born in Dartford Kent, England, in 1891 and died in 1967. When he first arrived in New Zealand he managed sheep stations with names such as Hakataramea, Orielton, and Geniti. He eventually left farming for the city lights and did any number of different kinds of work, including that of door-to-door salesman.

Ngaire's mother, Winifred Lea Draper, was born in Blenheim in 1901 and died in 1979. She was almost the opposite of her husband in that she was a professional pianist and sang in the opera. These differences, plus the fact that Walter Baker had a gambling habit, may have lead to the eventual breakup of the marriage in 1938.

Ngaire was fifteen when New Zealand declared war on Germany in 1939, and spent the war years in Wellington, where her mother and other families took in servicemen in order to give them a semblance of home life when they were not training for coming battles. Her mother took in, not only American servicemen, but Kiwis, Brits, and even men from Holland. A brimmed U.S. Marine Corps hat was kept at the house, and visiting servicemen signed their name in it almost as a substitute guest book. The story that follows is a story about a few of the names in that hat, and especially about one U.S. Marine, John "Jack" Erskine Place, who brought the hat to the Baker house and was special then and always in the life of Ngaire Baker, who now lives in Australia.

My father, known as Ben, came from England to New Zealand when he was a young man. He went to South Island and managed sheep stations for some time. My mother, known as Winnie, was born in Blenheim. She was a professional pianist and played for the silent films at the Palace Picture House in Blenheim. She was also a soprano and sang in many light operas, as well as in the Anglican Church choir.

Ngaire Duncan (née Baker) and John "Jack" Erskine Place: Jack, a U.S. Marine, survived the war but his relationship with Ngaire did not.

My father left the farming life for the city "delights" and worked as a door-to-door salesman for the Electrolux Company. My mother and father married in Blenheim in 1921. My mother was seven months pregnant at the time, and my brother, Brian, was born in December of that year.

The family moved to Dunedin later, where my sister Rae was born in 1927. Sometime later, we moved back to Blenheim, and also [spent] some time in Picton. We went from one boarding house to another. I started school in Blenheim, but also remember attending school in Picton, where we boarded again. Then back to Blenheim, another boarding house and eventually renting a house at 88 Maxwell Road.

My mother left my father in 1938, when I was fourteen, and took Rae and me to Lower Hutt to her sister's place, where I attended Hutt Valley High School. My mother took me out of school when I turned fifteen, so that I could work to help in our support.

In 1939, when war broke out, my mother, sister and I had just moved to Webb Street. American troop ships began to arrive in Wellington around 1942, as my photos are dated. I was nineteen and worked as a sales person in a department store — Kircaldie and Steines, on Lambton Quay. I worked there for about six months, and then went to RKO Radio Pictures on Willis Street. I loved to dance, having been trained by my aunt, Eva Draper, a dancing teacher. That was my passion. I had many New Zealand boyfriends, but nothing serious.

I remember the real threat to New Zealand was the likely invasion of the Japs, which sent fear and panic to the women who were left alone, their men having enlisted and either in camp or very soon to go overseas. I remember my mother saying the safest place would be in Queen Charlotte Sound — Picton, South Island. We knew it well, having spent many holidays there from Blenheim.

Most of the men in my office enlisted, leaving the women to run the show. The manager, W.W. Duff, was too old to enlist. Some of the girls had boyfriends who enlisted, so as each one went there were great farewells either at the railway station if they were going from Auckland, or down at the docks if they were leaving from Wellington. And then the letters; there was great joy when these arrived, and of course shared with all in the office.

Changing jobs at that time was risky. You had to have a jolly good reason, or you could be made to work in an "essential industry," like hospitals of all kinds, certain engineering, laundries and even cigarette manufacturing.

My friend and I volunteered to work in a cigarette factory in Courtenay Place after our day jobs, and we sat at a conveyor belt and stripped the leaves off the tobacco stalks. We used to joke that our war effort was stripping.

One of the essential industries was on the land — farming — and many women joined up as "Land Girls." These girls were given uniforms, so they could go to the service clubs when they were on leave in town.

Then the Yanks came! We must not forget that if it had not been for the American forces in the Pacific, we might well have had a Japanese invasion. Social clubs opened up in Wellington, namely the ANA (Army, Navy, Air Force), Webbies and the Spinsters, enabling them [servicemen] to meet the locals in a safe environment. At the time, hotel bars closed at 6 P.M. Ladies only could join these clubs under very strict conditions, signing a register at the door. They were to provide a safe and friendly environment for the girls and the forces. They were open several nights a week, and I think Saturday afternoon.

Hot and cold drinks were available, as well as cakes and sandwiches at the evening dances. The girls all had to wear evening dress to the dances and were not allowed to leave the premises on the arm of a man. So if I made a date, we met up the road. Alcohol was banned at these clubs, and if someone seemed a bit tipsy when they arrived they were refused entry. No hanky-panky here, please!

At public dances like the Majestic Cabaret on Willis Street, there was plenty of alcohol, and girls were persuaded to hide the bottles under their coats, as the girls were never frisked.

The Yanks were very popular because they were so polite and respectful, and they treated women like they were precious — always a corsage when dating, cigarettes, silk stockings, chocolates, and fur coats! Not every girl got a fur coat — probably only girlfriends of officers. I just remember it as a bit of a joke as to what they had to do to get one. I will say the American forces were paid a lot more than our servicemen and could spend up large on the girls. It was always a sore point with our boys, and there were many fights.

One Christmas Day, a troop ship docked in Wellington, and the men were all allowed off, but had to walk from the ship through the city, up Willis Street, across Webb Street (where we lived), down Cuba Street, and along Oriental Bay — one long, continuous stream of servicemen. People came out of their homes and gave them food and drinks. Christmas cake was popular, and we cut ours up and held out the plate for them.

I was dancing with a marine at the ANA when I looked up as a marine was walking around the mezzanine, looking down at the dancing. When our eyes met, I said to myself, "I'm going to marry you," and he followed my gaze, came down the stairs, made his way through the dancers, tapped my partner on the shoulder and said, "Excuse me." He took me in his arms and said, "Was that right?"

I said very shyly and with a beating heart, "Yes."

We chatted, had a cup of tea and left separately. We met up the road, and he walked me home — a ten-minute walk to Webb Street. We sat on the steps, talking. It was though we were meant to be. For me anyway, there was an instant bond, something at that age I did not fully understand. We were soon seriously in love, and that is where my mother stepped in, trying all sorts of ways to get us to stop seeing each other.

"These boys are only after one thing (it was never referred to as sex). They will all leave and go home and forget you. You are too young to know what love is, and you are too young to get married. He will never come back and get you." All the while my mother continued to allow him to call and take me out.

One time we all went to Queen Charlotte Sound for a holiday, and Mum invited Jack and John De Vall [one of the names in the hat] to come with us. Jack and I were walking along the beach, when we came across a mass of lilies growing wild. He picked a huge bunch for me, and John took a photo.

Jack took me to see the Knuckeys (see previous oral history). We had fun on the farm, riding horses — a first time for me, and I managed to stay on.

One day Jack and John met me after work. Jack was very upset about something. As we walked, he told me he had sent to his aunt for her to send an engagement ring for me, but somehow between leaving Silverstream and getting to me, he had lost it. So he said that as it had arrived safely, he would get his aunt to send the real one, the one his mother wore.

THE HAT: Jack found the hat in the street as he was coming up to my place, and he signed it as a kind of statement of ownership. It was always in our living room, so became a focus of amusement, and everyone signed it for fun. Some who signed it would have been buddies who came with the ones we actually knew and who came often for the family atmosphere. My mother was a very friendly person and loved to cook.

My brother was in the New Zealand Air Force, and often came home on leave, with or without permission, so he met most of the boys as well.

My mother dated one of the names in the hat, Sherman Laudermilk. Then she met an Australian airman, Alan Andrews, who played a trumpet in a band. They dated for some time, but my mother never married again. Then, of course, Jack and I were an item.

I do not remember most of the names in the hat, as they came and went. The ones I went dancing with are the ones I remember most. Charles Tecklenburg, Robert Johnson, Pep Martin, Bob Conrad and Wade Ackinson were all good dancers.

A bit about Jack: His parents were killed in a car accident when he was young, and he and his brother, Eugene, were brought up by his aunt. Jack was studying to become a lawyer when war broke out and he was either drafted or enlisted in the marines. He had a girlfriend in the States, but they were not engaged.

After the ring episode, I had another upset with my mother, who was trying to get me to stop seeing Jack. I told her about the ring, but of course she did not believe any of it. She managed to wear me down, and one night I told Jack that I did not love him and would not see him again.

It was a terrible night. We were both crying and not believing what I was saying. I eventually left home and went to live with my Aunt Eva in Lower Hutt, and Jack and I resumed our romance, but he was very cautious, never mentioning marriage again. I had hurt him so cruelly, and he said that we would keep in touch, but that if ever I went back to my mother's he would never contact me ever, and he kept his word.

Jack eventually left New Zealand on a ship from Auckland. I went up to see him off and that was the last time I saw him. I was heartbroken, lonely and confused. And after months of no letters, people began taunting me about him being just another marine here for a good time.

I left Wellington for Auckland, a city in which I knew no one. I was boarding with a family and met a man who fancied me. He said if I married him he would take care of me. That's what I did. I did not even know his age, and I did not know he was a gambler (horses), and two weeks before we married he put his shirt on the nose of a horse that ran second. The name of the horse was "Cross Roads." It was a loveless marriage and ended after two years, when I came back to Wellington, and resumed my life as a single woman. I married twice later, with a daughter from each marriage. These marriages also ended.

The Knuckeys kept in touch with Jack, and he followed what I was doing through them. Six years after leaving New Zealand, he married Anne and I think they had a son. That's when the Knuckeys visited him. He became a lieutenant colonel, and sometime in the 1960s Dallas Knuckey wrote to me to say Jack and Anne were making a visit to New Zealand, and Jack was hoping to see me. But it never happened, because his doctor wouldn't allow him to fly. He had emphysema. He was a smoker, as they all were during that time.

I can't remember the year that the Knuckeys wrote to tell me that Jack had died. Maybe it was in the 1980s. I suppose Anne would have informed them.

Those war years in Wellington were, for me, the best time of my life. The boys who came to our house never spoke about the war or what they had endured. Some, including Jack, suffered from malaria, having been in the jungles of Guadalcanal. The navy men would have endured a few horrors as well, but never spoke about them either. They lived for the day, spent up large, and enjoyed every minute of every day, probably knowing that when they eventually left New Zealand it could all end very suddenly.

Some years later, I went to Hawaii and visited Pearl Harbor, and the shrine to the men who lost their lives when Pearl Harbor was bombed by the Japs. Oh, dear, I really felt as though I had been there at the time; it was so realistic and moving.

14. Maori Elder:
Georgina Kiripuai Aomarere

When U.S. forces first arrived in New Zealand early in the war, there were tensions between Americans, especially those from Southern states, and Maori. There were racial slurs, fights, and at least one full-blown riot. As a result, prominent members of the Maori community, especially Princess Te Puea of the Waikato region, made efforts to soften American attitudes and bring some understanding of Maori culture to Americans serving in New Zealand.

Although Georgina Kiripuai Aormarere was Maori, her experiences were anything but confrontational as she recalls those heady days when the U.S. Marine Corps stormed New Zealand.

Aomarere was born in 1916, in Otaki, North Island, New Zealand. She is of the Iwi Ngati Raukawa, Hapu Ngati Huia, Marae Katihiku, on her father's side, as well as six other Marae, if one includes her mother's ancestry. Her father's name was Whitu Aomarere, and her mother's name was Rahapa Reupena. Her father and oldest brother died during the pandemic that followed World War I, when Aomarere was only two years old.

Aomarere was the youngest of seven children, and all of her siblings had grown up by the time she started to school. She didn't start primary school until she was seven years of age, and attended Otaki Primary for six years before continuing her education at a boarding school. However, because of the Depression, she ended her formal education after two years at boarding school. After the war, she had a child and worked for a garment factory for thirty years before retiring.

There was a reason why I didn't start school until I was seven years old; my mother told me that because I was such a naughty girl that if I went to school I would get the strap all the time. Of course, she scared the wits out of me and so naturally I didn't want to go to school. She was a person who didn't believe in corporal punishment. She was a person who tried to scare you out of your wits by telling you what you should be doing and shouldn't be doing, and how naughty you were and all.

Luckily, a girl from across the roadway said to me, "Why don't you want to go to school?"

I said, "Because Mother said I was naughty, and if I went to school the teacher would spank me all the time."

She said, "Oh, look, the teacher won't spank you because you're a nice girl." So that is how I started to school, and the first day I thought any minute the teacher was going to rush up to me and whack me! But as each hour passed and it came to playtime, nobody had hit me. Lunchtime came, and I went home for lunch and told Mama, "Nobody has hit me yet, so I guess they don't know you."

The day went by, and I thought, "Oh, what a wonderful place, and all this time I thought...." Yes, I thought school was the most wonderful place, and after that [first day] I would be up at cockcrow and be ready for school. I thought school was a fantastic place!

After primary school, I went away to boarding school, but it was the Depression, and my mother couldn't afford it, so I only went for two years. I came home, but there were no jobs — no work at all — so I was home for nearly two years before I found a job at the princely sum of twenty-five cents a day.

Living was quite different in those days. People didn't always have jobs. You know, there was an abundance of seafood — plenty of fish to catch — and everyone had big gardens, so that's how we lived. Where we lived, there was an acre-and-a-quarter, and we had a draft horse and a cart. We would collect wood and seafood and things like that. The horse would graze in the front of the house, and the whole of the back part we had in vegetables. And in the back of our section there was a creek with nice clean water, and you could catch eels. Eels are very good food to eat, and down at the beach we could get shellfish — *pipi* and *tohemunga*.

I give people three chances to pronounce a Maori word correctly. If after the third chance they persist in mispronouncing it, that's when I tell them off. Maybe because you weren't born in New Zealand I might give you one extra chance. This is what I noticed about Americans; if I said, "Would you mind if I told you the correct way to pronounce that word?" "No ma'am," they would say.

To me, that was a very courteous thing. I tell *Pakeha* people, "Look, if you were living in any other country in the world — France, Italy, wherever — and you mispronounced their words, you wouldn't be very popular."

My mother died in 1947. She was a slim little woman, and very hard working. My father was a Roman Catholic and my mother was an Anglican, but we were all baptized Roman Catholics, and the nuns used to come around every year and say, "It would be nice if Georgina would come to the convent school." And my mother, with the best of intentions, would say, "Yes, I will send her to the convent school next year."

That's what she hoped I would do, but when it came time, I would say, "No, no; I'm not going there."

When the war started, I was working at the sanitarium for people with tuberculosis. That was 1939, and I worked there for four years. The matron used to refer to us as "scrubbers," which I didn't think was very nice, but anyway....

First of all, I went to work in the laundry, and then I became a part-time launderer and [part-time] scrubber. Then I came to the most exalted position — "second cook." Relieving cook — that is what I actually was — a relieving cook.

The cook worked from six in the morning until ten [in the morning], and after that I came in and the Maori patients said to me, "If we go out and get some *puha* [eatable thistle], will you make it for us for tea [the afternoon meal]?"

I said, "All right," and then the other patients said, "Usually on Mondays we have grilled chops for our tea, could we have some chips as well?"

I said, "Well, I'll try."

And then they said, "Can we have pikelets [small pancakes]?" So I had a very busy time, indeed, but I thought it was worth it because never having been sick or in hospital I could just imagine how boring it would be if you knew that every week, well, on Monday you were going to have this or that. It would be nice to have a little change — a nice little surprise.

The cook's bedroom was just above the kitchen, and she would be the first one to smell the pikelets. She would come down and say I was a mug — a fool — for making those pikelets. She would say, "You know, you are supposed to be taking time off," and then she would go back to her room with a half dozen pikelets to have with her tea.

Then on the days when I went back to being a scrubber, the patients would say, "Ah, look, that was so lovely; those grilled chops and those chips..."

The first time I ever met a marine, my girlfriend and I — we had been saving up and went on a shopping spree. We bought the very latest in coats, ones with epaulettes. We both had these on and were walking up to the hall by the railway station. There was a big dance on there. Some Americans in a jeep stopped and said they were looking for the dance but had lost their way.

We told them that they had passed it, but if they turned around and went back they would find it. Then they asked us where we were going, and we said, "Well, that's where we are going." And they offered to give us a ride in the jeep. Fantastic, a ride in a jeep!

They thought we were dressed quite nice. I don't know, maybe they thought we would be in grass skirts or something. Then one of them asked, "Are you May-ories?"

"Yes," I said, "but do you mind if I correct your pronunciation?"

"No, ma'am."

I said, "It's not May-orie; it's Maori."

My friend had much lighter skin than I, and one of them said, "Are you both Maori?"

I said, "Yes."

They were very polite, and we went to the dance with them; and that was a bit of all right. They had a Marine Corps band playing. Oh, that was fantastic music. And from then on we thought the marines were a bit of all right. They were different from New Zealand men that we had any contact with in a romantic way — lovely flowers and chocolates, and they told you how beautiful you were. It was a very nice time.

In 1943, my friend and I left the sanitarium and decided to join the army. We thought all we had to do was send in our names and in a couple of weeks, at the most, they would call us up, but that's not what happened. In the meantime, we ran out of money, so we had to go look for another job.

There was a man looking for people to pick flowers to send to the market. It was a cold job; it was in the middle of winter. We asked him if we could begin about an hour later because frost is on the flowers, and it was cold.

"It's mind over matter," he said. "If it is cold, you say, 'I'm not cold, I'm hot.'"

We decided we weren't going to stay there any longer, so we went to work for a Chinese gardener, and he was a real dear. Each day, he would go uptown and buy us a madeira cake — just a plain cake — and cook us a meal.

Then I went to stay with my sister for the weekend, and she said, "Why don't you come and work here?" She had just started working at Willis Tobacco Factory. That was in Petone. Well, I thought I would just work there until I was called into the army. But after I started working in the tobacco factory, they made it an "essential industry."

It was an essential industry, absolutely, because every month we had to send tobacco to the boys overseas, so I wasn't allowed to leave, and I hated working there. I stayed there until the war was over. But that's where all the action was — lots of marines!

Now, if you had a date with a marine, this is what you had to do: From the time you got to the factory, you had to tell the matron, "Oh, I'm not feeling well. I have this pain in my stomach, and a headache. I don't feel a bit well." So when 5 o'clock came around, you couldn't get home fast enough. You had to wash your hair to get the tobacco smell out of your hair, get yourself all together, and hop on the train.

At the factory, there were six of us working at a table, three on one side and three on the other. We were stemming tobacco leaves, and there was an Italian lady there.

I said to her, "Maria, tonight I am going to the pictures with an American Marine, and he's Italian." And she said, "Ah, ver-ry nice."

I said, "Would you tell me something very nice to say in Italian?"

She said, "Ye-es, Ye-es; I tell you something. When you see Amer-rican, you tell him, '*Dame un bacio.*'"

I said, "That's not swearing, is it?"

"Oh, no, no, no; I no tell you swearing."

So when I saw him, I told him that I work with an Italian lady, and I told her I was coming to the pictures with you tonight. I asked her if she would tell me something to say to you, and this is what she told me, "*Dame un bacio.*"

"Any day," he said. It meant, give me a kiss.

I used to come home every Friday to see my mother, because while I was away to work she was alone. So, I would come home on weekends to mow the lawn and things like that. And in those days, not many girls drank liquor. When we went to parties, it was to sing and have a good time. If we drank, it was lemonade, or something like that. I'm not saying that people didn't drink. The men did, but very few girls did.

Anyway, I invited this one marine home with me one weekend. His name was Eugene, and he was from Texas. I don't know if he was killed in the war, but he was here for a while. My mother wasn't very happy about my bringing him home, not at first anyway. I think she was a bit nervous, but after she got to know him she thought he was a very nice person, and had no objection to my going out with him. He came back only one other time, because the rest of the time I was in Petone. But there was a Marae down there called *Tainui*, and they used to have parties there for the marine they had become friendly with.

I don't have a nasty thing to say about Americans, because they were always very polite to us and treated us very well. I know other people may have had different ideas about them, but I'm just going by what I saw.

I think there was some green-eyed jealousy. There were some [New Zealand] men who worked on the railway at McKay Crossing, and the marines would whiz past in their jeeps. I think one of the marines must have said something, because when they came by again, one of the workers pulled down his pants and slapped his ass. So after that, when the marines drove by they would yell at the workers, "Black ass! Black ass!"

I don't think some of the Maori men were too happy about Maori women going out with the marines, but when you went out with a marine they brought you flowers and treated you as if you were someone special.

If a Maori boy wanted to take you to the pictures, he might say, "See you inside."

Things got very quiet after the Americans left. It was very exciting when they were here, you know, especially in a small place like Otaki, because you didn't really go far from your area in those days. It wasn't like now when people have cars.

One of the things that happened to me after the war was I became pregnant and had a child, but not by a marine. I think I should tell you this because if my daughter should read this she might think that her mum is ashamed of her. She was born in 1946, and my mother died in 1947, so I didn't have a very easy time of it.

15. The Nurse:
Louise Heffer Carkeek

Carkeek was born in Hastings, Hawke's Bay, on the east coast of North Island in 1922. She grew up on a farm as so many Kiwis did, being that New Zealand's primary economy was agriculture. And although New Zealand has diversified greatly since the war, it is still very much agrarian. Living in a rural area, which so much of New Zealand still is, Carkeek took correspondence courses until the age of ten. In order to go on to college, or high school, as it is known in the U.S., she had to take a "Leaving Certificate," and in order to do that she had to go to a Maori mission school to take the exams. Having passed her exams, she then had to travel thirty-five miles by train each day to the nearest district high school in Waipawa. And in order to get to the train station, she had to ride horseback for six miles, morning and evening. Classes started at 9 o'clock in the morning, but the train didn't get in until 9:30, which meant that Carkeek, and others like her, had thirty minutes taken off her lunch hour in order to catch up. She did this for five years.

After graduation from high school, Carkeek was accepted for training as a nurse at Wellington Hospital in 1939, just after war had started in Europe. Her boyfriend, later husband—Huia Tahiwi Carkeek—was half Maori and served with New Zealand forces during the war, but did not go overseas. He was a member of the Raukawa Marae. They had four children together, and Carkeek continued with her nursing career after the war and retired in 1975. She lives in Otaki, North Island, where there were a large number of U.S. Marine Corps camps in 1942-43.

Thirty of us girls arrived for training. We stayed in a hotel near the hospital that had been commandeered by the government after war had started. I think the first group of Americans arrived [in Wellington] in early 1942. They were a very young lot — not very old. A [American] camp was formed, and besides our nursing duties we were asked to give time to the American club on Willis Street. We used to give two hours to

Louise Heffer Carkeek, and her then boyfriend — later husband — Huia Tahiwi Carkeek. Louise was a nurse during and after the war. Huia served in the New Zealand Army, but did not go overseas.

wait on tables. We did that twice a month, but sometimes we were too tired.

One of my girlfriends became engaged to one of those marines, but he was killed on Guadalcanal. She had a baby by him. She [Sonya Davies] later became a member of parliament, and wrote a book called *Bread and Roses*.

During the war years here, there were restrictions on drinking — women drinking in hotels. I think it was 1940 when a law was passed changing that, but I know Maori women were still not allowed to drink in hotels.

There was this episode with my husband; his sister was much darker than him, and he invited her and her girlfriend into the Waterloo Hotel, and the barman said, "I can give you a drink but not the girls."

My husband said, "Why not? She's my sister." So they were asked to leave the hotel, but my husband wouldn't leave. But in general, women didn't drink much in those days; it wasn't the thing to do. It wasn't womanly.

I remember when I passed my first state exam when I was training as a nurse; the girls said, "Let's go out and celebrate." Well, I had never had a glass of alcohol of any kind, and when it came time to asking me

120

what I was going to have, all I could think of was what I had read in books, so I ordered a martini. It was all I could think of, and it was the most awful drink I have tasted.

There was some discrimination against Maori at the time, and then some. When I got married, my family wouldn't accept it because my husband was Maori. They came around in the end, and my husband was doing all of my mother's finances. But no Maori worked in banks, and any government job was quite difficult to get for Maori. There were no unions for women, and it wasn't until after the war when the first hospital to go on strike was in Hastings. Sonya Davies was one of the first to fight for unions for women.

You know, we had very strict rules. Our matron was particular about meeting these American boys before we went out with them. Later, some of us were sent to Otaki to nurse. The marines used to come into Otaki a lot, and the old picture theater, which was down by the railway, was made into a dance hall. Invitations were always sent to the nurses' home for us to go to these dances, and our matron used to go through the invitations to see who had sent them before we could accept, and our home was out of bounds to the marines.

A special van would be sent to pick us up to take us to the dance hall, and there we would meet the marines who had sent the invitations, and they had to be there to meet us. There were many, many happy times I had there in the dance hall. Some of them [the marines] asked me to marry them, but I was engaged and my boyfriend was away in the New Zealand Army. We also had big barbecues on the beach. Those were happy times too, with big singsongs.

We had a group of nurses who formed a musical group. Two of them in the group were Maori girls by the name of Keepa — Thelma and Erina. Thelma had the most beautiful singing voice, and Erina was a fabulous pianist. We had these evenings at the nurses' home and the matron said the girls could invite their boyfriends to some of these evenings around the piano, and some of these girls had boyfriends who were marines, but they were closely supervised. But then there was an episode and the marines were not allowed to come to the nurses' home after that.

Evidently, one of the marines — and I don't know all the details, because we weren't told — attacked a nurse, and she was quite badly beaten. She had a lot of facial injuries. He had used his belt on her. So from then on all the marines were banned from coming to the nurses' home.

The marines knew that we were strictly supervised, so they would hide in the lupin [a tall weed] at night and wait for the nurses to get off work, and the lupins were quite high, and thick too. And of course during that period, we didn't have torches [flashlights], and no lights at night. Electricity was for daylight because of the Japanese being out to sea — blackouts. After daylight, we had these jam cans cut down, with candles inside them and the nurses would go out into the lupine with these, looking for their boyfriends. In fact, we lost one of our patients in the lupine one night — a little Negro man — and here were all the nurses and porters with their jam tins out looking in the lupine for him. He had been a resident in New Zealand for some time. There were quite a number of Negroes in New Zealand at that time. They had come out to work in the mines. He was one of our geriatric patients, and one of the things he used to do at sunset was sing Negro spiritual songs.

There was another girl in the home, Frances Ngatere, who unbeknownst to us had developed TB — tuberculosis. I contracted tuberculosis and was in hospital for about five months, and then I was asked to go home to recuperate. While I was away, Frances died.

We had what they called the "military block" at the Wellington Hospital, which were wards twenty and twenty-two. Also, there was the American hospital there where most of the [American] patients went, but if they had complications they were sent to the public hospital, and they were the worst injured.

There was one case that was really sad to me. He had lost one arm and one leg; he was a marine. He had lost his brother, as well, but he was the most happy-go-lucky guy. He came from Pennsylvania, and all he wanted to do was go back home to his mother and get help for his wounds.

Sometimes, we had American nurses come in to experience nursing at our hospital. They wanted to catch up on our methods, I think, and then they would go back to their hospital at Silverstream.

At one time, I went to the hospital in Auckland, and there I nursed some Americans, but they were army. A lot of them had skin problems. Some of them were caused by ticks. You have to remember that antibiotics had just come in about then. Some had wounds that were infected, and they took a terrific long time to heal.

We worked long hours. We were so exhausted that we just fell into bed. Looking back, my whole life [then] revolved around my work — what was going on in the hospital.

A lot of the marines I knew in the Otaki area were friendly with the Maori girls. One I knew in Hawke's Bay married a marine. She was a very pretty girl. Another one was here [in Otaki], Petel Webster — I don't know if they ever became engaged before he went away.

John V. "Baldy" Harwell was a marine that came back to New Zealand in 1975, and had a big dinner in a local hotel for the Maori family that took him in. He had become friendly with my in-laws, and they had taken him in [during the war]. He was with them for about three weeks, and he never forgot the kindness that was given to him. He stayed with us for a fortnight, and he told me that when he left New Zealand [after the war], he went back to his hometown in Texas, where he set up a pretzel factory, and that is how he made his money.

He seemed to be on a lot of boards — head of a bank. He opened the hotel for all of the town [Otaki]. He also gave my husband $1,000, and told him to distribute it in the town however he felt. My husband gave half of it to the church and half to the Marae. He [Harwell] took two of my husband's sisters for a trip right through South Island, and paid for everything. He said it was a thank-you to my husband's parents who had since passed away.

When he [Harwell] came back — I think it was in 1988 [the second time] — we gave him a thank-you party at the local Returned Servicemens Club, and I think he realized that that was his farewell to New Zealand, because he never came back again. We kept in contact for a number of years, and then I guess he must have died.

The Americans brought in a lot of Camel cigarettes, I can tell you that, and chocolate. And another thing that they gave to the nurses were silk stockings, and if you could acquire silk stockings, that was like a piece of gold.

I also thought Americans were very courteous, and perhaps more generous than our New Zealand men. I think that was mainly because our men had been through a depression, and a lot of unemployment, and that is why they were very careful with their money. But the Americans were also different in that they gave flowers and gifts, and they were more outgoing. New Zealand men were more reserved. Maybe it was the way in which they had been brought up. I don't think you could blame them for being so reserved; I think it was part of the times — Victorian attitudes.

Some donut houses — something we never had before in New Zealand — were opened just to accommodate the Americans. And New Zealanders opened their homes to the Americans. I didn't have much opportunity to go home because of my work, but my parents did take in some American boys for two or three weeks, and I must say that they [the Americans] were grateful for what was done for them. I mean they were only young boys. They had happy times in New Zealand, but they knew it was temporary, and I don't think they really knew what they were going into when they left here. So many of them lost their lives. They were very homesick — a lot of them — and a lot of them have come back on reunion trips.

16. From Whangamomona to Wellington: Wyn Muirson Stockwell

Wyn Stockwell was born in 1917, in Manaia, a small farming town in the south Taranaki region of North Island, New Zealand. Her father immigrated to New Zealand from Bedfordshire, England, in the latter part of the nineteenth century, and her mother came to New Zealand from Melbourne, Australia. Stockwell's father bought land in Whangamomona, which at the time was bush, and hacked a stock and dairy farm out of it. The only access to Whangamomona in the early days was a dirt track. People and supplies going in, and farm products going out, had to rely on horses pulling sledges, not wagons. Later, much later, those dirt tracks were replaced by dirt roads. The road that leads to Whangamomona today is paved and known as the Forgotten Highway; and like many other towns in New Zealand, it boasted a much larger population during the brief years that small family farms made up the region. Today, the population is less than fifty.

Stockwell left Whangamomona for the big city of Wellington in 1940, in order to start her nurse's training. She trained and worked in Wellington throughout the war years, and after the war — in 1945 — was posted to Fiji, where she worked in a tuberculosis hospital for two years. She then lived and worked in Australia for a number of years before returning to Wellington to work. Some years later, she moved to New Plymouth, where she had family. The farm in Whangamomona had been sold years before.

My mother's father came over from the north of Ireland. He was a schoolmaster, and went around New Zealand teaching in various schools. There were no high schools in those days, and very few [grade] schools. So he went around from school to school, and ended up in Whangamomona. In those days in New Zealand, the schoolteacher would pick out the brightest pupils and educate them sufficiently that they could then be called "pupil teachers," and that had to suffice until New Zealand got high schools and universities, which came many years later. You see my parents came out here in the later part of the nineteenth century.

There were ten children in my family, and I was the eighth. But remember, there was a war [World War I] and then a slump — the Great Depression — and then another war, so there was very little progress financially. It would have been all right had the government kept its promise to give access to the back country, but there was only a track to our property. To get produce out you had to have access, so it was a lost cause really for the twenty-eight or thirty years that my family lived there.

When the Labor Party came into power in 1935, Bob Semple was the Minister of Roads, and he said, "The back country farmers will now get access to their property." They were then able to get a four-wheel-drive vehicle over the road. It was just a mud road. Before then, you could only get in and out on horseback; and the cream, which would come out three or four times a week, was brought out on a sledge.

My mother was a teacher, and after many years of trying, persuaded the government — Mr. Polson, the Minister of Education from Stratford — to finally give her a school built on our property. It was one room and held five or six desks. It was registered as the Astwood School. That would have been in 1910—1912 — something like that. Astwood was the capital of Bedfordshire in England. So I went to school there until I was about nine.

The railroad came through in 1931, and there were about 2,000 or 3,000 people in Whangamomona at the time. Films used to come once a month. Somebody would come with a projector, and put a film on. And I recall very clearly when I was about twelve or thirteen; there was a wonderful film with Grace Moore with a

Wyn Stockwell grew up in the small farming town of Whangamomona, which was hacked out of native bush by European settlers. In 1940, she left the only life she knew to study nursing in Wellington.

beautiful voice — an American film. The film was *One Night of Love*. It was very romantic, very lovely. We were five miles out on an awful road, and I had to nag my mother until she took me.

There were shops: a butcher and a baker, a hotel, tennis courts, and a Ministry of Works that looked after the roads — that's all gone. We were all big families in those days out there. We were not the only family with ten. Every family had ten or twelve [children]; some even had more.

Once the war broke out that all died. The men went away, but strange as it may seem, wars always bring prosperity. The next-door [neighbor] bought our farm, and so it went on; and people started having [only] two or three children. So naturally villages like Whangamomona died. The population of Whangamomona now is about forty.

War was declared in 1939, and I went to [nursing] school with a class of eighty in Wellington. It [Wellington] was a bombshell for me, a country bumpkin. I had had a very free and lovely life in Whangamomona, and then suddenly going to a city like Wellington was quite a shock, and I think the Americans coming was another big shock. Our boys had all gone, or most of them anyway. I think we — about eight of us — were going to the Majestic Theater — to a film — and all these Americans swarmed towards us. They wanted to take us to the film. We were scared stiff! No, no, no!

That was my first encounter with the lovely American boys. I met with some of them later, of course. I did have one good friend, and I think his name was Dale, but it was nothing serious. I used to write to his mother. He was probably killed in action.

There were a lot of dark boys amongst those Americans, and there were a mighty lot of little babies born to them. I used to go on duty [at the hospital] at night. There was a certain place they [the babies] were kept, because they were up for adoption. I don't know what became of them. We were so busy; we were so short of staff, because most of our senior staff had gone overseas — our senior nurses. Those of us who had just started our training had to take a lot of responsibility.

We were of an era when [nursing] was a dedication. You went in not for the money, because that was what we never got. We got three pounds a month when I started training. We bought our books and clothing with that, but that was about it. You didn't have any money to get dressed up, but when the Americans came in that was lovely. It was absolutely lovely! Cigarettes — goodness me — they seemed to have masses of them, and they would give us masses of them — and silk stockings....

They were wonderfully generous, and there was one other thing about the Americans; if you had a pram, they all had to stop and see what you had in the pram. They seemed very interested in children. Yes, that is something I remember about them — something very nice about them.

There was a lot of misery too. People were not faithful — a lot were not. It's all a bit hazy now, but I can remember stories about people who had sent their engagement rings back or wrote Dear John letters. There were girls I was training with who said, "I'm writing a Dear John letter," but we were young and I don't think it always hit home what that entailed. And there were women who were not faithful to their husbands while they were overseas.

In 1943, a lot of our boys came home on a rest period, and a lot of them didn't want to go back. They felt that the Americans had sort of taken their place, but what they forgot was that if they [the Americans] hadn't come we would have had a bunch of almond-eyed children around us. The Japanese were perilously close to taking over. And there was a lot of fighting; a lot of brawls went on, and I presume that is what it was all about. But it was an equitable time, and we as a country were so grateful.

Having the Americans here during the war changed us. We became — young people became much more outgoing. I think we lost a lot of our sober habits. The Americans were very outgoing — "Come and have a drink at the pub."

We were never allowed to go into a pub. No, women never went into a public bar; it was not allowed. It was the old English way of women behaving. The Americans didn't change the law; they just made it all right — nothing wrong with it.

The first time I went into a pub, I was invited, and I felt most uncomfortable; and it wasn't an American who invited me. But I think the Americans had that different attitude to life from ours. We were prim and proper, definitely.

When we first went to training, we had to be in by 8 o'clock. Mind you, we did sneak out now and again — put a dummy in the bed, and down the fire escape. But mostly it was discipline, discipline, discipline; and we accepted that. I don't want to say the Americans changed us, but they did show us that there was another way. They were so friendly and open; that was the difference. And I think since the war years, women have become more liberated, and maybe more militant than they were. Before that men always took the lead. We accepted that.

Women [during the war] became quite liberated in another way. They drove the busses; they drove the trams — things we had never done before the war.

There was an awful lot of osteomyelitis in those days — TB of the bone. TB was rife in those days, and gonorrhea and syphilis; and this was before the Americans came. I will always remember this little boy; he was a beautiful little boy, and he had this painful dressing that had to be done. I can remember saying to him, "Now, which of us would you like to do your dressing?" He was about nine years old, and he said, "Nurse, I can't say because there would only be a fusion."

What he meant was that everyone would get confused.

Another patient, Mary, had been in hospital for twenty-five years. She wouldn't get that now. I don't know what was wrong with her, other than she was the size of a house, and we had to do exactly as she wanted. She was an enormous woman.

Then we had the Japanese prisoners of war out at Featherston. Oh, that uprising they had I remember very clearly indeed. I was on night duty, and coming on duty at 11 o'clock at night and finding all these beady eyes looking at me. They had all been badly knocked about. They couldn't speak English, of course, and they didn't let on if they did. It was the most eerie feeling, because I had never had any dealings with Japanese ever before. We had to care for them; I had to wash them, and they hated that. We had to feed them, get them up, make their bed; but I didn't feel comfortable with them. I didn't like them; I still don't like them. I can't like them, not after what they did to our prisoners of war.

A boy from out the back country, Ron McCarty, was a prisoner of the Germans, and he was badly shot up and mentally very disturbed. He had to be hospitalized for many months after he got home. It was the skeletal look of the men who went away young and beautiful coming home like that. No, I can't like the Japs — sorry about that.

After we finished our [nurse's] training, we owed the hospital a year, so in 1945 six of us were sent to Suva [Fiji] to open a TB hospital, which the Americans had built there at Tamavua. There was another hospital at Lautoka, and other outlying posts, and mostly New Zealand nurses went there. I was there for two years. We went over on a little ship called the *Viti Levu*. We took six days to get there in pounding seas; we were all so ill. We didn't eat anything, because we couldn't.

Marge Haase was a nurse in Fiji, and she got involved with a Maori who was in the air force out at Lauthala Bay, and she was immediately sent back to New Zealand. That is how prim we were, but Marge married her Maori boyfriend.

There was a very strong prejudice in those days. Maori were not allowed in the bars to drink until many years later. Now we fraternize, but there was a class distinction in those days. There is no good in saying there wasn't. We were told very clearly when we went to Fiji, "No fraternization with Fijians or dark fellows, or you will be sent straight home."

There was another incident I can give you. Cliff Adams was a dentist, and he was sent over to Fiji. His wife was part Maori — Diana Wharahuia [sp?]. They were married, but he couldn't bring her. That's how we were. I remember that very clearly — Marge being sent home and Diana not being allowed to come.

17. Farming in Ohura, an Essential Industry During the War: Melvin Alfred "Ike" Watts

Watts was born in 1916, in Taumarunui, on the North Island of New Zealand. He knows little about his father, other than that his father dropped out of school at the age of twelve and went to work as a farmer in Ohura, which was a small town in those days, and even smaller today. And like his father, Watts spent most of his working life in Ohura as a farmer, and during the war years farming was considered an "essential industry" that could keep an individual from serving in the active military. Watts farmed in Ohura until he retired in the 1960s.

Peggy Martin Watts, Ike's wife, immigrated to Ohura from England with her parents at the age of two, and saw little if anything outside the Ohura Valley until her husband sold the farm and moved to New Plymouth.

Ohura, like so many small towns throughout New Zealand, served a population made up mostly of small family farms. Today, there is little left of small farming towns like Ohura, as those small family farms were bought up to make big family farms. As late as 1956, Ohura and environs boasted a population of over 2,000. It had a cinema, a war memorial hall, a bowling club, a rugby league, and a high school. The main road in Ohura remained dirt until it was first sealed in 1951.

After having interviewed Watts, my wife and I drove to Ohura, which is two hours by car northeast of New Plymouth. The last thirty-seven kilometers was on a winding gravel road through the mountains. When we finally arrived in Ohura, we found only one shop open, and that was the general store. The bank had shut down years before and is now the home of a retired pilot whose wife was originally from Ohura. There are a couple of other shops on the one and only main street, but they were closed that day.

Melvin Alfred "Ike" Watts lived most of his life in Ohura. He was able to avoid active military service due to the fact that he was a farmer, and farming fed the soldiers and sailors who did the fighting.

One of the Watts children told me that during the war years conscientious objectors were sent to work in the local coal mines, all of which are now closed. However, the woman and owner of the general store told us that although people are still moving out, the government is looking at reopening the coal mines.

My earliest memories are of riding to school on the back of a horse with my older sister. That lasted for a while until I was old enough to ride me own horse. But I was such a puny little bugger that they took me out of school until I was seven.

We were just country folk, that's all. My father was a dairy farmer — a few sheep. He used to milk eighty to ninety cows in those days. We didn't have any power [electricity] in those days. We used to buy our petrol in four-gallon tins — two tins to a box. That used to come in with the cream cart when they collected our cream. The petrol was to run the milking machines. For light, we used candles and kerosene lamps.

There were no tractors in those [early] days; it was all horse work. Ohura was just a big wide-open street, all mud. There were big stables for the horses and coaches.

Ohura, in those early days, consisted of a shop, a bakery, a butcher; and that was it. But it was a bit of a thriving place; we had our own football teams, and our basketball teams for the girls, and all that; but during the war years all that went. Today, there is nothing left. There is one lousy little store — no bakery, no nothing. It's all gone down the drain.

In the early days every man had a hundred acres, his cow and his pigs; we lived off the land. But as time progressed and the roads got better all these little farms got swallowed up by their next-door neighbor, and then the next-door neighbor, until today Ohura is owned by about three people.

There were hardly any roads in those earlier days, just tracks — bullock wagons and horse coaches. In my day, there were about a hundred families [in Ohura]. Just to give you an idea, as progress went by, at one time we had three school busses running in that area. But when I went to school, I had to go about a mile by horse. I started when I was seven, and left when I was about 12½ or 13. I helped my father on the farm. I stayed at home until I was sixteen. My father leased the one farm and started a "junk farm" on the other side of Ohura — just an unimproved place out in the bush. I took that over and haven't been home since. I took over the working of it. That was my career, you might say — right from the word go — right through to about 1960, I suppose.

The railway came through in the 1930s — early 1930s. Yeah, the railroad came right through from Stratford. It was a big thing, the railway coming through. The tracks are still there, but I can't remember when it stopped running.

We were married in 1938, and it wasn't long after that that the war come along. Almost all the young men from Ohura went, you might say. Some got killed in the war, and some came home. Two of the Risk brothers didn't come back. They [the veterans] scattered when they came home. The government offered them land when they came home.

We were married about twelve months [when the war started], and I was just a one-man band, milking my cows. I never joined [the military]; my brother joined and went and got himself a prisoner of war for three years over in Crete.

Farming was essential work; they wanted all the butter, and all the foodstuffs they could get. I didn't volunteer; I was called up. I went for the medical and all that, and passed all that. In those days, they gave you a form [to fill out] if you wanted to object. So I put in a claim to object — told them I was milking cows. I got out of that, but had to join the Home Guard. We used to have parades in the town, and we used broomsticks for rifles. Yeah, we used to parade up and down the street and so forth.

Eventually, they issued us — some of us — with rifles and just one magazine full of bullets. What the hell were we supposed to do with that?

I guess they reckoned someone would land on the beach out in Mokau, and walk inland over what we called the Waitaangi Road, which was only a bush track in those days. And as the Home Guard, we had to block this road with a big tree, and then hide up in the bush and use sniper tactics. I think only about nine of us got issued with '03 rifles.

The army didn't commandeer any horses [from Ohura] during the war, but they did commandeer a lot of trucks — just took them away, and I don't know that they were compensated.

The local carrier, they took one of his trucks and left him with one. He had two trucks — old Model A Fords. When I say "carrier," he used to get the goods from the train and deliver them around town, and pick up wool bales and take them down to the train. Don Stewart was his name, and that is how he made his living. Everything else we did with horses and wagons in those days.

Now, during the war years Ohura came to life because we had opencast [open-pit] coal mining — three opencast and one underground. There is a lot of coal up there, or round abouts, and they wanted the coal to run the factories; and heating was all coal. And once the train got to Ohura, well they used to send out whole trainloads of coal. They [the coal mines] are all closed now.

We had some Americans come to Ohura on convalescence. There was a family there in Ohura by the name of Borthwicks, and they took in a lot of these boys to spend a holiday and recuperate. I got to know them, but I've forgotten them now.

There was a girl by the name of Flora Borthwick, who married a Percy Gindi. The wife was from Ohura, and he [the husband] must have come from Wellington. They were just outside of where these people were convalescing — these Yankees, we called them. They were a big family — a very motherly family — and they [the Gindis] used to send up some of these boys for a fortnight holiday with Flora's family. They [the Borthwick famly] only lived a half-mile from where we did.

There were a lot of Maori back in there in those days, a lot of Maori. They were mostly laborers. But they have all scattered now; they're all gone. And I had a chance to sell my farm to a next-door neighbor, so I did that and built myself a new house on twenty acres. We were going to retire there, but got sick of that, so we sold that and came here [New Plymouth]. Our life was busy, but nothing spectacular; but I've got my memories.

18. The Lady and the Batsman: Joan Masters

Mrs. Masters was born in 1920, in Napier, a city on the east coast of North Island, New Zealand, and survived the Napier/Hastings earthquake of 1931 that killed over 250 people. Her mother was born in Thames, on the Coromandel Peninsula, North Island, New Zealand, and was a widow when she met and married Joan's father. Joan's father immigrated to New Zealand from Wales shortly after his return to the British Isles, having served in the Boer War. When World War I came along, Joan's father volunteered again, apparently a man who loved the excitement of military service. He was decorated for heroism and made an officer before the war was over.

Before leaving for his second war, he left his wife with a young son, and a daughter was born while he was away. Joan was the youngest of the children in her mother's second marriage. A half brother, Colin, was killed in World War II as a motor torpedo boat captain trying to escape the Japanese as they closed in on Singapore. He was fleeing with a boatload of women and children, none of whom are believed to have survived.

Masters went to school during the early years of World War II, trained as a school dental nurse, and practiced as such throughout the rest of the war in several small towns on the North Island.

Joan dated a young man she met in college by the name of A.O. "Cappy" Masters before he was called up to fight in the war. He trained as a fighter pilot in the Royal Navy Fleet Air Arm, later becoming a "batsman," or what would be called a landing signal officer in the U.S. Navy. In his seventies, "Cappy," as he liked to be called, wrote a book about his life in the military titled The Reluctant Batsman.

Joan and Cappy married in 1945, shortly after his return from the European Theater of war, and only a couple of weeks before he reported to duty aboard HMS Indefatigable, *which made up part of the British Pacific Fleet.*

Cappy left the service soon after Japan surrendered, and took up run-

Joan Masters trained and worked as a school dental nurse during the war. In 1945, she married A.O. "Cappy" Masters, who had been away serving in the Royal Navy Fleet Air Arm, first as a fighter pilot on British aircraft carriers, and then as a "batsman," or landing safety officer. He spent the last year of the war serving as such aboard HMS *Indefatigable* in the Pacific.

ning the family hardware business in Stratford and New Plymouth. Joan, now a widow, lives in New Plymouth, New Zealand.

My father did all sorts of things when he immigrated to New Zealand. He worked in the kauri bush [kauri being a tree native to NZ, and valued for its timber and gum], and managed a store near Dargaville, where they paid in kauri gum for their goods. So he knocked around a bit, and then he met a widow in Thames, who was [to be] my mother.

He had a good brain and rose to become the manager of the Kauri Timber Company. But then the First World War came along, and he loved being a soldier; so he went off to the war, leaving my mother with my brother, who was about twenty-one months old. When he returned, his job at the timber company was gone to somebody else, so he looked through all the newspapers. There was a vacancy for a repatriation officer, settling men who had come back from the war. He got that job and moved to Napier, which my mother hated because she had been living in Thames, with the native forest up behind her. Four years later a position opened for secretary of the Hospital Board, and he was determined to get it. He dashed out and bought some books on accountancy, studied them, and out of a big number of applicants was again successful. He said he walked in like an officer and made a good impression, and he kept that job twenty-five years, until he retired.

The 1920s was a strange sort of decade. Skirts went up above the knees, hats looked like flowerpots, and women smoked long cigarettes; but there were those who were very poor. Around 1929, I have been in houses where the floors were hard polished earth, but beautifully clean. There were people over the road who had very little food, and there were children who came to school, their feet blue with cold. Boys had no underpants, and very few children had a handkerchief; it was very basic.

A lot of men would come around; we would call them "swaggers," or tramps; and my mother always gave to them. They were First World War veterans. Some of them had been affected mentally, probably, but were always well spoken and grateful.

The Napier/Hastings earthquake of 1931: When I was ten, I was at Taradale School. There were about forty children in the room, and it was a wooden building. The teacher said, "Stand, children."

We did, and I remember the scraping of all the desks, and then the

137

floor went up, down, and then sideways. There was the most terrible rumbling noise, and we all went crashing to the floor. We were clawing and fighting each other to get out the door, and I remember a boy yelling out, "It's the end of the world!" And I thought it was. It was 7.9 on the Richter scale.

My father's office was in a beautiful new building — a Spanish/Moorish style, with arches, and it was three stories high. He escaped that day, pulling his typist behind him, but the two young men who worked in the office were killed.

We thought my father was dead, because we had heard that the building had fallen. It was only one year old, but badly built. My brother rode his bike up there, and it was just a heap of rubble. Someone told him that he had not seen my father, but he turned up later at 5 P.M. The earthquake happened at 10:45 A.M. in the morning. He had been organizing the patients from the hospital out to the Green Meadows Racecourse. They were mostly under canvas, and the doctors were already operating under the grandstand. It was wonderful organization. That was in 1931, and the earthquake made the Depression worse for some people because all the chimneys fell, and those who were already poor were badly affected. But Napier rose very quickly, and there was work for everyone, repairing and cleaning up. And when it was rebuilt, it was a beautiful art deco city, and is now very popular with tourists.

I remember coming on 1934 — I was fourteen then — and my mother saying, "Ted" — that was my father — "is very worried about what is going on in Germany." I know that people who read a lot and who were interested in world affairs were worried.

My brother, John — six years older — had six years at high school during the Depression. He was a clever chap, but couldn't get a job anywhere. New Zealand had just started its own air force, RNZAF. Before that, our men had gone to England — to the RAF. About 1936, John joined the air force as a sort of mechanic type, and stayed in for a career. He wasn't a pilot, but went up to the islands during the war, and as an aero-engineer serviced planes almost nonstop. Early in the war, he was transferred to Singapore, and escaped there just ahead of the Japanese.

In 1939, I went to Wellington to train as a school dental nurse. It was exciting in a way, because there were soldiers everywhere. From our hostel, we could see these huge ships come in, and we knew the names of them. There was the *Andes*, with three funnels, *Empress of Britain*, a dark one with four funnels; and they would come and go every few months. They would load up with supplies, and then hundreds of men. Some of them we had met at dances, where a few of the girls met their future husbands.

The Americans hadn't arrived yet, and I don't think I would have done much work if I had been there when they came. I heard after I left Wellington that the Americans lined up at the door for the girls to come out at 4:30.

My husband [to be] was studying at Victoria University to be an accountant. In July 1941, he left by train for Auckland for the Fleet Air Arm. I saw him off, and he was sort of my best boyfriend then, but I had met a lot of soldiers and said goodbye to them as well.

Cappy went to Auckland to board the *Dominion Monarch*. They sailed to Portsmouth in England for their early training, and then on to Ontario, Canada, for further training. He was a fighter pilot. He left in '41, and came back in '45.

In 1941 I was sent up to a place called Wairoa, between Napier and Gisborne. I spent two happy years there. A lot of Maori families farmed up there, and it was wonderful there — wonderful Maori families up that east coast. Further up the coast, there was a [Maori] family member who won the Victoria Cross. Moana-nui-a-Kiwa Ngarimu was his name. I don't think he came back.

After two years in Wairoa, I was sent to Huntly. The nurse up there was not getting along with the coal miners, and they thought if they sent two friends we would get on better. I went with my best friend, who had been stationed way up near East Cape. At Huntly, together, we got on fine with the miners. They were the salt of the earth. A lot of them were from England, and every few months I would go out to the sub-base on the train. A sub-base means a small clinic out of the area. I would see all the school children, but the people in this village were shy. They thought I might be a city slicker. It was a little place called Pukemiro.

Children had good teeth in those days, because they had these dental clinics all over New Zealand; and when they closed the service, which was in the last twenty years or so, their teeth deteriorated. Now, they wish they had never done away with it.

It was while I was in Huntly that I met my first Americans. Up until then, I only knew them as well-dressed servicemen who whistled and called out things like, "Hey, pretty legs!" That was 1944. New Zealanders were coming back from the Middle East, and there were lots of fights in Auckland, so some of the men at Papakura — a U.S. camp — preferred to come south rather than go into Auckland. They would go down to Hamilton by train, the way to go then because of wartime petrol rationing.

We went one day to Hamilton. A Maori king lived near there, and this was a day when they had a regatta. My friend and I were there, just standing there and watching, because the royal barge was going to sail down the river.

People made a big fuss over the Americans, and two of them were invited on board the royal boat. They saw us and called out, "Hey, hey; you two come too!" So we got on this boat and went down the river, and these crowds of people were waving to us. You see, Americans could get away with anything. They were guests, you see.

Anyway, that's how we met these two Americans. They were both married men. One of them had gray hair. His name was Huck Lawless, and his friend's name was Rusty, from New Jersey. They started coming to Huntly to see us. They weren't very good dancers, but they were fun.

I didn't smoke, but my friend did, and the Americans brought us "candy," they called it, and cigarettes. And one day they invited us to go to an American football match at Otahuhu, a big suburb south of Auckland. We went up by train, and they met us and took us to this match, and it was hilarious, really. They were playing against a local rugby league team, and it was packed with American Army personnel. They had a little band that played quick music every so often when there was a lull.

It was a great outing. Then our friends decided to take us into Auckland for a meal. I was appalled, because we had to climb into an army truck for the drive into the city; and only days before I had become engaged by a surprise cable from London. There were about fifteen soldiers in the truck, and I said to my friend, "Goodness knows what cars behind us will think of this. What if someone sees me and recognizes me?" I was horrified! But we only saw Rusty and Huck a few times, and then they moved out. It was all very secret.

My father used to have a big map on the wall, and he followed the war with little pins, and followed it every inch of the way. He tried to go back into the military, but he was too old. He was born in 1882. He liked war; he did! He was a fearless man in the earthquake too.

Cappy and I had become engaged by cable. In the cable, he said, "Will not take No for an answer." We had been corresponding regularly, and when he went to London on leave with a friend called Archie Foley, he said he was going to the post office to send a cable to me. Archie said, "Whatever for?"

Cappy said, "I'm going to ask Joan to marry me."

Archie Foley said, "Don't be a fool; we're never going to get out of this!"

But he did send it, and he had had a few drinks; and that's how it all came about, and I was engaged.

I was in Huntly when my husband came back. That was quite romantic. He was in Ceylon, when he sent a cable saying he was on his way home. Then I received a telegram, saying he was in Auckland. I met the 5 P.M. Express, which stopped at Huntly. I was so nervous my knees were shaking. The train came in, and all these naval men were hanging out the windows and whistling, and out stepped this splendid naval officer, and he was bigger and strong. He walked over to me, and we were both speechless. I thought, "This is the man I'm going to marry?" I didn't even know him very well. We just said, lamely, "Hello, how are you?"

We walked up to our flat, and when we got there, he said, "I suppose I better kiss you." And everything was all right after that.

We had a little wedding in Napier. His naughty friend, Archie Foley, who said they would never make it, was his best man, and then we went away to Lake Waikaremoana. Cappy wore civilian clothes, and we had ten days there, the war forgotten.

One morning the phone rang. It was the Navy Department, and they said he had to report immediately, even though he had two more months of leave. I heard him say, "Don't be bloody ridiculous! I've been away for four years, and I've got another two months to go." But he was told that he was the only available batsman in the South Pacific.

My husband was quite angry when they made him a batsman, but they threatened to send him to some awful little place called Adis Atoll for naughty boys. He knew he had no leg to stand on; he had to do what he was told.

He left Easter, 1945, and my friend there in Huntly had gone and married. I was there on my own, and I went a bit strange, I believe. I did my work, and then I would sit there and write a letter to my husband. I would stay there as long as I could before I went to my flat in the evening.

Eventually, he was sent down to Australia to train in night flying, which was very dangerous. Then the Bomb came, and he got home quickly, but after the war he was absolutely dedicated to the Fleet Air Arm. They had wonderful reunions, but a lot of those brave men are dead now.

PART III

Voices of Americans
in New Zealand

19. Sick and Hungry on Guadalcanal; Fat and Happy in New Zealand: Leonard E. Skinner

Skinner was born in the state of Oregon in 1924, and graduated from high school in 1941. After the Japanese bombed Pearl Harbor in December of that year, Skinner wanted to enlist right away. However, he was still only seventeen and his parents hesitated to sign for him, but finally did. As a result, in January 1942, Skinner enlisted in the U.S. Marine Corps, but was not called up until the following March. He did his training in San Diego, and upon completion of boot camp was assigned to K Co., Third Battalion, Second Marine Regiment, Second Marine Division. However, at this early stage in America's entry into the war, the four regiments that made up the Second Marine Division were scattered as far away as Iceland and Samoa. On 1 July 1942, Skinner and his fellow marines boarded USS President Adams. *After several weeks, they reached Fiji, before heading for the Solomon Islands, arriving at Guadalcanal on 7 August 1942. They met little in the way of resistance from the Japanese that first day, but the marines that landed across the channel on the islets of Gavutu and Tanambogo did. So on D+1, Third Battalion was sent over to help out. Skinner was slightly wounded during this battle but remained with the battalion for the next six weeks before returning to the main battle that raged on Guadalcanal.*

In the early part of 1943, Skinner and the sick and wounded surviving members of the Second Marine Division were relieved and sent to New Zealand.

In July 1943, Skinner was one of fifteen men in his company selected to rotate back to the States on leave. He rejoined the Second Marine Division after it had arrived in Hawaii. This time he was assigned to the Eighth Regiment, Headquarters and Service Company, and made landings on Saipan and Tinian in the Marianas, and again later on Okinawa. Skinner's next landing was supposed to be the Japanese mainland, but never came to pass as the result of Japan's surrender.

Skinner belongs to a unique club of survivors. He was there on the first day of the land counteroffensive against Imperial Japan — Guadalcanal — and the last one — Okinawa.

On 6 February 1943, we arrived in Wellington Harbor and boarded trains for our camp, which was at McKay's Crossing outside of Wellington, in Paekakariki. The camp consisted of four-man huts, and although there was just enough room for four cots, we thought it was luxurious living compared to what we had been through during our six months in the Solomons. Also, the weather [in NZ] was so refreshing. The weather in the Solomons was so hot and sultry. And having been so long in the jungle, we were in extremely poor physical condition, plus our casualties had been very high. We were in pretty sorry shape when we got to New Zealand.

Our sea bags were there, so we dug out our winter uniforms because it was rather cool, and had liberty just a few days after our arrival. The first thing I did —

Leonard Skinner was a young U.S. Marine — a survivor of six months of fighting on Guadalcanal — when he met Peggy Harbottle (née Seerup). Leonard left New Zealand with the rest of the 2nd MarDiv and survived multiple island battles. Leonard and his family, and Peggy and her family, have remained friends to this day.

like most of the other fellows — was caught the train bound for Wellington. When I got off the train in Wellington, I started off through the station and was really looking forward to my first liberty in several months. Suddenly, I met two very attractive girls coming my way — two girls about my age. One was a blonde and one was a redhead. The blonde especially caught my eye, so I stopped and talked to them. I found her name was Peggy Seerup, and the other girl was her sister, Pat. They were at the train station because Peggy was catching the train to her home in Ohura, which was a small town about 250 miles to the north.

The girls didn't have much time, but we stopped at the milk bar and had a soda. Then they went on their way and I went on mine, and I didn't think much more about it for a while.

Our life in New Zealand was absolutely the greatest! The people were extremely friendly. Of course, they had good reason to be because they knew that New Zealand and Australia were the next ones on the list for the Japanese, and the Japanese had been sweeping everything before them up until the Solomon Islands. And the trouble was that New Zealand was unable to defend itself because almost all of their men were over in North Africa fighting the Germans. So the Japanese could have taken New Zealand fairly easily had they had the opportunity to get on down there.

One of the reasons that New Zealand was so nice during the war was the fact that our money went so far. My pay had gone up to $50 a month, which wasn't much compared to what civilians made back in the States, but it was more than what the New Zealand servicemen made. Our $50 a month went a long way in New Zealand, and my favorite meal when eating out was steak and eggs, and that cost about twenty-five cents.

We got along extremely well with the New Zealanders, and they bent over backwards to make us feel at home. And there were girls all around, and we hadn't talked to girls for months, and there was plenty of beer and wine to drink. In fact, New Zealand looked just like Oregon down under. The climate and everything was so similar. Even the towns were like home. So I have always had a warm spot in my heart for New Zealand, and I always will.

A couple of weeks after our arrival, I got a ten-day furlough. The first several days I spent in Wellington enjoying myself, but then I decided this was a wonderful opportunity for me to look around a foreign country, but I didn't know where to go. Then I remembered that blonde I met on my first liberty, and she had said that she lived 250 miles north in a place called Ohura. That sounded good to me, so I walked down to the train station and bought a ticket for Ohura.

I traveled up the west coast of New Zealand, and I met a New Zealand soldier on the train who had just come back from North Africa, where he had been severely wounded. He and I got acquainted while on the train, and he told me he would not have to go back into combat because he was too badly shot up. But he knew that I was just starting my career in combat, so he took a little ivory elephant off from around his neck and handed it to me. He said that that was his good luck charm, and that it had brought him through the North African campaign, and he wanted me to wear it. I put it around my neck and wore it for the rest of the war. I guess that luck held good for me too, because I came through three more years of combat without getting even a scratch.

The train stopped at every little town we came to, and the conductor approached this New Zealand soldier and I and said that everybody on the train was very interested in the two of us. He was one of their first servicemen to get back home, and I was one of the first Americans from the Guadalcanal campaign that had been up to that part of New Zealand. He said people wanted to hear us talk, so every town we stopped in from then on, this New Zealand soldier and I would get on the platform in the back of the train and make a little speech to the people who were present. That was quite an experience for both of us.

We had to change trains in Stratford — at least I did — and I found out it would be midnight before I reached Ohura. I didn't want to walk in on this Peggy, who didn't even know I was coming, so I spent the night there [in Stratford]. Everywhere I went the people couldn't treat me any nicer. I went into a restaurant and ordered a meal, and all the cashier wanted was my autograph. She said the meal was on the house, and when I went back outside the Salvation Army band was waiting for me there on the sidewalk. They played the Marine Hymn when I stepped out the door.

I then went up to a hotel up the street, and people stopped me every two feet for the whole way. When I got to the hotel, the manager insisted on carrying my bag up, and told me the room was free. Everything was free; all they wanted me to do was sign the guest book.

The following morning, I caught another train and did go on to Ohura. Arriving there, I looked Peggy up, and you can imagine her surprise when a marine she had met for about ten minutes a couple of weeks before showed up on her doorstep. Her and her family was extremely nice;

they took me in and I spent about three days there with them before I had to return back to my camp. They and everybody in this little town couldn't have treated me any nicer.

Shortly after I got back to camp, I was promoted to Pfc. I had been in the Marine Corps for close to a year. But most of the fellows in my outfit were in very bad condition. Everybody had gotten malaria up in the Solomons except me. For some reason, I was just born immune to malaria. The doctors told me that about one person in a thousand seem to be born immune — they don't know why. But the rest of the guys in my outfit were having one malaria attack after another, so they couldn't give us much in the way of training because any little exertion would bring on another attack. Our guys were constantly going to and from the hospital.

A typical day for most of the time we were in New Zealand, we would get up in the morning, have roll call, and then have breakfast. And breakfast was always very good because for a change we had all the food we could eat after having starved for so long up in the Solomons. In fact, we were told one time on Gavutu to be prepared for a second Corrigedor, because they didn't see any chance of bringing in any supplies or reinforcements to us. The Japanese were sending more men in every day.

After breakfast, we were given liberty almost every day, and would catch the train right there at McKay's Crossing and go on into Wellington. We had a hotel room there in Wellington that about four or five of us had gone together on so we would have a place to go to, and from my hotel room there was a girl I could see working in her office in the building next door. She looked pretty nice, so I met her when she was leaving work and we got acquainted and I went with her for the rest of the time we were in New Zealand. Her name was June Pearce. I would go out to her home, and her parents were very nice. I would eat dinner there with them almost every night. The only bad thing was that we had to be back to camp at night. We hardly ever had overnight liberty.

On one occasion I had a three-day liberty. I took advantage of that and again went up to see Peggy. It was a real fast trip — one day up on the train, one day with her and her family, and a day coming back. It was a brief relationship while I was in New Zealand, but it is amazing how long it has lasted. It is now about sixty-four years later, and we are still in contact with each other all the time. We have visited her over in New Zealand a couple of times — when I say "we," I mean me and my wife, Joyce — and she has been to see us a couple of times.

A number of years ago, Peggy's daughter, who had just completed nurse's training, stopped by to see us on her way to England, and we just fell in love with her. She married and had a baby over there, and we went to visit her. We timed our visit to match one that Peggy was making from New Zealand. So Joyce, my wife, and Peggy and I all got together at her daughter's home.

It is amazing what a short visit with Peggy Harbottle — which is what her name is now — turned into. Her family and our family have both been close ever since. The last time I went to visit Peggy's daughter and her family, she had moved to Australia and my son and his wife went with me. Of course, they have long known Peggy's family from previous visits.

That other girl I mentioned [June Pierce] also wrote to me throughout the war, but after the war I got married and she did too. However, I have lost contact with her. However, I have been back to New Zealand several times — my wife, Joyce and I — and I think it is a great country, with a great climate and absolutely fantastic people. I have never met a New Zealander I did not like, and if I had a choice besides living here [Oregon], I would hope it would be in New Zealand.

Looking back, Skinner says he is lucky to have survived all of those island campaigns, because the casualty rate in the Second Marine Division during the time he was there was close to 150 percent.

20. The Marine and the Farmer's Daughter: Clifford Charles Carrigan and Sylvia P. Carrigan

Carrigan was born in Canada in 1924, but spent most of his early life in Chicago. He enlisted into the Marine Corps on 8 December 1941. Carrigan went to boot camp in San Diego, California, and did follow-up training at nearby Camp Elliot and other areas in Southern California before being shipped to New Zealand.

After eleven months in New Zealand, Carrigan, along with the rest of the Second Division, left their home away from home and headed for the Gilbert Islands. The brief but terrible Battle of Tarawa followed. He was a member of Boat Teams #27 and #28 that were scheduled to go in ahead of the first wave on Tarawa. However, this suicidal landing was canceled at the last moment. They were later sent up to the lesser-defended atoll of Apamama.

After the Gilberts were secured, Carrigan and the rest of the Second Marine Division were sent to Hawaii to regroup and train for their next objective, Saipan and Tinian, in the Mariana Islands. Tinian was Carrigan's last battle in the Pacific. Years later, he enlisted in the U.S. Army, and finally retired from the military in 1975, after having served in both the Korean War and the Vietnam War. He now lives in Otaki, on the North Island of New Zealand.

Sylvia Whitehouse — now Carrigan — was born in 1926, not far from where she now lives in Otaki. She was a high-school girl living with her family on their farm near Titahi Bay, when the marines first arrived and started building camps and training facilities in the area in 1942. Her family, like so many others in New Zealand, adopted some of these young American servicemen, the majority of whom were teenagers, homesick and far from home.

Sylvia's father died suddenly of a heart attack in 1944, after these young

151

marines had departed for distant island battlegrounds. She was then forced to take a job in a dentist's office to avoid being "manpowered" to a job not of her choosing. In 1948, she was working for a dentist when she met her first husband. She stopped working to raise her children, and in 1965 went back to work, this time for the New Zealand Broadcasting Corporation, retiring in 1981. Sylvia is of English, Scottish, and Maori ancestry.

Carrigan: I was born in Canada, but raised in Chicago, Illinois. I was rejected from the Marine Corps in October of 1941, because the quota for the state of Illinois was five marines. On Sunday morning [7 Dec. 1941] I heard about the attack on Pearl Harbor, and Monday I went down and enlisted. I enlisted in the Marine Corps because I had a stepfather who was a German, and when he got drunk he would be yelling, "Deutschland uber alles!" And then my mother would pipe up, "Yeah, but you couldn't beat the marines," and that kind of stuck in my head, so I guess I always wanted to be a marine. I was the first kid in the neighborhood to go.

Sylvia Whitehouse Carrigan as a teenager, and Clifford Carrington as a young U.S. Marine. Both photographs were taken in New Zealand during the war. Note the old '03, A-3 Springfield rifle Clifford is holding. This was prior to his being issued the newer M-1 Garand rifles, the mainstay of U.S. ground forces during World War II.

After boot camp, I was sent to Camp Elliot, where they were form-ing the Second Marine Division. In Marine Corps boot camp, there are about sixty men to a platoon, and at the end of so many weeks' training they had what they call a "scatter sheet." We were standing in a big open field with all of our belongings — seabag and rifle, and whatever — and there is a fleet of empty trucks. They start calling out names and sending people to these various trucks, and that is how they fill out the regiments. They kept calling names, and our platoon kept getting smaller. Pretty soon, I'm the last shithead standing there. I found that because in school I had had half a year of wood shop, they put me in Headquarters Company.

Monday morning I'm carrying a carpenter's toolbox and following a civilian around while he changes hinges and doorknobs. I said, "God damn, I didn't join the Marine Corps to change doorknobs!" That noon, I went to the orderly room and saw the First Sergeant and said, "I didn't join the Marine Corps to carry a toolbox, while some civilian changes doorknobs. I want a transfer!"

He says, "Where do you wanna go?" Then I went to the tent I shared with a bunch of fellows and said, "I'm gonna transfer, but I don't know where," and they were yelling, "Second Scouts! Second Scouts!" Others were yelling, "D Company, Second Regiment!" So when the First Sergeant asked me, "Where do you wanna transfer?" I said, "Second Scouts." My first job in Scout Company was on a Monday morning. I was asked, "Did you ever drive a motorcycle?"

I said, "No."

"Well, can you ride a bike?"

"Yeah," I says.

"That's it — same thing."

These two guys were hung over and they showed me this old Indian [motorcycle], and they said, "This is the brake and this is the gas, go ahead." So I got on the damn thing and went about forty feet, hit a tree, popped the tire, bent the rim....

About 1 o'clock that afternoon I reported to the First Sergeant's office. He was raising hell with me, and I said, "I didn't know how to work the thing."

"Well," he said, "you had two good instructors."

"Oh, yeah, they were both hung over," I says, so they made a scout car driver out of me. At this time, I only weighed about 115–120 pounds. The scout cars weighed six tons.

We had armored cars in Scout Company, and we had to go to the docks and load our own gear on the ships to go to New Zealand. We landed at New Zealand in November 1942, and went to Titahi Bay. It was about 0330 or 0400. There were no lights, or nothing. All I can remember was gray-black hills all over, and I thought, "Where the hell are we?"

We pulled up to the docks and nobody was there. The New Zealand dockworkers were on strike, so we had to unload our own ships. We had a guy in our outfit we called "One-jump Kanilli" [sp?], because he fell out of his bunk one night — the top bunk — in boot camp; he wanted to be a paratrooper. During all this unloading, he steals a truck and got in line with some other trucks where they were unloading these big slings of beer. He got a whole load of beer in the back of this truck and drove it out to Titahi Bay, and told us it was a present.

The roads were so small that they couldn't take our tanks, and they couldn't take our scout cars, so we just practiced hiking and snoopin' and droopin' in the hills. Then we traded our scout cars to the New Zealand Army for gun carriers; we called them the "knuckle buster," because to turn you had to lock the tread on one side or the other. We used to see these young New Zealand [army] girls driving these gun carriers all over. We would take them up in the hills and turn them over. It's a wonder nobody got killed.

We were in New Zealand for eleven months [prior to going to Tarawa]. I didn't get into Wellington very much because I wasn't making much money. But this one night we were walking back to the main entrance to our camp at Titahi Bay; I was with two other guys at the time. There were no lights on this road and we see three shadows coming down the road. They are three women. They are coming this way, and we are going that way. We told them we were going to walk them home to make sure they got there all right.

One of them was Sylvia's mother, and she said, "No, we are all right."

One of the marines was named Spinks [sp?], who always wore his hat sideways, and he latched on to Sylvia, and I had Sylvia's aunt. I forget the other guy's name, but he had Sylvia's mother, and Sylvia's mother is protesting all along. We took them to where the steps go up the hill to their house and said good night to them.

Miller, yeah, that was the other guy's name — Miller gave Sylvia's mother a kiss good night. I don't know how she reacted to that; it was dark.

SYLVIA: The three of them turned up the next evening and knocked on the front door. My youngest auntie answered the door and came back to Mum and I with big eyes and said, "Those three marines are here."

Dad says, "Let them in."

So they came in, and we had a nice evening; and from then on members of the Scout Company came over regularly, but they didn't all come over at the same time.

CARRIGAN: There were 120 men in Scout Company.

SYLVIA: Being that we were farmers — we had a very large ... I suppose you would call it a ranch, and some of the boys [marines] were farm boys. They would come up to Mum and say, "Where's Whitie?" That was my dad.

She would say, "Up on the farm," and they would catch a horse and go up and spend the day there and do whatever he was doing. And some days they would just come over and talk.

Dad was great, and he was young; he just took them in. And they [the marines] would come over and have meals with us, and play the piano. And Mum didn't protest after that. Mum was great. She washed their clothes, cooked for them, made them welcome. She treated them like one of her sons — the older ones like a brother.

Mum was only about thirty-eight or thirty-nine. Dad was forty-two. For me, it was like having a lot of brothers or uncles coming to the house, because that is how they treated me.

CARRIGAN: Spinks wouldn't leave Sylvia and I alone.

SYLVIA: No, he was just being protective, like a big brother. All the boys were. I remember one night in particular; there had been a party at Tawa Flats. Mum and Dad had gone, and I stayed with my two younger brothers. At one stage, he [Carrigan] showed up. We hadn't been alone very long when some of the other boys [marines} showed up too.

We weren't in any romantic — well, possibly romantic, but my grandmother was very good at telling me about the facts of life, and....

CARRIGAN: No sex!

SYLVIA: ...the facts of life, and I was no fool. And I knew they were all going off to war at some stage, so...

My parents kept a pretty good eye on me. We went outside the door one night to say good night, and the door opened behind us and we were both pulled back in by the neck, and my Dad asked, "Where do you think you are going?"

I said, "We are just saying good night."

Dad said, "Inside is a good enough place to say good night."

I was sixteen at the time, and living in the country, I wasn't very sophisticated. In those days both Titahi Bay and Porirua were tiny villages, so no matter where you went, before you got home your mother knew where you had been.

CARRIGAN: She was going to the girls' college, and when we were getting ready to leave [for Tarawa], I went and got her out of school. We were at the docks in Wellington, and I came and got her out of school.

SYLVIA: I went to college [the U.S. equivalent to high school] in Wellington, because they didn't have one where we lived. We were in assembly at about 3 o'clock in the afternoon, and my form mistress, who was a very strict lady, came and tapped me on the shoulder and told me I had a visitor, and to collect my things and to go home. I had to promise her that I would walk down to the station and catch the train home.

When I get out there, he [Carrigan] is leaning on the fence waiting for me. He had just come right into the college. He walked me down to the train, but wanted me to stay in Wellington with him. But I caught the train home and told Mum and Dad that he [Carrigan] wanted me to go back to Wellington with him. Mum and Dad said, "No way!" So I cried. Then Dad said, "Well, okay, if your mother comes with you."

We went back to Wellington — down to the ship — and asked for him. He and one of his mates came down. We walked up Wellington Street for a while, and went to the pictures. About halfway through the film, there was a tap on his shoulder. It was an MP, and he had to get up and go, and when the lights came on there was an almost empty theater, with just a whole lot of women crying. That was the last time I saw him until 1981. We exchanged letters for a while; that was until after Saipan.

CARRIGAN: After Saipan and Tinian, I stopped writing because I figured my number had to come up. That was my third island — my third invasion, so I just stopped writing.

SYLVIA: Yeah, I thought he was dead, but life goes on. I left school and got a job, but I always wondered what happened. He did write to my mum in 1947, but she never told me about that one. I was engaged then.

Mum used to write to his mum, and I used to write to his mum and his sister. Then the letters just stopped. By then, he had married, and I was married, and our lives went on. However, we did talk about him a lot because he had been a part of our family. He came up [in conversation], and some of the other boys would come up [in conversation], but after the war they got on with their lives too. It wasn't until we [Sylvia and Carrigan] were married and I started going to some of the reunions. I opened my mouth and I had so many marines around me that just wanted to hug me and kiss me because I was a New Zealander. That's when I realized how much we really meant to those boys who were out here.

CARRIGAN: I made about $5,000 or $6,000 in the stock market and decided to take a trip and go back to New Zealand. I told my wife, and no, she wasn't going to New Zealand — no way! So I said, "Well, I'm going."

I flew down and checked in at a hotel in Porirua. I showered and shaved, and got the telephone book. There were two names that I remembered, Jones and Whitehouse. Under the Joneses — Jesus Christ, there must have been 200 of them. So I went to the "Ws" — Whitehouse. I called the first one, and it was her sister-in-law, who had a beauty shop right across the street from the hotel.

I said, "Don't hang up; I know this is a weird conversation, but I was here with the marines."

She said, "Well, who are you?"

I said, "Carrigan."

"Oh," she said, "we often talk about you."

Then she said come across the street to the beauty shop. When I walked over there, there were all these women looking out the window. Then she jumped in the car and took me out to her house. Her husband had had a heart attack and wasn't supposed to drink, but we opened a bottle of scotch and had a couple of belts.

I asked about Iris — Iris Jones, another girl I knew, and he said he would take me to her. She was at the RSA [Returned Servicemens Association]. He called down there first, and when we pulled up all the windows were open and all these people were looking out to see who the hell this marine was coming back here. It had been thirty-eight years.

I was drinking in there and the place is getting crowded. I had gone back to the toilet and some New Zealander said, "You God-damn Yanks were over here doing our Sheilas, and damn if you ain't come back!"

I didn't say nothing; I walked by. But on the way back I tapped him on the shoulder and said, "What you don't realize is that thirty-eight years ago we had all these girls under contract, and every thirty-eight years they have to be reserviced."

Later, we called Sylvia from her brother's house.

SYLVIA: I worked for a TV station then. I was a production library supervisor, and we were doing research for a program on New Zealanders in the Vietnam War. I had been dealing with the U.S. Embassy, getting film I couldn't find, and this American voice came over the telephone. I thought, "Oh, they got back to me quickly." Then he [the voice] said, "This is Carrigan," and I nearly fell through the floor. The girls said I changed color.

I went home and told Bob, my husband, and he already knew about Cliff because we always talked about him. Then I said, "Well, what do I do now?" And he said, "You better go get him."

My mum was staying with us then, so Mum and I went and picked him up. He stayed with us for a week, then went and stayed with Iris and her husband for a week, and then came back and stayed with us, and then went back to the States.

Bob and he corresponded quite a bit. I didn't want to. I was married to Bob, and I loved him very much. I wasn't going to mess things up there. Then Cliff came back again in 1986. Bob and I owned an RV, and were traveling around with our daughter. Cliff was coming over and they said, "Why don't we go over and pick him up?"

We traveled around the top of North Island for two weeks together, and then dropped him off at Whangarei. Bob and I then just traveled around until Cliff had gone, but he [Bob] wasn't going to take me back home until Cliff had gone. You see, Cliff had been divorced by that time, but it didn't have anything to do with me.

My husband died in 1989. He was quite sick, and just before he died — the day before he died — he said, "Find somebody else after I am gone and do the things that you want to do." Then he looked at me with a silly look on his face and said, "But it doesn't have to be that Yank!"

Anyway, Bob died and my daughter kept saying to me, "Did you let Cliff know?"

I said, "No." I wasn't going to write.

She kept nagging at me to write to Cliff, so I wrote to him to tell him that he hadn't heard from Bob because he had died. About a week later, the phone rang. It was Cliff and he said he was coming down. That was 1990, and it went on from there. He came back for a month, and then I went back [to the States] for three months. Then Cliff came back with me for six months, and I went back [to the States] with Cliff for six months, and in that six months we married.

We traveled back and forth for a while, but in Tucson there is no sea; it's not green, and then there is the heat. I also had my family here. That was okay for Cliff because he had traveled all over the world [in the military].

In 1993 [the 50th anniversary reunion of the 2nd Marine Division in NZ] two of his friends came and stayed with us.

CARRIGAN: Dave Perry and Kenny Wyman [sp?]. I saw Spinks last during the Korean War. I was at Camp Lejeune, North Carolina. I was going some place in my car on base. I saw this short guy and he's got his hat on sideways. I went up to him and it was Spinks. He had stayed in the Marine Corps; he was a private. He would get promoted, and then he would get drunk and miss formation or something and get busted.

SYLVIA: It was sad; he [Spinks] was about twenty-six when he first came out here. He was divorced and he spent a lot of time with my dad.

One time I rang up Schulte; he was the piano player. I never knew their first names; everybody went by their last names. Another one was Bilska [sp?]. Cliff called him "Frenchie." He was the trumpet player. He used to sit with his arm across my shoulder and tell me all about his wonderful wife. I tried to find him but couldn't.

I think it was in 1959, or maybe it was in the 1960s sometime that I heard that the marines were coming back [for a reunion], and they came back every five years after that.

After I left Otaki, I called Cliff and Sylvia several times on the phone. Cliff, especially, had more he wanted to tell me — anecdotes about his time in the Marine Corps — funny things about the people he knew. Sylvia wanted to talk more about the marines who married local girls and stayed or took their war brides back to the States, the Maori girl who married a Mormon and settled in Utah, and the marine who married first one Kiwi, later got a divorce, and then married another. He died in New Zealand just a couple of years ago, she told me.

21. Marine Corps Combat Photographer: Norman T. Hatch, USMCR (ret.)

Norman Hatch, like so many Americans, was a product of the Great Depression; and like my father and several of his brothers, he felt fortunate to have been accepted into one of the military services upon graduation from high school in the 1930s. And like my father, Norm was born in 1921, and graduated from high school in 1938. My father and one of his brothers enlisted in the U.S. Navy; Norm enlisted in the U.S. Marine Corps.

After completion of his training, he had numerous interesting assignments before being accepted to train as a motion picture cameraman. After America's entry into the war, Norm was assigned to the Second Marine Division. He spent the early part of the war in New Zealand, and like all the U.S. servicemen who were stationed there, he has nothing but wonderful memories of that unique time. However, after eleven months of training and holiday living in New Zealand, Norm, along with the rest of the division, headed for the bloodletting of combat on the small Pacific atoll of Tarawa, in the Gilbert Islands.

Norm, and a team of other photographers, took most of the still and movie picture footage of that battle. It was then taken to Washington for screening by the Joint Chiefs of Staff, thence to Hollywood, where his film footage was turned into a documentary that received the Academy Award for the Most Outstanding Short Subject for 1944. The award was presented to the U.S. Marine Corps as its first and only such combat film award.

Norm's next combat assignment was Iwo Jima, in the Volcano Islands, south of Japan. Iwo Jima was the bloodiest battle in U.S. Marine Corps history. Norm survived that battle, and as all U.S. Marines who did, refers to himself as a "survivor."

The training he received in the Marine Corps served him throughout his life. After the war, Norm worked for various photographic equipment com-

Corporal Norm Hatch being taught a traditional Maori dance by Peggy Kaua. The photograph was taken during the 1942 Christmas holidays in Gisborne, North Island.

panies, and as the principle audio-visual advisor to the Secretary of Defense. He was a consultant to the White House Press Office during four administrations, and continued to serve the U.S. Marine Corps and Defense Department. Norm, at the age of eighty-six, is too busy to call himself a retiree. He is still involved in film, and was an advisor to a member of Clint Eastwood's Malpaso Productions during the production of the movie Flags of Our Fathers. *After a total of forty-one years of both active and reserve duty, Norm retired from the Marine Corps as a major.*

I joined the Marine Corps in July 1939. I was eighteen years old, a child of the Depression, looking for work, and the military service seemed to be the best thing available. There were a lot of people to come out of the Depression who served in the army and the navy, as it provided them with a roof over their heads, three meals a day, and something to wear. That's how I came to join the Marine Corps.

I went to boot camp at Parris Island, South Carolina. It didn't bother me very much because during three years of high school, I had mandatory army ROTC drill. After boot camp, I volunteered to teach English at the Marine Corps Institute. This was through correspondence courses. I held that position for about six months, and then became an associate editor of *Leatherneck Magazine*, the magazine of the U.S. Marine Corps. Then my next job was to work in the Office of Navy Public Relations, at Headquarters Navy, which was also the headquarters of the Marine Corps. I learned an awful lot about the art of public affairs, which stood me in good stead for many years to come.

While I was at the Navy Department, I had applied for, and was sent to New York in October 1941, to learn the art of motion picture photography and the telling of stories with film. *March of Time* was a noted newsreel of the day. It was a monthly [newsreel] magazine that was about a half an hour in length, and ran in all the theaters in the country. It was also shown down in New Zealand. I was at the *March of Time* when Pearl Harbor was hit. I was also at the Capitol when the president came to the assembled House and Senate to announce a declaration of war. I was up there with a *March of Time* crew, doing a little handheld shooting.

My training then took me to Quantico, Virginia, where I worked on training films for a number of months. But then the Second Marine Division was forming out in San Diego to get ready to go overseas, and they shipped two of us who had been trained at the *March of Time*—Johnny Ercole and me—out there to join the Second Marine Division. We were there for several months, and then we were put aboard a ship, code named "The Bo-Bo Spooner," which was actually a McCormick ship, and its real name was the *Mormacport*. We spent somewhere between 20 and 30 days en route to New Zealand, which was to be our home for nearly eleven months before we went into combat. En route to New Zealand, we were provided with a handy little book titled *Meet New Zealand*, which told all about the country, how it was formed, and what its main efforts were in dairy farming and sheep farming. It was interesting in that there were only about 1,600,000 white inhabitants and close to 91,000 Maori.

We did not have a senior officer in the photographic section of the Second Marine Division until we got to New Zealand. We had a warrant officer in charge of us by the name of Leopold; but after we got to New Zealand, a captain came out from Quantico, who we had worked with before. His name was Captain William Halpern, and he was with us for about six months. He had been an actor and a sort of third unit director on *Gone with the Wind.* Then he was relieved by Captain Louis Hayward, the actor. He had been in *The Man in the Iron Mask*, and other swash-buckling films. Johnny Ercole and I had a good relationship with him.

Another interesting person was Major Jim Crowe. He was the bat-talion commander of Second Battalion, Eighth Marines that landed on Red Beach Three at Tarawa, and I was with him. I selected to go with him because he had a terrific reputation from Guadalcanal of being the type of guy who would go out looking for trouble and find it. I figured that if I was with him I would get the good film I was looking for. He was noted for having a handlebar mustache and carrying a shotgun in one hand and a cigar in the other. That was the kind of a Marine he was.

As we approached the island after about a month aboard ship in very cramped quarters, you can be sure the troops were willing to get off the *Mormacport* as quickly as possible. As soon as we tied up, there was a mass exit. Aboard this ship was most of the headquarters battalion for the Sec-ond Marine Division, and most of our efforts were located in town [Wellington]. In fact, our division headquarters was the Windsor Hotel, so I was very fortunate, as were the other photographers, in being able to take over what must have been at one time either the restaurant or maybe the ballroom of the hotel on the ground floor. But for living and sleep-ing, and that sort of thing, most of us went up to Central Park, which was pretty much at the end of the main drag of the city, which was the capi-tal — Wellington.

The Second Division started to consolidate. It had men on Guadal-canal, and other points throughout the Pacific. They finally brought them all together and located them at McKay's Crossing, and other places. Our particular problem in the photographic section was to document all that went on. As the men began to form up in units and get organized, there were wonderful opportunities for training because of all the beaches. A lot of training was done there, and we photographed it all.

We arrived on November 9, 1942, and so were pretty close to Christ-mas. One of the young fellows who worked for us as a beginner in the motion picture business and was my assistant, Bill Kelleher, met a girl in Wellington. As time went on, her mother invited him to Gisborne for

Christmas vacation. He came to me to ask if it would be okay to go. I jokingly told him, "You can't go alone because you are too junior in rank, so you will have to take the complete motion picture section," which was a total of four people. He didn't realize I was joking, and said, "Okay, okay," and walked away.

He approached the mother of the girl, Mrs. Oakden, who was a very enterprising woman, because she came to Wellington, and saw the general — General Marston — and got an okay from him to take about sixty people to Gisborne. I realized that we couldn't leave the whole section unmanned for ten days for a holiday, so we turned it into a story idea. I got our captain, William A. Halpern, to approach the general with the idea that if we get people out of Silverstream Hospital [mostly sick and wounded back from Guadalcanal] and up to Gisborne, "Wouldn't it be a good thing for them?"

Mrs. Oakden went to Silverstream and picked out sixty names — both sailors and U.S. Marines — and the next thing you know she had a rail car all set aside for us. We, as photographers, went along to document it. So because of a joke, a great adventure got started. We were well treated by New Zealanders en route. The train had to stop at several points. People knew we were coming, and when we had a chance to get off the train and stretch our legs, they had all kinds of things — coffee, scones, sandwiches, and the inevitable "tea"!

When we got to Gisborne, we were greeted by the mayor, and it had been arranged for everybody to go to certain houses to stay during the visit. There was a big notice board for us, and we would go through and pick out our names, and see whose house we were going to; and those were the people we would stay with during our time there. The people Johnny Ercole and I stayed with were the Allen Shackleton family. They had two sons, Colin and David, and their house was on the beach where Captain Cook first landed.

It was a very pleasant Christmas vacation for everybody. We intermingled in all the activities; there were parties galore, learning Maori dances, and [we] took tours around the city. Probably the culmination of it all was when we went to the Boxing Day Races. There were a number of us who knew how to ride, so on the spur of the moment I asked one of the people controlling the races whether or not it would be possible if any of the owners of the horses would allow us to run the last race, so to speak. We had about thirteen or fourteen people who agreed to ride, so we got the horses and we had our race.

Coming back to the city [Wellington], it was a change, and we were pretty much wrapped up in military matters. And the next thing of importance that came up was the farmers who thought that if they could get some of these sailors and U.S. Marines who were in the hospital into the countryside, and working and eating good food, they would heal much quicker, and get back to active duty a lot earlier. So a good number of them elected to leave the hospital and go to live with various farmers and shepherding families, and we thought this would be a good story to document for the people back home [the U.S.].

We went along and traveled all over North Island. We went to Rotorua and other [Maori] tribal areas, and while we were up at Rotorua, we decided we would do a little photography of local [Maori] singers, and I got to know the woman who at that time was the leading chieftess of Whaka [Whakarewarewa]. All I remember of her name is "Minnie," and she had a daughter whose name was Pipbo Eparimu. Her [Minnie's] husband had passed away, and she inherited the village, so to speak; and her daughter had been married to the senior son of the chief of Ohinemutu. The reason for that was to solidify for both families the ownership of property that was in both villages.

Pipbo was very unhappy with her husband, because he was with the Maori Battalion in Egypt, and he kept writing home about how great the Egyptian girls were. That didn't go over very well, but that is the way life was during the war.

She [Minnie] invited me to stay with her for the couple of days that we were there, so I could get a better feel for the life of the Maori. And right where they lived, they had hot water bubbling up out of the earth, which allowed them to put a basket outside the window and cook dinner. They had also diverted the hot water through a series of rock falls, which allowed the water to cool off in a larger pool, and that is where the bathing was done every day. And I will say that the ladies were a little surprised at my very white skin. Anyway, it was an interesting insight into Maori life of that day — and what great people they are. I can't over emphasize that.

Then from there, we ran into this big three-day *Hui* that was being held to posthumously honor a lieutenant in the Maori Battalion, who had been awarded the highest British wartime medal, the Victoria Cross, for having scaled a cliff with his troops to attack some German machine gun nests. They ran out of ammunition and were using rocks as weapons, but they had apparently done what they had to do; they put the machine gun nests out of operation. So for the first time, a Maori received the Victoria Cross.

It was the first time in many a day that the government had allowed such celebrations to be held by the Maoris, for fear of such celebrations escalating beyond the Maori reservations. The Governor General presented the medal to the lieutenant's mother. All in all, it was a very nice time — singing, war chants, dancing, eating and drinking.

On this tour, we also went to South Island, and saw Christchurch, which was a wonderful city. Everybody was on bicycles in those days. We called it the "Bicycle City." Our photographic officer at that time was [still] Louis Hayward, and Christchurch turned the town out for him, and that meant for us as well. We even went skiing on Mt. Cook.

It was an enjoyable time to be in that country. We were there for just about eleven months, and had excellent training and leadership. There has been made mention of the big fight on Manners Street [in Wellington], at the Allied Service Club, but it wasn't as bad as it was recorded to have been. It did wind up in the street, and it took the [U.S.] military police, the New Zealand military police, as well as the [civilian] police of Wellington to quell it. I've never been able to determine the true fault of it. Some say it was because somebody was uncomplimentary to a Maori, such as, say, a Southerner might be towards a Negro in that point in time. Or it was because some returning New Zealander saw his girlfriend having a nice evening with an American Marine. So those things did happen, but very little. The New Zealanders were wonderful in their reception of us, taking us in, and accepting a lot of our newer ideas.

When I first arrived in New Zealand, I was reminded of a Western town in the era of the late 1800s. In those days [in New Zealand], butcher shops didn't have any refrigeration, and a whole half-side of beef would be hanging outside the front door. That to us was a strange thing, because we [in the U.S.] had refrigeration for years. And of course, too, the stores were divided. If you wanted bread, you went to a bakery. If you wanted fresh eggs, you went to another store. We were used to going to one store for everything. And I think the biggest thing were the milk shake machines. Right next to the Windsor Hotel, a Russian gentleman opened up a store he called "The Hasty Tasty Hamburger Shop." He was quite a character, because he had a mouth full of stainless steel teeth, and it was always a surprise to see him smile and see those things gleaming at you. As we understood it, he had one of the very few, if not the only milk shake making machines in town, and everybody went there for milk shakes, and we showed him how to make them the way we liked them.

We had a visitor one day from the U.S. Office of Information in Australia. He had been asked by his boss to come to New Zealand, and get some photography of the only existing prisoner of war camp in the Southwest Pacific, which was at Featherston. He in turn asked for some members of the photo section to go with him — both motion picture and still — to document what was going on at the POW camp. So away we went, both Ercole and myself as the two cameramen and our assistant, Bob Opper, as a still man.

We interviewed several of the [Japanese] officers. There were seven Japanese naval officers in that group at that time, and they were under threat by the leading [Japanese] petty officer, who insisted that they commit hara-kiri. He thought it a tremendous disgrace that [Japanese] officers should allow themselves to become prisoners; they should have killed themselves. However, most of these officers had gone to school — college — in the United States, and they couldn't see any reason to kill themselves.

The camp was a little jittery at that point in time; we could sense it. I was standing with the sergeant major — Godfrey — of the camp, who was a reservist and had been in the British Army in World War I. He was a hell of a good man, and he was calling the morning roll call. Everybody was answering; nobody was missing. Then all of a sudden, a shot rang out behind us! He [the sergeant major] thought some of the Japanese near the back fence might be trying to break out, and we were surrounded by Japanese. Then somebody else fired a shot, and all the [Japanese] broke ranks and started running around the place.

I looked at Godfrey, the sergeant major, and said, "What the hell are we going to do now?"

He said, "Stand fast!" And that is what we did, we stood fast in the middle of about two hundred or three hundred Japanese running crazy all over the place, but none of them touched us, and finally order was restored.

When Eleanor Roosevelt visited New Zealand, I was detailed to cover her for newsreel release in the Untied States and the rest of the world. I did that, and a couple of times she said, "Sergeant, why are you taking so many pictures of me?" And I said, "If I don't, I will probably be court-martialed, because that is what my job is."

When she was about to leave, we had a group picture taken with the military police, Public Affairs Office staff, and the photographers, including myself— all the people who had taken care of her. When she got to her car, she turned around and motioned with her arm, but none of us could figure out who she was motioning to. She finally pointed at me. I walked over to her, and she said, "Sergeant, do you still like to ride on fast horses?"

That almost floored me, because 2½ years prior I had been part of the guard detachment out of the Marine Barracks in Washington, D.C., to protect the president when he went to Warm Springs, Georgia. One afternoon, I was out riding one of the horses from the Warm Springs Stables. I rode this one horse almost every day, and was coming around a curve at a full gallop to the main gate of the camp where all the U.S. Marines and Secret Service lived in tents. And right there in front of me was Mrs. Roosevelt and Missy Le Hand in the center of this dirt road. I guess I wasn't more than 35 or 40 feet away from them when I saw them. I pulled back on the reins, the horse went up on his hind legs, and I fell off— still holding on to one rein. I wasn't the steadiest man in the world at that moment anyway, and the president's wife was lying in a ditch on one side of the road, and Missy Le Hand, the president's secretary, was in the ditch on the other side. After I helped Mrs. Roosevelt and then Missy Le Hand out of the ditch, Mrs. Roosevelt said, "We could hear you coming, but we didn't know how close you were." Then she said, "Don't worry about it; no problem." And they went on their walk. After that, I walked the horse back to the barn, thinking how close I came to ruining my career in the Corps.

But I thought, "How could she remember something like that, and remember me 2½ years later, after all the things that she had participated in since then?"

They were getting fairly up-to-date movies out of the States, regardless of the war; and there were dances at the hotels. The Majestic was there, and they had a big dance hall. But I think probably the biggest thing in the relationships between young U.S. Marines and young ladies in New Zealand was when we arrived you could hardly find a [New Zealand] male over eighteen and under fifty-five. All of them were either in North Africa, or in the Pacific Islands. So this tremendous influx of young men, plus men who are earning more money than perhaps the average New Zealand soldier did, and had more money to spend, had a great deal to do with what happened in a relationship. And it was not unusual for a fellow [an American] on his first date to bring flowers or a box of chocolates, or something of that type; and come in a taxi. Well, as I understand it, those little pleasantries weren't generally the way the New Zealand men handled their dates, and this was all something new to the young [New Zealand] ladies, and they liked it.

A lot of relationships were started up. There were cases of children being born who didn't have married parents, but if you put 20,000 men into an area, that doesn't mean that everything is going to go right all the time. That happened, and there were marriages too. Sometimes, like we did when we went off to Tarawa — leaving a number of wives behind — a lot of those men were killed. It took a long time for the [New Zealand] women to find out whether their husbands were still alive or not. And those who didn't get killed or wounded at Tarawa, then went to the battles of Saipan and Tinian. There was a lot of danger to those men who had enjoyed their eight or nine months down in New Zealand.

New Zealand was almost like a second home to us. It is just hard to describe — the generosity of the people was great. People would invite us to dinner — people they didn't know. They would meet somebody on the street and ask them to come and have dinner with them, maybe even introduce them to their daughter. There are a lot of wonderful stories like that that came out of the war, and maybe a few not so good stories.

When it came time for us to go into combat, our commanding officer, Louis Hayward, came down with a serious case of asthma. The senior doctor for the division said he couldn't go into combat; he'd have to go home. That just about devastated Louie, because he had been like Errol Flynn, a dashing actor with a saber in a number of pictures, and he thought this would kill any chance he had of getting any good parts again, because he couldn't go into combat. Johnny Ercole and I thought we would do something, but we didn't know what. We went to the division surgeon and said, "What can be done for this man — anything that will change your mind? We would like to help him out, because he has been a good leader and everybody likes him. We want to do something for him."

He said, "Yes, I will tell you what you can do for him." (There were two-man huts for the officers.) "Tell the other man to get billeted some place else, and stuff up all the cracks in the place, and on the stove — I'll give you a bottle of Mentholatum. You take a big pan and put it on that

169

stove. When it gets real hot, put the Mentholatum in. This is going to create a mist through that whole hut, and he is not to come out of the hut except to go to the bathroom or to eat. Then he goes right back in again."

We kept him locked in the hut, more or less, for about five or six days, and when he came out his asthma was gone. With that, he went on to Tarawa, and won a Bronze Star for his handling of the photographic efforts. However, after Tarawa, he did not go on to Saipan. He had kind of an emotional breakdown after Tarawa, and went home. He just was not equipped for being in a battle zone for any length of time. I saw him when I came back from Iwo Jima. I ran into him at a restaurant in Hollywood — Mike Romanoff's — and that was the last time I saw him. I really liked him; he was a good officer.

Actually, in Hollywood during World War II, you couldn't do anything wrong. All you had to do was stand on a street corner and somebody would pick you up; it didn't matter if it was a man or woman. There was that kind of trust and friendship. Hollywood was like being in a big candy store.

I never attended any of the returned visits [to New Zealand] that the Second Marine Division Association had, because of my work at the Department of Defense, or something always interfered. So I never made one of those, but I have stayed in touch with people down under, especially the sons of the people I stayed with in Gisborne. All in all, it was a great time, considering that we were in the middle of a major war. New Zealand was a godsend! And I know we relieved them of the worry of possible Japanese invasion.

I had a lot of memorabilia concerning the Featherston POW camp, which I presented to the New Zealand Ambassador to the U.S., Jim Bolger, in 1999. I also sent a story and photographs of our visit to Gisborne to the Mayor [of Gisborne], Meng Foon, in 2003. This material resides at the museums at both locations.

22. The Marine and the Girl from Eltham: Joe Wetzel

Wetzel was born in 1918 in Monroe, Louisiana. Just like many New Zealand kids, he grew up on a farm and the depression years were difficult. The Wetzel children went without shoes and wore clothes made from flour sacks. After high school, he went to university for a few years and then joined the Marine Corps in 1939. During the war, he first went to Guadalcanal, and then New Zealand. He was with the Second Marine Division, Headquarters and Service Company, 2nd Battalion, and followed the division from New Zealand to the Gilbert Islands, Hawaii, and then on to the Mariana Islands — Saipan.

Before leaving New Zealand, Wetzel married a girl from Eltham, a small farming community in the Taranaki region of North Island. After the Mariana Islands operation, Wetzel was rotated back to the States on points, where he served out the war. Unlike most marines who served in the Pacific during World War II, Wetzel saw little in the way of combat due to the fact that he was the division postal clerk. Shortly after he arrived back in the States, his war bride joined him, and they eventually made their way to Louisiana, where their first child was born. After two years in the States, it was decided that they would return to New Zealand, where the couple had two more children. Wetzel's wife died in the 1970s at a relatively young age.

When I met up with Wetzel he was still living in New Plymouth, where he has resided since 1945. He is mentally and physically robust, and although retired, he stays active with charitable work in the community.

I was in my second year of university when I left to join the Marine Corps. I knew war was coming; they had already started calling up people, and I didn't want to be drafted into the army. I had a brother in the Marine Corps, so I joined the marines.

Joe Wetzel enlisted in the U.S. Marine Corps during the Depression years, and was sent to Guadalcanal with other elements of the Second Marine Division. He then spent about eight months in New Zealand before going on to Tarawa, Hawaii, and the Mariana Islands. While in New Zealand, he met and married a New Zealand girl. Wetzel has lived in New Plymouth, North Island, since the war's end in 1945.

One of my brothers, when he graduated from high school, decided he didn't want to go to work; he wanted to be a marine for thirty-some odd years. He said that was going to be his career, and he did thirty-two years. He's retired and still lives in America — Monroe, Louisiana. During the war, he was with the 155th artillery outfit that was stationed on Johnston Island. I think he spent most of the war there.

I had four brothers, and all four of us [*sic*] were in action somewhere in the Pacific or in Europe during the war, or towards the end of the war. One brother fought on Guam and we got together while I was on Saipan. We all survived the war, but I only have two brothers left alive.

We made practice landing at Tongatabu [Tonga Islands], and then went straight to Guadalcanal. I had an easy life in the Marine Corps, really, because I was the division postal clerk. I had a post office to carry around with me. Everybody in the Marine Corps is a combatant, but you have a second job as well. For example, when I landed on Saipan, I carried a little steel safe with me. I dragged that ashore with my rifle and all my gear, and had to drag it around with me wherever I went, because I had $20,000 worth of stamps and money orders in it. I never even got off the transport in Guadalcanal. It was USS *Crescent City*.

I first came to New Zealand from Guadalcanal in 1943 — February of 1943. My first impression of New Zealand was that it was bloody cold. We had come off of Guadalcanal, where we had been walking around in skivvy — shirts and shorts, and then we came down here and I had to wear my overcoat, it was that bloody cold.

My other first impression of New Zealand was that it was great because you could get all the ice cream you could eat. I can remember the ship tying up at the wharf, and hundreds and hundreds of marines over by a wire fence where you couldn't get in and out, buying ice cream and bottles of milk from some guy on the other side. The poor old milkman had to go back and get more, and come back, and go back and get more. He never got to finish his run because we bought all of his milk.

We disembarked and went out to Paekakariki. I was still joined to the post office. I went into Wellington each day to collect the mail and bring it back and sort it, and deliver it to the battalion mail clerks. When I had time off, I went into Wellington, but I never learned to drink so I didn't spend time in the pubs.

I had ten days of rest and recreation coming, so I went to the YMCA. I went to the person at the counter and asked questions about going to a farm, being I was a country boy. I was sent to a table where this young lady was answering questions, and she was from Eltham. We got to talking, and she said, "You come over for tea tomorrow, and I will call my father and see what we can arrange for you."

I said, "I apologize very much, but I don't drink tea."

She said, "I don't mean *tea* tea; I mean a meal."

I had to learn English all over again. Anyway, I went around to this young lady's place over on Oriental Terrace, and from there things developed, and we ended up getting married in July 1943. Her maiden name was Whiting — Peggy Whiting of Eltham. Her father was a builder.

When I went on my leave, I was sent to a farm on Mangatoki, which is outside of Eltham, to a Mrs. Gatenby. She was an elderly widow, but had a son and daughter helping her out on the farm. So I went to Mrs. Gatenby's for ten days. They made quite a fuss of me while I was there. I was always being introduced around as that marine from such-and-such.

You have to remember that in 1943, chaps were still being sent to the Middle East, and as they were being called up they always had a farewell function for them at the Mangatoki Hall, and I was invited to those. Generally speaking, the men were very friendly until we started taking their girlfriends. Later on, there developed a little bit of friction, but that was more in Wellington. I stayed in contact with Mrs. Gatenby right up until she died.

Like I said, I got married in July 1943, and we didn't leave New Zealand until October 1943, on the way to Tarawa. Peggy and her sister, Netta, were living in a flat, and when we got married the sister joined the [New Zealand] women's army. She went off to camp, so we lived at Oriental Terrace. We lived there until I left.

When I told my mother I had married a New Zealander, she was very upset. When I asked her why she was upset, she said, "I thought you married a fuzzy-wuzzy."

Nobody knew what a New Zealander was until the war came. I didn't know where New Zealand was when I came out here. I had never heard of New Zealand, and I studied history. My mother said, "I was so glad when you sent me a photograph of your wife."

There is that racial problem in Louisiana, and there still is.

There was another chap, Walter Nye; his job was to run the movie projector for the division. He got married while we were there, and some others did too, but I didn't know them at that stage.

One of Peggy's other sisters — she had five — had married a man who was the manager of the Bank of New Zealand in Wellington, so we used to visit with them and their friends. I more or less became a Kiwi right away, but I had a problem learning the language, of course.

Most of the division left before I did. I was rear echelon, and stayed behind to clean up the camp at Paekakariki. I was aboard ship at Tarawa. And after Tarawa, we went to Hawaii and set up camp there. We made practice landing there, and then went to Saipan.

On Saipan, I went ashore at about six the first night. We went over the side and into the landing boats, and my steel safe was lowered down on a rope. I was responsible for those stamps and money orders. I landed on the beach and crawled inland as far as I could go and laid there with my safe all night long.

At one point, I got arrested by the MPs for driving around in a Japanese car. When we got ashore, I had all the mail to deliver and the regiment was all spread out, and somebody had captured an old Japanese V-8 — a Ford V-8. I asked to have it to deliver the mail, and painted on the side of it, "U.S. MAIL, RD1" [RD — rural delivery]. The MPs stopped me, wrote me up a ticket, and took my car away from me. After that the battalions had to come and get the mail in jeeps. My post office was just alongside the road.

After Saipan, I went back home. I had had thirty-five months overseas. I didn't get back to New Zealand until after the war. I was sent back to the naval base in San Francisco, and I went to work in the fleet post office. And while I was in San Francisco at the fleet post office, I was advised that my wife was in Los Angeles. The Red Cross had put her up in a hotel.

Her brother [-in-law] was the manager of the Bank of New Zealand in Wellington at the time, and he was also on the Joint Purchasing Board. When I got my orders to be sent back to the States, I asked that a copy be sent to her in Wellington, so that she could then apply to come as a war bride. War brides were not allowed to go to America until their partners were back in America. I think strings must have been pulled, because she got there almost as quick as I did.

When I got my discharge, we went back to my home in Louisiana. I applied for university and went back to work for my old boss in a grocery shop. I didn't finish university not because I didn't want to; my wife got homesick. She got terribly homesick, and being pregnant she wanted her mother. And even though my mother was running around like a chicken with her head cut off—she was so excited about having her first grandchild—that wasn't the same as having your own mother there.

I had promised my wife when we got married that if she didn't like America, "We'll come home." She loved America, but she wanted to come home to see her mother.

We came back to New Zealand in 1945, and I was under the understanding that I was going to go to the university in Auckland, but there was no housing available for families — no place to live. And that was right after the war, and all the New Zealand men were coming home and they needed housing too. So I enrolled and went to the university for about three months, and lived in a one-room YMCA unit, and then came home to Eltham. I got fed up with that, because there was no transportation in those days — no bus service, no hitchhiking, so I just gave it up.

I came home to Eltham, and then shifted [moved] to New Plymouth. I got a job working for Burns-Phillips in a grocery shop. Then I worked for Social Welfare, and did that for about thirty years. And when we first moved here, we got all sorts of invitations to come and talk to school groups, and this kind of group and that kind of group, about America.

I thought it [New Plymouth] was a bit backwards at the time. The population had just reached 20,000, and had just become incorporated as a city. I was coming from a country where things were open seven days a week. I beg your pardon, but in those days, everything locked up on Friday evening, and didn't open up again until Monday morning. Nothing was open on Saturdays and Sundays, except petrol stations and chemists shops — drug stores. You couldn't go shopping; you couldn't go to the library; everything was closed.

Everybody had two days off. They were family days. It was better than today; you had more time for family life. Nowadays, a wife has to work — most wives have to work — to make ends meet. The point is that women didn't have work in those days.

We did a lot of our own preserving — fruits and jams. It wasn't until our kids were older that my wife took a job. I worked in the garden, and played sports [on weekends]. Indoor basketball was just starting up in New Plymouth in those days, and because I came from America everybody thought I knew all about the sport. I didn't know bugger-all; I'd never played basketball.

We got back here in 1945, and my wife died thirty-odd years later.

After she died, I went home — oh, I don't know — in the 1980s, I think was the first time. My mom and dad were still alive, and I wanted to see them. I got to see my father before he died, and then went back two or three more times to see my mother. My father died in his seventies, and my mother lived to ninety-six. I have never regretted moving to New Zealand. I wouldn't be happy if I went back to live in America now. The last time I went home I was told that when you go out in your car you lock the door when you get in, and you don't roll your windows down.

I said, "Why?"

I was told because when you pull up to a traffic light someone will jump in and steal your car, and push you out.

I've been home three times, but I wouldn't stay. I've loved every day I have lived in New Zealand, and I have had relatives come out and visit me in New Plymouth, and they have loved every minute of their time here. If I went back to America, I would miss my three children, my ten grandchildren, and my great-grandchildren. I've made a life for myself here, and I'm happy.

23. Defending Samoa from Japanese Invasion: Carl W. Matthews

Carl Matthews was born in Corsicana, Texas, in 1924, but spent most of his youth in Dawson, Texas. He enlisted in the U.S. Marine Corps before Pearl Harbor. However, shortly thereafter he was sent to Samoa in the South Pacific to defend against a possible Japanese invasion. Samoa has the only natural deepwater port in that part of the Pacific, and the fear was that if Japan occupied those islands, or any of the other strategically located island groups north of New Zealand, then the supply route between North America, and New Zealand and Australia would be jeopardized.

If Carl had not become ill with some undiagnosed tropical disease, he would have continued on with the rest of his regiment to fight in the Solomon Islands, along with other elements of the Second Marine Division. Instead, he was hospitalized in California, and when well enough to return to duty, was made part of the Fourth Marine Division. He then saw combat for the first time in the Marshall Islands, and then on Saipan in the Mariana Islands, where he was wounded.

Carl now lives in Dallas, Texas, but spends part of each year traveling to various parts of the world. The wanderlust that led him to enlist in the Marine Corps more than sixty-five years ago has not left him. In 2005, he made a nostalgic return visit to Samoa, and was warmly greeted by some of the high chiefs and many others.

It was a little after noon on the sixth of January 1942, when the Second Marine Brigade sailed from San Diego. The unit had been formed just a few days before, and it was the first American expeditionary force to leave the United States following Pearl Harbor. The convoy included Matson liners — *Lurline, Matsonia,* and *Monterey* — converted to troopships, two freighters, a tanker, plus a small navy escort, which included

Carl W. Matthews, shown here in 1943, was one of several thousand U.S. Marines rushed to the Samoa Islands soon after Pearl Harbor to prevent a feared Japanese invasion of those strategic islands. Carl was invalided home prior to his unit being sent to Guadalcanal, but later fought in the Marshall Islands and the Mariana Islands — Saipan — where he was wounded.

the aircraft carriers, *Enterprise* and *Yorktown,* part of the way.

The Matson liners had been fitted with 3-inch antiaircraft guns, and .30-caliber and .50-caliber machine guns, but we would have been no match for any Japanese attack. Fortunately, our convoy encountered no Japanese air, surface, or underwater units. They probably had no idea that American troops could put together such an effort in such a brief time period, and concentrated their offensive efforts elsewhere. Moreover, the sea-lanes we were traveling were on the outer range of usual shipping.

There were 245 officers aboard, and almost 5,000 enlisted men. We had no idea where we were headed, and were not told specifically until a day or two prior to reaching our destination. Small details of what we were to expect when we arrived at our destination were given out from time to time, and based on that information the scuttlebutt was that we were on our way to Samoa.

One of our men [by the name of] Strong, had a brother with the defense battalion [already] stationed in Samoa, and had become somewhat familiar with the location, harbor capabilities, natives, and so forth. And we were soon reminded that this was not going to be a pleasure cruise. There were morning details, exercise sessions, inspections to make sure rifles were thoroughly clean, abandon ship drills, gas mask drills, sessions on how to disassemble and assemble Browning Automatic Rifles while blindfolded, and so forth.

There was a PX that sold soft drinks and candy, but that lasted but a few days until the stock of merchandise became exhausted. Empty bottles were taken to the fantail and carefully broken before being thrown overboard, and all troops were warned not to throw anything overboard, lest a [Japanese] submarine pick up our wake.

As the scuttlebutt had spread earlier, we arrived at our destination, Pago Pago, Samoa. The day was January 20. We had been aboard ship for two weeks, had traveled 4,500 miles across the Pacific, and had encountered no contact with the enemy. Three miles wide and thirteen miles long, the island had been defended by the Seventh Marine Artillery Battalion and a small contingent of Samoan Marines. We were informed that Pago Pago had been shelled on January 11, 1942, by a Japanese submarine, and that an attack by Japanese forces was expected at any time. Our presence was to reinforce the existing defense battalions.

Our task was to unload the troops and equipment as quickly as possible, and set up defense positions. One of the first obstacles was the fact that Pago Pago had but a single dock, which created a logistical problem that had been anticipated by command.

One-by-one, the liners moved to the single dock and unloaded all passengers and equipment as soon as possible. Troops were quickly moved away from the docks to permit others to unload. When the liners were unloaded, the cargo ships, *Jupiter* and *Lassen*, took their turns at the dock, while some supplies were offloaded from ships anchored in the harbor into small boats.

Our ship, the *Luraline*, made its way to the dock, and I viewed Pago Pago from the upper deck. Rain was falling; and the combined smells of rotting bananas, dead fish, and diesel fuel, compounded by the high temperatures and humidity, deflated any idea that this was a tropical paradise.

Each company had been assigned an area well away from the dock. Our area was two or three miles south of Pago Pago, and located in a small valley with mountain peaks on three sides. The ocean road was on the fourth. We pitched our pup tents on the ground, making sure they were in a straight line and in military order. Trucks had brought our bedrolls, and we placed them inside our tents.

We were informed that the *Jupiter* would be docking in a few hours, and that we would be on a work detail to unload its cargo. We were told to get as much rest as possible. Cooks had set up big garbage cans as coffee makers, and prepared Spam sandwiches. We consumed our rations and crawled into our bedrolls for some needed sleep.

Command was very much aware of the vulnerability of the ships that remained in the harbor, so it was imperative that they all be unloaded quickly so as not to become victims of Japanese shelling similar to the one of the previous week. Each crew worked feverishly, and every man was exhausted at the end of the shift. While crews were unloading the ships, [other] marines were installing antiaircraft guns around the harbor, and several artillery pieces were positioned at strategic points on the island.

We had been in our bunks three or four hours when Schiller sounded his bugle, and we crawled from our downy bedrolls without having rested sufficiently. The *Jupiter* would be docking shortly, and we would be unloading it the minute we could get on board. Our breakfast was garbage-can coffee and C Rations. The *Jupiter* was waiting at the dock when we arrived, and the workmen had removed all the hatch covers and had booms in place to begin the unloading process.

The ship's boom — cranes — would lower cargo nets with large wood pallets into the holds, and we would place the items — ammunition, mortar shells, artillery shells, and so forth — on the pallets or into the cargo nets. When they were sufficiently filled, a signal was given for the boom to lift the cargo to the dock, where another crew would place the items on a waiting truck. Dumps had been designated along the South Road, and each truck knew precisely where to go to another waiting crew. The operation was very well organized.

Sometimes, items would fall from the nets while they were being lifted, and fall back in the hold. We learned quickly to stay well away from the opening when the cargo was being lifted. The heat and humidity in the hold became intolerable — unbearable very quickly. Thirty-caliber ammunition boxes, weighing 116 pounds — after several hours in the hold — felt like 200 [pounds]. I remembered that we had been told to expect another attack from the Japanese at any time, and I thought frequently about what would happen should those Japanese put a shell into that hold where we were working with tons of live ammunition. I had seen the devastation that the Japanese shells had inflicted on Pago Pago the previous week, and it impressed me.

It was near 3 A.M., and we were near the bottom of one large hold on the *Jupiter*. The 116-pound boxes of that .30-caliber ammunition had become heavier and heavier. I must have shown some evidence of fatigue when Lt. Martin Levett of Columbus, Ohio, my platoon commander, had me leave the hold and relieve another marine who was standing guard over our personal gear not far from the dock.

The fresh air on the freighter's deck was welcome, and I was grateful that Mr. Levett was giving me the assignment on the dock. The sergeant who headed the guard detail was a tall redheaded marine from B Company, who wasn't very smart; but after twelve years of service he wore three stripes. He was one of the most obnoxious individuals I had ever known, and had no friends in the company. He gave me an order to walk in a military manner back-and-forth where the rifles were stacked in groups of three, and where packs were laid in a neat row. Back-and-forth, forth-and-back, I marched, dressed in my khaki pants and shirt and wearing leggings. My head was covered with a World War I steel helmet. I had a gasmask and a belt filled with .30-caliber ammunition, a bayonet, and my '03, A-3 Springfield rifle, number 345343. The rifle had been issued to me in boot camp, and I had been required to memorize that number.

The morning hours wore on and I became more tired. There was no one on the dock, and I decided to lean for a few moments against a wire mesh fence. The next thing I remember was a redheaded sergeant yelling in my face that I had gone to sleep on guard duty in a time of war, and would receive a court-martial and be shot. He had me walking my post at a 120 steps a minute, and was still yelling and screaming when Mr. Levett came up and wanted to know what was wrong. The sergeant informed him what had happened, and what was going to happen to me as a result.

Mr. Levett told me to stand at ease, and after listening to what the redheaded sergeant had to say, began to dress the sergeant down unlike anything I had ever heard. The sergeant had never spent one hour in the hold of the *Jupiter*. In fact, he never did any real work at all, and Mr. Levett so informed him. He told him that this kid had worked almost sixty-three hours, with little more than four hours of rest, and was dead on his feet; and if that sergeant ever breathed one word of what happened that he — Lt. Levett — would personally kick the living shit out of his freckled ass! That was the end of that episode.

It was almost daylight when we were relieved. We climbed aboard the trucks back to our billet area. We were all looking forward to another Spam sandwich and some hot coffee, and most of all some needed rest in the comfort of our downy beds. The area had been a beautiful area the day before, and our tents had been pitched in neat rows. Two waterfalls could be seen on the mountainsides, and the area was a perfect picture of what one would expect the South Seas islands to be. That site would have been an ideal choice on the plains of Texas, where rainfall averaged forty-or-so inches annually, but the marine planners had forgotten that the average rainfall in Samoa was often five times that.

When we rounded the final curve to our billet area, ready for some quality sack time, the place was a disaster. Our soft, downy bedrolls and the pup tents were scattered everywhere except where we had left them. The heavy rain that had fallen during the night had raced down the side of the mountain, and the little stream we had seen the day before had overflowed and covered our billet area. The bedrolls had floated away until they had caught on a bush, or were stopped by equipment or boxes of ammunition. Some tents remained in their original location, held by ropes and tent pegs driven into the ground. We salvaged our tents, and once again secured them to the soggy earth, and slept until it was time for another shift in the hold of a freighter.

The troop transports and cargo vessels had been unloaded by January the 23rd and immediately headed for the open sea. The escort vessels were released, and we learned that while unloading the ships that the Japanese had shifted their priorities to Rabaul, where they had met little resistance from a small Australian garrison. The fact that the Japanese had captured Rabaul increased the possibility of the Japanese attacking Samoa before making any threat to New Zealand or Australia.

Five days after we had arrived, the island of Tutuila became a madhouse of tanks, trucks, and marines. We had brief glimpses from time to time of Pago Pago, which was not a large place at all. It consisted of a grassy oval, perhaps the size of three football fields. Little shops and a few residences faced the grassy oval on one side, and the harbor road on the other. Most of the shops had closed after the [Japanese] shelling. They had existed on tourist dollars when passenger ships stopped there on their way to Australia, but the new tourists had few dollars to spend, and even less time to spend them.

Behind the shops were small residences, and on the hill overlooking the harbor was a small cluster of white buildings with green rooftops that comprised the Samoa Hospital. I never saw any structures that resembled a hotel, and assumed that people who visited Pago Pago resided on the passenger liners while in port.

We were told that the Samoan Marines had used the green for parades and close-order drill. They were serious-minded young men, proud to be marines, and under the command of a sergeant from the mainland. Samoan

Marines wore *lavalavas*, a large piece of khaki cloth that was wrapped around the waist and extended to near the ankle. A white marine-issue T-shirt and khaki pith helmet completed their uniform. Each [Samoan] Marine was armed with an '03, A-3 Springfield rifle, and an ammunition web belt, with bayonet, surrounded their waist. Samoan Marines were barefoot, as were most of the natives.

The Marine Corps officer responsible for organizing the Samoan Marines was Capt. Maurice "Red" Gremillion, who was at the time — and probably still [is] today — the youngest U.S. Marine commissioned [a] captain in the U.S. Marine Corps. He had enlisted as a private at the age of seventeen in the Marine Reserve unit in Galveston, Texas. He was almost twenty-one when he was commissioned a second lieutenant. He was an avid photographer, and took many still and 8mm movie photos while stationed on Samoa. And he spent part of each day writing to a cute girl from Hubbard, Texas — my hometown. Red and Fran married, and Red remained in the Marine Reserves [after the war], and retired a colonel. He spent many years in South America, working in American consuls, and Red and Fran currently live in Dallas, Texas.

Pago Pago Harbor was small and was entered by a narrow channel. Palm trees grew in great profusion along the shore adjacent to the single road that went north and south from Pago Pago, and we soon learned that Samoa was a challenging base of operations.

January was mid-summer south of the equator, and it was as well the highest rainfall month of the year in Samoa — sometimes five inches in a single day. There were no paved roads, and the heavy trucks and tanks and rain soon reduced the roads to impassable, knee-deep mud. Jungle trails turned into a muddy mess after a few days, and we soon learned that sharp coral was always under the mud, and would create a mean cut to a leg or hand.

Work schedules were often twelve to fourteen hours daily, and most marines were required to stand four hours guard at the many listening posts scattered over the island. Mosquitoes, without doubt, multiplied based on the number of inches of rain per day, and they flew in formation to attack the marines.

The high command had issued secret maps that designated where each organization would set up a permanent billet. These permanent billets were located on either side of the single road that ran from Pago Pago to the south tip of the island, and to a shorter distance north of Pago Pago.

When the trucks arrived to move us to our permanent billets, we climbed aboard and the trucks headed south down the road.

The road was not wide, and had been covered at some point with crushed lava [lava or coral?] rock, a fine surface for small cars and foot traffic, but no match for the heavy trucks and tanks brought in by the marines. Potholes the size of foxholes appeared, and there were areas where soil had washed into low areas, creating a quagmire. Samoan natives lined the road, staring at us like we were strange creatures from another planet. We were strange to them, and they to us.

We passed several small villages, each with a circle of small oval, thatched-roof dwellings surrounding beautiful green areas. We learned that the thatched-roof structures were called *fales. Fales* were oblong structures, with a base of coral and small rocks. The finished floor was made of small pebbles, covered with woven mats. The use of coral and rock and small pebbles was [a] very practical means of dealing with water; and there was always lots of water in Samoa.

We found the Samoan people to be exceptionally clean — clean villages, clean houses, and clean bodies; and clean roads until the marines came. I was especially impressed with the beauty of each village green, and how the grassy areas appeared so manicured. I did not suppose they had lawn mowers, and presently we came upon a village where the villagers were cutting and caring for their green. A row of *lavalava*-dressed men, perhaps four or five feet apart, were in a line and each held a razor-sharp machete. As the men moved in unison, each man cut the grass at a precise level above the ground. A lawnmower could not have done a better job.

The marines were quick to observe that some of the women and girls who gathered to watch the trucks roll by wore brightly colored *lavalavas* that extended from the waist to well below the knee. Nothing covered their breasts. The bare breast was a way of life for the Samoans, and they thought nothing about the practice, but it was an exciting eyeful for the young marines.

Our permanent billet site was near the village of Pava'ia'i, located about halfway between Pago Pago and the south end of the island. The trucks stopped where a field kitchen was being constructed. We were home!

While we had been unloading ships, other marines had chosen sites for the eight-man tents that would be our home for some time. They were followed by another group of marines, who had constructed wooden plat-

185

forms, which would be covered by our eight-man tents. The wooden platforms were some distance from the main trail that led east from Pava'ia'i, and were widely scattered to lessen casualties should bombs be dropped on our area. Campsites were also chosen well under a canopy of trees to prevent being seen from the air. The platform crews, out of necessity, created crude trails to each of the tent platforms, and the entry to each trail bore a sign.

"Smitty," the supply sergeant, was waiting with the huge eight-man tents, wood folding cots with mosquito netting, an area map which showed the main trail and directions to each of the tent platforms, and [a list of] who was to occupy each tent. First Sergeant Ruth informed us that we were not to create any light at night; that steel helmets, gas masks, rifles, ammunition belts, and bayonets would be carried at all times by all marines; that we were not to interfere with the native population in any manner; that listening posts were created around the perimeter of our camp, and a list of listening post duties would be posted on a bulletin board at the company office on the main trail.

Sergeant Ruth had also mentioned that we had been given shower privileges at a community water spigot that served each village. Water that served the spigot came from high in the mountains, and had been piped to the village by the U.S. Navy. The spigots ran continuously into a concrete vat. It was at the community water spigot that all members of the community came to bathe, and Sergeant Ruth had stated that it was agreed that marines could use the facility at certain hours in the late afternoon and early evening. He was very careful, however, to emphasize that we were to shower with our pants on.

Meals consisted of Spam, bread and butter, canned peaches, and coffee. Marines sat on the ground to consume the meal. Some inverted their steel helmets — World War I issue — and they became dining chairs. And we learned that a palm tree base was an excellent dining area, with the trunk serving as a seatback. More than one marine was to become victim to falling coconuts while having a meal. Marines soon learned the technique of eating with one hand, and fanning flies with the other.

Following the evening meal, we all rushed to our tents, picked up towel and soap, and made for the concrete vat. Some members of the village — male and female — were still using the facilities when we arrived, and were taking their showers, modestly covered with their *lavalavas*. Men and most women wore the *lavalavas* from the waist to below the knee —

nothing above. It was amazing how the ladies would manipulate the *lavalava*, concealing their most private parts, and yet bathe completely.

I might add at this point that the bare breast ogling became short lived as the female population became aware of the stares from the marines, and began to cover [their] breasts with their *lavalavas*.

The natives soon quickly vacated the concrete vat, and the vat was soon filled with young marines attempting to shower with their pants on. It soon became apparent that the *lavalava* was a practical item, which lent itself to showering in public. Long G.I. pants created all sorts of difficulties with regards to showering.

As time went on, the pace would slow a bit and we would be given a day off now and then, and we began to make friends with some of the natives. One family lived not far from our tent. A man may have lived there, but I never saw him. There was a mother and three daughters — one about twelve, one about fifteen, and one perhaps seventeen. The mother did laundry for the marines, and sold little pies from time to time. The two older girls lost no time in finding marine boyfriends, and they had dates in the jungle. One of the older daughters appeared to be very much with child by August of that year.

The inhabitants of the village of Pava'ia'i were very gracious, and attempted to do everything possible to make the presence of the marines pleasant. They often reminded us that we were there to protect them against the Japanese. And there was an infusion to them of cold cash. Once the chiefs, and others in the village, decided to have a *sivasiva*, a community dance for the marines. It would have been impossible to have a dance for all the marines, so it was decided that only noncommissioned officers be invited.

A band of sorts was brought from Pago Pago, and older girls and young single women were recruited to participate. The band played several tunes, but I remember hearing "You Are My Sunshine" while resting that evening in my bunk. I was told that the girls were overly chaperoned, which was just as well; and the marines were requested to remove their shoes before the dance on the village green. There were no refreshments, but the entertainment was surely way ahead of playing poker, sitting around shooting the bull, or sleeping.

Three months had passed since we had arrived, and no ship had arrived in Pago Pago Harbor. We had a plentiful supply of small-caliber ammunition, plenty of mortar and artillery rounds, but food was beginning to get critical. The field kitchen began to cut down on portions served, and even Spam began to have a respectable taste. Some people might not believe this, but the marines on Samoa in 1942 were given that famous hardtack that had been left over from World War I. When it was first served, I assumed that it had been recently made, but one day I was on a work detail to pick up supplies for the field kitchen. The hardtack was packed in large, sealed tins; and would you believe it was stamped "1917"?

The first ship to arrive was from Australia, the one that brought the huge bottles of Australian beer. The ship also brought mutton, flour, and sugar. A few days later it was announced that a ship from the States with provisions would arrive. Mail was among the initial items unloaded and quickly routed to the various units throughout the island. The entire island exploded like Christmas; this was the first mail we had received since we left San Diego. Three months earlier, Mother had sent cookies that were nothing but crumble, but they were the best crumbled cookies I ever ate.

One night I showered, and felt on the bottom of my foot a break on the sole of my foot. I washed it carefully, and I always wore fresh socks. A few days later, the condition became worse, and I was limping when I requested permission to go to sickbay. The navy medical corpsman who examined me promptly informed me that I was another of the many who had come down with "jungle rot." The lesions on my one foot soon spread to the other and grew larger. My feet became so swollen that I could barely hobble to the aid station.

One of the medical corpsmen noticed that huge blisters had formed on my feet and hands, and that my temperature had become elevated. He immediately called the medical officer on duty, who decided that what I was experiencing was not jungle rot. After the medical officer examined me, I was placed in one of the green field ambulances and transported to the regimental hospital. I was placed in an isolation tent, and my hands and feet were wrapped in gauze. The fluid that leaked from my body onto the gauze created a terrible odor. Later, I was moved to the Samoan Hospital in Pago Pago.

Soon, I was the senior patient. The lesions on my hands healed completely and my feet were beginning to clear. I had lost several pounds by that time, but was able to be up and about. Beds became a premium, and after three weeks' stay I was discharged and told that I could return to the camp, but I never returned to full duty. The blisters on my hands and feet returned in a few days, and walking to the field kitchen was again a problem. First Sergeant Ruth called the aid station, told them I was on my way over, and not to send me back to camp until I was completely fit for duty.

My condition worsened each day, and my hair began to fall out. My temperature rose to 102 [degrees] and stayed there for days. I was hoping that my strength would return and I would return to normal duty, but that was not to happen. A Dr. Truitt informed me that a ship was coming from Australia, on its way to Long Beach, California. It would be making port in Pago Pago, and would accept a limited number of ambulatory patients for transport to the States. I had been a bed patient for several weeks, and my feet were still raw. Dr. Truitt explained that if I could just walk up that gangplank, and down to where the bunks were located, I could go home.

I was determined in about two seconds to take that stroll. Dr. Truitt obtained some oversized shoes, and I rolled two pair of socks over the bandages on my feet. Several fellows brought all of my belongings from the camp, and they said their goodbyes. The next morning, a navy corpsman placed me in a wheelchair and rolled me to a waiting field ambulance. When we arrived at the dock, the ambulance driver maneuvered the ambulance as close as possible to the gangplank. I stepped out of the ambulance and made my way toward the gangplank. Each step was torture, but I climbed each step to the ship and down into the hold where our quarters were located. I collapsed exhausted on one of the bunks and did not move.

The trip back to the States was uneventful. The ship was the USS *Brazos*, a navy tanker, and when we docked at Long Beach, California, ambulances were waiting at the dock.

PART IV

Voices from the Next Generation

24. The Missing Bit: Alfred Vaughan Leach

Alfred Vaughan Leach was born in Hastings on the east coast of North Island, New Zealand, in February 1945. He was one of many children born to New Zealand mothers and American fathers during the war years. The exact number is not known, but according to official records, approximately 2,000 children were born out of wedlock in New Zealand during the war years, and Vaughan — as he likes to be called — was one of them.

His mother, "Beth" Leach — née Devonshire — came from a large family, and her father made a living as a farmer. After the war, Vaughan's mother married a New Zealander, but had no more children. Vaughan took the name of his adoptive father, which was Leach, and didn't learn until he was sixteen that his biological father was an American serviceman. And as I have discovered, people who grow up not knowing who their fathers are share something similar with people who are related to men declared Missing in Action. That something can best be described as a need to know.

Discovering that he had a biological father somewhere in the world may have been a factor in his leaving home at an early age. He married early, had two children, and is a retired schoolteacher. He is still married to the same woman, has a close relationship with his wife, his grown children, and his grandchildren; but not knowing for sure who his biological father is still haunts him.

My mother's side is an Irish/English sort of mixture — Devonshires, they were — and intermarried into Maori — Ngati Muaupoki and the Broughtons. Yeah, that's my mother's side. I know the tribe and iwi, and the names of some of my ancestors, but off the tip of my tongue, I couldn't tell you. I haven't had a lot to do with them.

My mother had eleven children in her family [siblings], so I had lots of uncles and aunties. I had sixty-five first cousins, and I was an only child, so I was a spoilt little bugger. I had everything, or so I was told; I had a mother and a father, and we used to go to big family does down in Foxton and that area. My father — well my stepfather.... I thought he was my father until I was sixteen. You see, all these family gatherings I went to I always felt different, because I was an only child and all the other families had more than one child. But there was something else, and I knew it and I felt that other people knew it too; but I could never put my finger on it. And it wasn't until I was about sixteen, and I was with other relations from my stepfather's side that I first heard someone come into the room and say, "That's Pip's — that's my stepfather's nickname — stepson."

That word went straight into me because I knew what it meant. As a sixteen-year-old, I knew what that meant. This was in Foxton when that happened. Yeah, that hit me like a sledgehammer! I couldn't wait to get on the phone to Mum. I said, "I just heard a guy call me Pip's stepson. What's the story?"

Alfred Vaughan Leach is one of many hundreds — if not thousands — of individuals in New Zealand born to New Zealand mothers and American fathers. More than sixty years later, it still bothers him that he does not know who his father is.

So that is where it started, and she opened up and told me all about it; and I had always wondered why my stepfather had treated me so strange. Whenever this American stuff came on TV, he went BANG! He just went crazy; he got upset. See, it must have been hard for him, because he couldn't have children. But my mother was very good about it; she still is. She tried to explain it all to me; and as I found out, during those times things like that were covered up.

I was probably a bit young to take it all in, and I

194

went a bit off the rails. I wanted to try and find something out, and I went to see a lawyer in Palmerston North to see what he could do for me. I was too young, and didn't have anyone to help me, so I couldn't do anything for several years. It wasn't until many years later when I became a schoolteacher and it really started to hit me. It was then that I started to write a series of letters to my mother, and she wrote back, giving me all the information she could. But unfortunately, she destroyed everything. It was one of the conditions of marrying the other fellow [his stepfather]. She had to get rid of all the photos — all the letters she had from my real father. So she had no evidence; she had nothing to give me except her memories.

My relationship with my stepfather was never much good after that. When I was younger, he was just my father and I didn't know any different. He was a hard father, and he used to belt me if I misbehaved, but I think he cared for me when I was younger. But when I got older — when I got into my teens — I think that is when he got jealous of me; he resented me. I didn't want to be in the house with him, and I wanted her [his mother] to leave him. I didn't like him any more, and he didn't like me. He couldn't handle that; he didn't know how to talk to me about it.

My mother told me the truth, I imagine. I've never been sure if it is the complete truth, but she seems to be so consistent. I read all the letters that I got from her about thirty years ago, and I had a talk with her again recently. I told her this father thing has come back to me as it always does; it never leaves me. It's been good for both of us.

Now, the story is that she was in a service job — working in a tearoom, I think it was. She started with a blind date with this fellow — Fred Rondell was his name — Sergeant Fred Rondell. He was twenty-six. Anyway, she had an affair with him and became pregnant. He was in the army, based at Pukekohe. He was based at Camp Pukekohe Racecourse, and my mother visited him there. They had a relationship that must have gone on for a few months — a fairly loving relationship it sounds like. Yeah, she got pregnant, and he got shipped out two months later. The historical records show he would have been in the 43rd Division, 169th RCT [Regimental Combat Team]. Then when I was two weeks old, her friend who had also gone out with these Americans, got a letter from one of Fred's friends. She contacted Mum and said, "Oh, I've got some bad news. Evidently, Fred has been killed in action." And that is all she knows. There is no confirmation, and that lady is now dead as well.

If killed, most likely he was at Luzon in the Philippines, where 952

U.S. soldiers were killed between January and June 1945. My mother received letters from him in the Philippines for a while.

He had a sister, and they were from Boston; that was his hometown. He must have been here at the beginning of 1944, because that is when he met my mother. I was conceived in May 1944, so I imagine that they knew each other for a wee while before I was conceived; who knows. Then he left when Mum was about two months pregnant, so he must have left about July [1944]. Auckland, they would have been shipped off from, and Mum thinks they were going to the Philippines. It was another seven months before notification came to her that he was killed.

Through some of the things I have done trying to trace my father, I have come across people who have told me, "Hey, come on; that was a common story." If somebody already had a family back home, and they knew they were heading back home, or they couldn't get back to New Zealand, they got one of their mates to say they had been killed in action. It was an easy way of getting out of any paternity [obligations], or anything like that. So I thought, "Maybe that's true." There is no proof either way for us — none at all.

I've done many things over the years; I've even rang America — all the Rondells in the phone book. I've talked to people called Rondell, and they've said, "No, I can't help you," and they hung up. And I would think, "I wonder if that was one of my relations?" — because what would you do if some guy from another country rang you many years later and said, "I'm trying to track down a person."

The big problem for me was that in 1973 all the personnel records for the [U.S.] army were burnt in some fire they had in their headquarters. The last time I tried to find something I did it through the Internet, and it sounded quite promising for a while. This was September, last year [the Natl. Archives], and they said they couldn't trace anyone under that name. So then I said to my mother, "Are you sure this is his name?" Of course, that is another question, but she named me Alfred, so she believed it was. My name is Alfred Vaughan, but I call myself Vaughan. But as far as she is concerned, the name is correct. But I have often thought, "Yeah, you know how fellows are," and he was twenty-six, so there was a good chance that he was married and had family at home. So that is why I think there is a good chance that he wasn't really killed; it was just his way out.

This is something that has always been there; it's hard to describe, and Mum says, "Why is it still bothering you?" She can't understand, because it is a chapter in her life that she cut off a long time ago.

I said, "I can't shut it off, because he is my father and I don't know anything about him except these very little facts, and that is the part that makes it so difficult; and it always comes back."

I have tried to shut it out, and have for periods of years, and then all of a sudden it will come back and hit me hard. I get emotionally upset, and had a breakdown when I was about forty and had to give up teaching. I don't handle stress very well, and this is something that I get emotional about all the time.

I think our children have had a great life. They were raised the best possible way we could. But I have a marvelous wife, so I don't want to take too much credit. And now I have two granddaughters that I just love to bits, and they love me to bits. And then I start thinking; "It's a shame I can't give them anything from my past about my family." When I see my little granddaughters loving me as granddad, and then I can't even get back to my own father or any of his relations, and both of my children are in the thirties — or one is forty now — and they are both quite interested to know. So that's the other thing now, I can't tell them much.

The other night at dinner, my son was over and I said, "I might have to go to America, if I know where to go, and try and find something out." And he said, "I'll come with you."

Yeah, so the family is very important; it's that one bit that is missing — the missing bit. I don't have to find out much to satisfy myself, I don't think. If I could see a photo....

25. Lost Opportunities: June Margaret Baudinet (née Taringa) and Tanya Savage

June was born in Wellington, New Zealand, in June 1944. Her mother was a "Cook Island Maori," and was one of several women from the Cook Islands, who went to New Zealand during the Second World War to work. She, along with a number of other women from the Cook and other Pacific island groups, met and fell in love with an American serviceman who was stationed in New Zealand at the time. Some of these women married their American boyfriends, and others did not. At the same time, there were some American servicemen in the Cook, as well as other island groups to the north of New Zealand.

The Cook Islands are south of the equator, with Rarotonga being the largest. During World War II, two of these islands served as bases for U.S. forces — Aitutaki, which is directly north of Rarotonga, and Penrhyn, which lies north and slightly east of Rarotonga. Liaisons were formed and quite often children resulted from these relationships. At war's end, a couple of these American servicemen returned and married their island girlfriends. In more recent times, others have returned for a reunion of sorts, and have met for the first time the children they sired during the upheavals of war.

June Baudinet was raised by her maternal grandparents and has been looking for her biological father ever since she knew she had one. Her daughter, Tanya Savage, likewise has been involved in the search. As she told me during her interview, "Once I had children of my own, it became important for me to find out who my grandfather is."

June, in spite of being teased as a child for looking different from other island children, excelled in both sports and academics. She later won a scholarship to study in New Zealand, where again she did well both athletically and academically. She later returned to her island home, taught school for several years, and then started her first business. She has expanded her business

June Baudinet (Taringa), and her daughter, Tanya Savage. June has lived all her life wondering who her American father is, and Tanya has been helping in the search ever since she started having children of her own.

holdings over the years, while at the same time raising a family. She remains an active member in Cook Island affairs, and in 2006 was recognized by the Queen of England for her contributions to sports and business in those islands.

Tanya was born on Rarotonga in 1969, and studied business management in Auckland after graduating from high school. She lived in Hong Kong for two years before returning to Rarotonga to help her mother run her many tourist-oriented businesses, as a sales and marketing manager.

JUNE: My maiden name is Taringa, which is my grandfather's name. I was born in Wellington. My mother, Tairi, was a Cook Islander, and it was her parents who brought me up. I believe my father was an American who was in Wellington during the Second World War. I was two months old when my mother had to send me home [with her aunt] to my grandparents.

My aunt, Pa Ariki, was the paramount chief of our district here in Rarotonga, Takitumu. She went to New Zealand at the age of twelve, or maybe a little later, when her parents died. She was sent to school in New Zealand to be educated, and then when she was twenty-one she was to come home to become the paramount chief of our district, and she is the one who brought me home to Rarotonga.

My aunt never called me "June." She always called me "Tearikivaine," which means Queen. *Teariki* is "king," and *vaine* means "woman."

She knew my father very well. In the evenings they [she and her cousin, June's mother] would dress up and go out together. My aunt, if I am correct, told me that my mother was working for this family in Lower Hutt — the McKenzies — and later on she worked for the Gracie [sp?] family on Bowen Street in Lower Hutt. And it was much later that I discovered a note that said my mother was working for the Oddland [sp?] family in Wellington.

I don't have any correspondence from my mother. Once I received a letter when I was thirteen. I really wanted to be with my mother, and I wanted to know about my father, because as I grew up on the island the children at school gossiped that I was the American bastard, and all that nonsense. And every time my grandmother would lose her temper with me that is exactly what she would say to me, and I would go under the mango tree and have a good cry.

Anyway, I think I was thirteen when I discovered my mother was getting married, or had gotten married in New Zealand. I think he was from a Scottish or English family. But as I was saying, I wrote to my mother and said I wanted to come and live with her because I really wanted to be with her. I guess it is a normal feeling in every child. Every child that I knew at school had a mum and dad, and I didn't. So I always had this very hurt and very lonely feeling of not knowing what real love between a mother and a father and a child is. I always felt empty, and it didn't take very much for me to be hurt. She wrote back and said, "June, when you become a woman you will understand that Rarotonga is better than New Zealand."

I think right at that moment the only feeling I had was, I hated my mother so much! I felt she didn't want me to go and live with her. It was like a knife going through my heart, so I ran under the same mango tree and had another good cry.

Then my stepfather wrote and said, "Don't ask those questions of your mother any more," meaning, don't ask about my father. "You have hurt your mother so much."

I was shocked; I thought, "I never wanted to see these people." Sometimes I would sit on the bus going to school and think about it and my eyes would well up in tears; but I would snap out of it and think to myself, "I just have to be strong."

I felt that I had to be better than all the other girls at school, because I felt they had everything and I had nothing. So I excelled in everything I did. I don't know if it was my own determination or if it was in my genes that I excelled in athletics, in public speaking — I had that drive inside me. For years, they called me the fastest girl on the island. But I'm not sure about school, because I didn't speak English at all until I went to primary school.

I didn't have any books except the Bible. I was brought up as a Catholic by my grandfather, who was a very staunch Catholic. He came from the island of Atiu, and my grandmother was [from] a very promi-nent Rarotongan family — Raina. And you will notice that everything I have done in my life I have dedicated to my grandmother. All of my busi-nesses are named after her, Raina Beach Apartments, the *Are o Raina*, which means the House of Raina.

At school, I was good at math and things like that, but my English was shocking. Whenever we had exams, I was not at the bottom, but I wasn't very far from the bottom in English. It was my worst subject. So in the end I started to read, and I haven't stopped since. And when chil-dren were asked to read in class, I always put my hand up and I could hear the [other] children laughing in the background. They thought, "Oh, there she goes; she can't read." But I ignored that, and that is how I improved my understanding of English.

When I turned sixteen that was a memorable year in my life. That was 1960, and there was a public speaking contest at the school, and I won. I can almost remember my speech; the topic was "What is the world we want?" It went something like: "The world we want is one of peace, where all men and women can live without fear."

I think I based that on the feeling that I had no parents, and war was something I hated. Whenever I look at a movie that involves war, I think, "Now, isn't that just meaningless, because men go out to fight, to kill, and for what?" So that was the feeling I based my speech on.

It was after Christmas, I think it was — the High Commissioner and the Director of Education came to our house to ask me if I wanted to go to school in New Zealand. There were two of us who were selected to go on scholarships. I was absolutely stunned and excited. It was a big day in my family; it was a time of happiness and at the same time there were tears, because my grandmother realized that I was going to go away from them.

My grandfather had just had a stroke, so he couldn't talk very much, but he understood what was going on. And then it dawned on me, "Oh my God, I am going to see my mother!"

The day I left the island, my grandfather was in the hospital; and, of course, I went on a ship, the *Moana Roa*. I went to say goodbye to my grandfather in the hospital. The stroke left him paralyzed, and he couldn't speak. He held my hands, and right now I can still feel those hands holding mine, and he just cried, and cried, and cried. I cried too, because I realized, and he realized also, that we were probably never going to see each other again.

A doctor had to come and separate our hands, and he said, "Papa, June has to go because the ship is waiting." So I went down to the wharf, and the whole island was there because the two girls — Daphne Herman and me — were leaving. We were covered with flowers, and of course my grandmother was crying. It was a sad day for me.

The trip took five or six days to get to New Zealand, but for the first three days we did nothing but spew our guts out. It was three days before we could manage to keep any food down.

When we got to New Zealand, I realized I didn't know what my mother looked like. I was having all these feelings of not knowing what to expect and how I was going to react, or how she was going to react. At the same time, I was so anxious to meet her and hug her, but didn't know if I could do that. I don't know how we found each other, but there were tears, and yes, we did hug. Then there was the Director of Education from Wellington — a Mr. Davies — waiting for Daphne and I.

Going on the train was another experience. It seemed like it took forever, because we didn't realize how far Auckland to Wellington was. It took all night, and I remember thinking, "Where is Wellington; how far before we get there?"

Finally, we got to Wellington, with my mother. My stepfather was waiting for us, and I had an uncle waiting for us there as well. We went to my mother's home, and she named it "Akapuao," which is the name of the land of my grandmother — Raina. I was amazed that she put that on her house. It means "the place of gathering," and it was where all the children, and cousins, and uncles would meet whenever they came to Wellington.

I think we had two or three days with my mother before Daphne and I had to go to Wairarapa College in Masterton. I didn't approach my mother about my father at that time. It was never discussed in the house. My sister — half-sister — hated me because every time I went to Wellington on school holidays, and my sister was naughty, my mother would say, "Cathleen, why can't you be like June?" So I guess that didn't help.

The day I finished my exams I was so excited I ran all the way back to the hostel where I was staying in Masterton, and when I got there the matron was standing at the door, waiting for me. She said, "Your parents rang up, and they want you to go to Wellington tonight." This was a Thursday, and I said, "Why do I have to go today? Why can't I go tomorrow?"

On the way down on the train, I couldn't stop thinking about my grandfather. I guess I have always had these strong premonitions about things, and that is all that I was thinking about on the train, that something has happened to my grandfather. When I got home my mother told me that my grandfather had passed away. Wow! I think I screamed so loud, and I cried and cried and cried. I think I cried for two or three days; I couldn't stop crying. Then I realized that my grandmother was on her own, and who was going to take care of her?

At the end of the year, I went to Auckland, to the teachers' training college. I trained to be a home science — home craft — teacher. I stayed there three years, and my last three months I went to stay with my mother and stepfather before I returned to teach here [in Rarotonga].

When I finished my training all I could think of was to come home and look after my grandmother. I really never had the courage to ask my mother about my father. Every time I wanted to ask her I remembered what my stepfather had said, so the days just went by, and then I came back home. That is when I realized that I really, really wanted to know who my father was. So one day, I approached my aunt, the paramount chief, Pa Ariki, who brought me home. I sat down with her and said, "Auntie, please tell me about my father."

"Yes," she said, "you look like him, you walk like him, and yes, I know about your father." So she told me the story about my father, and then I asked, "What was his name?" That's when she said, "June, that's not my place to tell you. I think you need to ask your mother. That's her right to tell you who your father is."

So I decided, "Right, I'm going to ask my mother," but I guess the courage I didn't have, and it is probably the biggest regret in my life, because a couple of years later my aunt died suddenly. And then I was very determined; I must ask my mother. I was having my last child, my son Brett, and I paid my mother to come home to keep an eye on Tanya and Cleveland while I had my baby, and I wanted to ask her about my father. I don't know what happened. I didn't have the courage to say out of my mouth, "Please, Mum, tell me about my father." So back to New Zealand, and I still didn't know.

Then I met a gentleman who said, "I think I know somebody who knows your father." His name was Don O'Brien, but I don't think he was an American. I think he was a Kiwi, but he is long dead now. He married one of our relations from the island of Mitiaro — one of our very small islands. He came on the island [Rarotonga] one day, and I approached him. We went and had coffee, and while he was talking I was crying. He said, "June, I would do anything to be your father, but your father died." He said that my father died during the war, and: "Yes, your mother was very much in love with your father." And that was that, and I think I was too devastated when I learned that he had died. I was hoping he was still alive somewhere.

Then I remember the first time I went to Hawaii, you know the feeling of anger and hurt, because they tell you American citizens this way, and non-citizens that way. And then you go through immigration, and they ask you, "What are you doing here, blah, blah, blah?" You feel like you don't have any rights. I guess there has always been a lot of anger inside of me all my life because I was denied my rights.

Then I was coming home from Australia; I arrived in Auckland where I was overnighting to come home. I couldn't ring my mother because the phone in my house was broken, so my husband had to ring his mother in the middle of the night, and his father had to come and wake me up to tell my mother had died.

I was so stunned, and then flew to Wellington. My sister and her husband came and picked me up, and as we turned down the street to my mother's house I just screamed, because I realized that I had lost my mother and I would never know the truth. It was like part of me had been chopped off forever.

When we buried my mother, and as the coffin went into the hole, I sat on the ground. It was freezing cold and I never cried so much. People thought I was crying for my mother, but I was actually crying for the fact that I would never know who my father is, because I lost my aunt and now my mother. The pain was too hard to explain — the emptiness....

When we came back to the hall where they had a big feast for my mother's family, I got up and made a speech and described how painful it was to want to be with my mother. I didn't talk about my father at all, because I couldn't express my feelings about that in front of all those people. But really, that was the worst pain I felt that day. I felt so cheated about never being able to know the truth about who my father is.

I knew that there were a lot of old photographs that my mother had, and I was hoping that my sister would take them, but she never went back to the house. Then my stepfather sold the house, and I asked my sister, "What happened to all my mother's things?"

She didn't know.

I came home in 1966, and my grandmother died in 1967, a year later. She wasn't even sick. She complained about a toothache, and went to the dentist, and they pulled all her teeth out. Well, I don't remember how many they pulled out, but they shouldn't have pulled out more than one. When I came home, I realized she had been bleeding all day. She had to go to the hospital, because she couldn't eat and the bleeding hadn't stopped. They took her to the hospital, and when they did a test they realized that she had lost too much blood. They gave her a blood transfusion, and when I went the next morning to see her, she was all blue, and she never recovered. Three months later, she died.

Three years ago, I heard about Amy Whittaker, one of the women who went to New Zealand during my mother's time. I went to visit her, and she knew who I was. She told me about my father, and about her husband, how they spent time together in Wellington. Talby was an ex-commissioner of the Cook Islands, and he would invite all the Cook Island girls — there were six or eight of them in Wellington — every weekend to his place. They would get together with their guitars and ukuleles, and singing and dancing; and their boyfriends would come. She said, "June, your father was there. I knew your father, and we were all looking at your father, but he only had eyes for your mother."

I said, "Auntie, what was his name?" And she said, "Oh my God, I'm over eighty now, and I can't remember anything. I can't remember his name."

Then she told me that she, her boyfriend [later husband], Richard

Gilling Bolus, and they had one child, born in June 1944. I realized that she [Amy's daughter] was the same age as me. We were born the same month, and I wanted to talk to Amy, because she said her daughter contacts her father.

Amy gave me the number and I rang her, and we were both so excited to know that we had similar stories in one way or other. She wanted to talk about it, and I asked her about her father, and that is when she said, "I stopped writing to my father twenty years ago."

At the same time, my daughter [Tanya] has been doing some investigation. Last December, she said, "Mom, I think I found your father," and she was so excited that she couldn't wait to tell me, and called me at six o'clock in the morning.

She went through all sorts of things, all sorts of names; I don't know.... She got papers and papers, and all sorts of stuff. She had been talking to people, and narrowing it down to a list of people around that time in Wellington, and looking at photographs. She found this photograph and thought, "My God, that looks like me!"

TANYA: I grew up knowing that he [her grandfather] was an American in Wellington during the war, and that's where he met our grandmother; but unfortunately we had no information as to his name or his ranking, or whatever he was. It wasn't until I started having my children that I realized how important it was to know these things, and started looking into it.

It got to the stage that — apart from my grandmother — the people who knew who my grandfather was, all eventually passed away. But while they were still around, my mom would ask them what his name was, and they felt it was not for them to give that information. That was for my grandmother to say, but then she passed away along with these other people who knew.

We would sit down and talk about it once in a while, and with technology the way it was in those days, we were limited in getting information. It wasn't until about seven or eight years ago, when I discovered how important it was to know who my grandfather was that I started searching. Now, with the Internet and e-mail, the search has sped up on my part. And now that we have broadband on the island, things have sped up [even more]. Before that, with cable, it was very slow and limited. Today, the information I can get in one evening used to take me two weeks a couple of years ago.

I was told he [her grandfather] died shortly after my mom was born. My mom knew that from the various people who were in close contact with my grandmother, but when it came to a name she was not given that. All she knew was that he was tall, good-looking, and high in his ranking.

When I started researching, I started off with 400,000 men, and I thought, "Wow! How am I going to narrow this down?" Then I started looking at the camps [around Wellington during the war], and then I got it down to 6,000 men. Eventually, I got some names. I would write them down, and then look them up; and if there was an image then I could tell straight away if there was no connection — no resemblance.

As time went past, I finally got to who I think is my grandfather. As soon as I got an image of him I came to a halt. I could actually see myself in this photo. I pulled out some of my old modeling photos from a couple of years back and I thought, "There is some resemblance." And I could see my son and some of my nephews in that photograph.

I searched for anything about U.S. Marines in New Zealand — basically in Wellington during that time frame — and once I got a name I did a little background research on this person, and have looked into getting in contact with any family members. I have gotten a whole lot of responses from people, which has encouraged me, because I was about ready to chuck the thing in the bin. They have given me a lot of support and told me to keep going.

I found a sister in Colorado; I've written to her, as well as a brother who has passed away. His daughter forwarded my e-mail to another brother of my potential grandfather. He contacted me, and we have been corresponding ever since. It's been about six to eight weeks, now.

He has old letters from the war, and has on file information from his brother, which he has kept. Some names are mentioned, and places and people; and he is aware of some relationship his brother was in. He is aware of my wanting a DNA sample, but he wants more information from me first to make sure we are on the right track. The names I have given him so far do not match what he has on record. At the moment, that is as far as my story goes.

26. Looking for My Father: Shirley Ann Winistoerfer Fairest

Shirley Ann was born in June 1944, in Auckland, New Zealand, approximately eight months after her father, a U.S. Marine, left for the invasion of Tarawa. Before these events, however, her father, Francis "Duke" Wilbert Winistoerfer, survived the fighting on Guadalcanal with the Second Marine Division before joining up with the rest of the division in New Zealand in February 1943, where he met and became engaged to Shirley's mother. He was with the Third Battalion, Tenth Marine Regiment of the Second Marine Division, and after Tarawa was sent to Hawaii, where the division regrouped and trained for the invasion of the Mariana Islands — Saipan and Tinian.

Winistoerfer survived the war, and returned to his hometown of LaBadie, Missouri. According to Shirley, her father remained in contact with her mother until Shirley turned four. After that, the letters stopped coming. Shirley's mother eventually married a New Zealand man and had three sons by him — Shirley's half brothers.

At a time when having children out of wedlock — especially to American servicemen — was a social stigma, Shirley's circumstances were not discussed, except in whispers. However, at some point during Shirley's early years, she learned that her birth father was an American serviceman, but that was about all. As a result, Shirley describes her life as one of pent-up emotion, one where she felt somehow different from her half brothers, although she prefers not to use the term, "half brothers." At the same time, this did not prevent her from having a close family life. She was especially close to her youngest brother, Gary, who was a well-known New Zealand mountaineer, who died in a climbing accident in the Himalayas in 1993, not long after Shirley discovered her father's family in Missouri.

Unfortunately, because of limited information on her father due to family secrecy, privacy laws, and bureaucracy, it took Shirley a lifetime to find her father's family, her father having died eight years earlier.

Shirley has been married twice and has five children. She has worked as

a cook in a restaurant, worked in a factory for sixteen years, and now works
part time in a nursing home and is support for a Maori dance band out of
Taupo, a resort community in the center of North Island, New Zealand.

My mother was born in Australia. She came to New Zealand I think
when she was about seventeen or eighteen. She has not been back, not
even for one day. She is a bit of a closed book, my mom, but I think she
came to New Zealand because of her family. I think she came from a strict
upbringing.

My mother chooses not to discuss my past. But my stepfather died
just before Christmas [2006], and it is quite strange; since then, she [now]
talks quite a lot, and goes back in time about the marines and the war.
My mother and I have never been very close. My aunt and uncle brought
me up. I think I went there at about six months, and stayed there probably until I was about seven. It was then that my mother met and married Des, who adopted me and brought me up. I had three brothers from

Shirley Anne Winistoerfer Fairest,
as she looks today, and her father,
Francis W. Winistoerfer, as he
looked as a young U.S. Marine.
Shirley discovered who her father
was only after he had been dead
for eight years.

him, but spent most of my life thinking about this awesome father I had that was an American.

I always knew that I was different, because I am nothing like my brothers in New Zealand. And I don't know how it came up, but I know it came up through my aunt. My mother was saying something to my uncle one day about me, and my uncle said, "It's only history repeating itself."

I asked my aunt what he meant, and my aunt said, "You've got an American father." And when she said that, my mother wouldn't talk to my aunt for fifteen years.

I was brought up to believe that girls in that era who had children out of wedlock by American servicemen were lower than low, so I guess that is why my mother never discussed it.

I don't remember how old I was, but I have been looking for my American father since I can remember. I used to make up all these stories when I went to school about this awesome American father I had, and I think in my own mind that he was somebody like John Wayne.

When I was older, my aunt and my nana [grandmother], I think it was, said, "We have this name, 'Winistoerfer.'" And trying to spell [correctly] a name like Winistoerfer was hopeless. And I think it was about 1978 that I wrote to America — the American Embassy in Wellington. I had the name spelled wrong; everything was wrong. This letter came back saying, "Because of the Privacy Act, blah, blah, blah...," and that was it. But also over the years, I got married and divorced and married again, and had five children, so looking for my father went on the back burner.

Then one day I was talking to my brother, and at the time my brother [Gary] was New Zealand's top climber. He is my half brother, but I call my half brothers my brothers. I never refer to any of them as my half brothers. Gary lived on the South Island, and he said, "There is this guy, Denys Bevan; he has written a book about the American services." [*United States Forces in New Zealand: 1943–1945*.] My brother bought me the book, and from that day on I really started looking for my father. My brother was killed in the Himalayas in 1993, so it must have been before that.

Yeah, so I read this book, and then went down to the American Consulate in Auckland, and they still couldn't help me because of the Privacy Act and what-have-you. Then, strangely enough, my mother said she had read this letter in the *Women's Weekly* about this guy Stan Martin. "He has all these names and addresses for all these marines."

I didn't say anything, and I don't know why she told me that, but I got in touch with Stan Martin, and once I got in contact with Stan, he sort of put me on the right track. He gave me the address of the Second Marine Division. It was the *Follow Me* magazine [Official Publication of the Second Marine Division Association].

I wrote everything I knew about my father to this address, and said that I thought he fought as a boxer for the marines during the war. I also mentioned his nickname, "Duke."

Then I get this letter back saying they would print my story in the next edition but blocking out this, this and this; and I thought, "Oh, my God, they blocked out his name, they blocked out that he was from Missouri. How is anybody going to find him?" Then the marines came to New Zealand on a reunion tour in 1992-93, and just out of the blue I picked up the phone one day and this man said, "Are you Shirley?"

I said, "Yes," and he said, "I read your letter."

He had recognized what he thought might be my father, by being a boxer and his nickname of Duke. His [the caller's] name was Rod Sandburg from Bixby, Oklahoma. I was so excited, and said, "Where are you?"

He said, "We are in this hotel in Auckland, and we are taking off first thing in the morning."

I said, "Where are you going?" And he said they were all going to Wellington. So I told my husband, "Look after the kids, I'm going to Wellington."

I met him [Rod Sandburg] in Wellington, and meeting him I thought, "I wonder if he is my father?" We talked, and he had this little wee notebook with which he wrote in as we spoke, and he asked me what I knew about this man I think is my father. Then he said that when he got back home to Oklahoma, "I'm going to ring this family that I think is your family."

I spent the whole week with them [the marines], going everywhere with them. It was probably the best — no, second best week of my life. Then they took off back to the States, and I was being a bit negative, I guess, but I thought, "Will I ever hear back from him?"

I think from the time they left it was only ten days later that I got this letter from LaBadie, Missouri. It was from my Uncle Joe [her birth father's brother], and as soon as I opened it this photo came out. When I looked at the photo I just cried, because looking at the photo was like looking in the mirror. And my Uncle Joe said, "Yep, this is your father. You are Duke's daughter."

211

I rang Stan Martin to say I got this letter from my family but that my father had died. I started crying, and my husband had to finish the conversation. From then on I just planned to go to the States and meet my family.

I had my fiftieth birthday in June 1994. My daughters all gave me a birthday party, invited all my friends and family, and said, "Mom needs to go to America. Don't bring any presents; please bring American dollars to help her go."

My friends all came to this party and gave me $1,600 in spending money. My husband gave me a credit card and I bought an airline ticket. Stan and June Martin, and another lady — Pat Wilson — they were all going, and I had never flown before in my life. They were going and said there was a reunion [2nd MarDiv Reunion], so I said I would go with them.

I told my family that I wanted to go to this reunion to be with these veterans first, and then my younger brother [Jimmy], and my older brother [Gary] were going to meet me after the reunion. These were my American brothers.

The reunion was at the King of Prussia Hotel in Valley Forge, Pennsylvania. And that was probably the best month of my whole life — going to this reunion with all these veterans — and they were so proud that I had come to look for my family.

I can't remember too many of their names, but they welcomed me. One man that I do remember was Eddie Albert from the TV series, *Green Acres*, who up until then I did not know was also a marine. It was awesome. And when we went on a bus tour somewhere in Pennsylvania, we got off the bus and had lunch. We all sat around having lunch and talking, and when everybody got up to leave this man came over to me. He said, "You know, I have been listening to you," and that is when he told me that he had been stationed in Japan. He said after listening to me, he was sure that he had left a child behind and he wanted to go back and find him. I really felt sorry for this man, as he said he had never spoken of this, even to his wife. How sad to have lived with this secret for so many years.

I said, "Well, don't put it off because it might be too late." We talked until the bus got ready to go. I gave him a hug, and I am sad that I never got his address so I could stay in touch with him and see if he was successful in his search.

When I left Pennsylvania, I went to Missouri by bus. When I got to the bus station, all around the walls were photos of kids. I asked about this, and was told that a lot of kids go missing. That was quite an eye-opener for me.

I got on this bus, and that was something different for me too. I had never seen a bus with a toilet, and the driver locked the door after I got on. Then he announced that there would be no smoking of drugs and no drinking of alcohol on the bus, or whoever did would be put off at the next stop.

There were a lot of Negro people on the bus, and they were spread across their seats like they didn't want to have to share with me, and I was thinking, "Where am I going to sit?"

I walked down the aisle, and there was a Negro girl with a baby on her lap. I asked her if she minded if I sat there, and she said, "No." It was about a nineteen-hour bus trip, I think. I smiled at the baby several times, but the mother and I never spoke. She got off somewhere, and then a white lady got on and ended up sitting in front of me, and I think she was Amish, because she had on a bonnet and a long dress. We were the only two white people on the bus, and I felt a little bit scared because in New Zealand I was brought up with Maori and Pacific Islanders, and we inter-marry. But these people on the bus seemed hostile to me.

It wasn't until one of my American brothers came out to New Zealand that I realized what a color barrier there was in the States. For example, one day we stopped at a restaurant to have something to eat and the girl who served us was an Asian girl because it was a Chinese restaurant. She was a nice girl and asked Gary and his wife what they would like, and I just got these vibes from my brother that were not good. As she walked away from the table, he said, "You know, it wasn't long ago that we were killing them in Vietnam. Now, they are bringing me my food." Mind you, I guess his time in Vietnam had made him this way also.

When Gary came to visit me one year after I met him in America, I was so proud of him, and I invited the whole factory I worked with to my house. Ninety percent of the people I worked with were Pacific Islanders, Indians, Maori, with a few Pakehas thrown in. Gary stayed out in the garage with my husband drinking beer, and I said, "Come in and join everybody."

It took a while to get him in, but he said, "We wouldn't even have these people on our property at home in Arkansas."

I was proud of my brother, but I wasn't proud of the way he saw things. But then again, that was the way he was brought up, and I guess you can't change the habits of a lifetime in five minutes. And I saw that sort of thing several times when I was in America — the way some people were towards black people. I didn't like that, but I was there to meet my American family, and that's that.

But getting back to when I got off the bus in Saint Louis, my younger brother, Jimmy, met me along with his young son and his wife, Kelly. I was fifty at the time, and Jimmy was twenty-nine. I was old enough to be his mother. We were all hugging, and it was so lovely. We spent the night at his home, which had been our dad's home. We looked at old photos, but because of the age difference, World War II didn't mean anything to Jimmy. He was a veteran of Desert Storm.

So that first night I just met Jimmy, his wife, Kelly, and my little nephew, Nicholas. But the next day, we were all going down to LaBadie for this big family hoedown. We would call it a barbecue here. Then the next thing I hear is Jimmy saying, "Oh my God, here is Gary!"

Now, this is my other American brother, Gary, who at the time was forty-six, and Jimmy says, "We haven't seen him for nine years!"

I had been corresponding with Gary, and he said he would wait until I got to Arkansas to meet me. He walked in the door and said, "Shirley." Jimmy and Gary had not seen each other since our father's funeral, and Gary said, "I just couldn't wait to see my sister." He had even left his wife behind because she wasn't ready, but she followed the next day. He gave me the biggest hug; I just couldn't get rid of him. It was totally awesome!

Gary was a quiet man, and when I left he said, "I would like to give you something of value, but I haven't got anything that is valuable. But this meant a lot to me," and he gave me his dog tags from Vietnam, and I still have them. They are one of my most prized possessions. He also brought the American flag that had been on our dad's coffin, and gave it to our younger brother, Jimmy.

So we all got on Jimmy's truck and went to LaBadie, but on the way we had to go past the Bethel Cemetery. We stopped there, and that was a very emotional time for me. That was where the family was buried. My father was there, and my grandma and my grandpa. I had a wreath specially made in New Zealand with New Zealand flowers — artificial flowers. They left me there and I talked to my father for a while. The feelings I had this day of the meeting with my father will stay with me always. Then we went to this hoedown; it was probably only a mile down the road.

There were sixty-eight family members there, and I met them all individually. I have a tape of it somewhere, and I play it now and again. It was absolutely brilliant, and they were all saying, "We didn't know."

Then I met my Uncle Joe, my dad's brother. He had been in the American Navy, and he was chewing tobacco. It was something I thought was disgusting; something I had never seen or heard of in my life before. He even gave me some to take back to my husband in New Zealand. But he [Uncle Joe] knew about me; Duke told him about me after the war, and I said, "Why didn't he come back for me?"

Uncle Joe said, "Shirley, it was the end of the war; there was no money. We had no money."

My father worked for the county; he drove a truck. That is all there was around there, farming and laboring. I was a bit sad about all that, but actually mad at my mother because he had corresponded with my mother until I was four years old, and yet she never told me. Gary was four years younger than me, so I figured that Duke had remarried by then, or wanted to put that part of his life behind him. Who knows?

While we were at the barbecue that day, the three of us were sitting together — me, Gary, and Jimmy — and Jimmy said to me, "You know, out of all of us, Shirley, you are surely the only one of us who travels in the old man's smoke." He said, "You are him, more than all of us put together!" I took that as a compliment whether my dad was a rat bag or not. And why I say this is because many people told me over my search that to be nicknamed "Duke," one had to be very handy with their fists!

I also heard people talking about Aunt Iris, how she couldn't come that day, and I knew there was something wrong. It was getting towards the end of the day and young Jimmy said, "We'll head out and go down to Aunt Iris's house." She is my dad's sister.

We went up to her house, and it was still daylight. Jimmy went to the door, and I was hanging back a little bit, not sure of what was about to happen. Then this lady opens the door and comes out. She looked straight at me and I looked at her, and she said, "Shirley." She looked again and said, "Francis." Francis is my dad's name. She said, "Francis," again and then started to cry. She gave me a big hug, and took me inside. You only had to look at her and I; we were almost identical. Everything about us was so alike. She cried and told me about my dad, what he was like and when he went to the war. She said he came back a different man. She said life had been difficult for him; that he had several marriages. She said the best part of his life had been with Pat, his latest wife — his widow. But he used to drink heavy, and tended to get in fights. She gave me a lovely gold chain that my father had bought for her before he went to the war, and some other jewelry that belonged to the family.

After that, I went back with Jimmy, and then went to stay with my dad's widow, Pat. That was a nice time too. She was only five years older than me, but had been married before, and had four children from that previous relationship. Then she and my dad had Jimmy, my youngest brother. She gave me all the photos and everything that was my dad's, and said that his war years were more a part of my life and his than they were hers.

We laid in bed and yapped all night. She told me that her life with my dad had been good, but quite often the sheriff would ring her up because he would be drunk and driving his truck, and sometimes he had a shotgun with him. As I think back now, maybe my dad had me in his mind, as well as the years he was fighting in the Pacific, because he told my brother Jimmy once, many years ago, "If you ever want to go to a beautiful country, then go to New Zealand."

Perhaps he had wanted to find me after all.

I was in Missouri for not quite two weeks. I was away for just over a month, and Rod Sandburg came over from Oklahoma to Missouri to pick me up, and he and his wife, Carole, drove me all the way to L.A. to meet the plane. We took a week to get back to L.A., but I saw the most wonderful sights and had the greatest time of my life.

Looking for my father has had a sad conclusion, finding that he had passed away; but I have met some awesome people along the way. I came home with all this stuff— all these photos and memories — and then I went to see my mother. I told her about this awesome family," [Shirley's American family] and she said, "I can't believe they accepted you."

I said, "Well, why wouldn't they? They are my family. You have to come out of that time warp."

I was rapped when I got home because everybody I knew wanted to talk about this trip and my family. And then my American brother, Gary, wanted to come to New Zealand and meet all of his New Zealand nieces — my children. I was really proud to have him here and show him off to all my family. The colored issue didn't become a problem, but I was always a little anxious that he was going to say something to hurt one of my friends.

After I got back, I received a letter from a girl saying, "I've seen your article in the *New Zealand Herald*, and I'm looking for my American father too." I had been interviewed by our national newspaper and a woman's magazine, and she said that she was Maori, and she believed her father was a Negro. She apologized for being Maori, and I just thought, "Humm-m-m...."

I wrote back to her and said, "Well, from my understanding I doubt that your father would have been a marine, because I had heard that there weren't any 'coloreds' in the Marine Corps at that time." I never heard from this girl again, but I told her to go through the American Navy.

Some marines have sent me photos of ladies they went with during the war, and they have tried to find them. This one guy was writing to me, but he has since passed away, and I think it had got to the stage where we had found this guy we thought might be his son but the New Zealand Privacy Act said, "No, somebody adopted that child, so sorry...." And it was quite sad.

It's funny, it seems it is mainly the girls who are looking for their [American] fathers, but some men are too. But on the other side, Kiwis trying to find their American fathers found families that didn't want them to know, because the American children didn't want them to get their dad's inheritance. And it is sad, too, because there are these old men looking for their [New Zealand] children; they knew they fathered children here.

The search and finding of my [American] family was probably the making of me; it made my life better. It gave me a sense of finally being someone, and being a part of this family, which I knew was mine. I know I have become a different person — hopefully a better and more tolerant person. And I'm not too sure of what sort of life we do actually have after this one here on Earth, but if there is another life then I know I surely will meet my dad then.

27. My Father Was
a Marine: Clint Libby

With so many Americans being in New Zealand during World War II, there resulted between 1,400 and 1,500 war brides. Some of these couples moved to the U.S. after the war, while others remained in New Zealand. Some of these marriages failed, while others lasted a lifetime. Clint Libby is a product of one of the latter cases. Libby was born in 1946, in Levin, a small town on the west coast of North Island, New Zealand. His mother, Jean Denton, was a Kiwi and one of four girls. She met Libby's father, Robert Clinton Libby, known as "Bob," in Levin during the war. He arrived in New Zealand in early 1943, after having survived six months with K Company, 3rd Battalion, 2nd Regiment, Second Marine Division, in the disease-ridden killing fields of Guadalcanal. During the eight months that he spent in New Zealand, before going on to Tarawa, and then Saipan and Tinian, Bob Libby met and eventually married Jean Denton.

After having survived four major island campaigns, Bob Libby was rotated back to the States, where he trained new U.S. Marines at Camp Pendleton and Camp Elliot, in California. After the war, he returned to New Zealand to retrieve his war bride. Jean, however, refused to live in the United States, so Libby elected to stay in New Zealand. He returned to the U.S. only once during the rest of his life, and passed away in 1995, aged 73.

Clint Libby worked most of his life in law enforcement, and is now retired and living in Wellington.

On my dad's side, his dad was an army sergeant during the First World War. He was Oliver Libby from Maine, and he married Lucy Jane Knight, from a well-known family in Boston. Her family was not in favor of the marriage, but they married anyway. There were two [children] from that marriage, Doris — my dad's sister — and my dad. When he was about two, his dad left and was never ever seen again by the family. It wasn't until I researched the family history in the last five years that [I learned that] after he left he went back up into Maine and cohabitated with a woman up there and gave her a son, so my father had a half brother that he didn't know about. It was after he died that I found that out.

After the marriage breakup, he was fostered out. His sister stayed with the mother, but he was fostered out over the greater Boston area. He went to the Federal Building in Boston and joined the marines on 27 August 1940, aged 18.

My mother was basically a country girl. They lived just south of Levin on a farm, and when she left school she went and worked at clerical positions. One was in a butcher shop, and then she left there and came to Wellington, where she worked for a department store. From there she joined the New Zealand Air Force, and saw the rest of the war out in the air force just doing clerical duties.

Her father's family, the Dentons, arrived in Lyttelton, Christchurch, in 1850, on [one of] the first four colonial ships. They were farmers. Her mother's father, Tate, was a seafarer and arrived here in the late 1870s.

My father joined the marines before the war [before Pearl Harbor].

Clint Libby's father, Robert Clinton Libby, was one of many American servicemen to meet and marry New Zealand women during the war. He was also among those who survived multiple Pacific island battles and returned to New Zealand, making it his home. He returned to the U.S. only once after that. Clint is held by his father in this photograph.

He got out in 1945, and came back here to collect my mother, who he married in 1943. She wouldn't go with him, so he was left with two choices: One, either he went back on his own, or he stayed here; and he decided to stay here. So he spent his life here, except for one trip back in 1968, when he went back and saw his mother for a few weeks. Other than that, he spent the rest of his life in New Zealand.

Dad never talked about the war unless there was a reunion and they all had a few drinks. Then their tongues loosened up and they started telling the war stories, but I was just a young fellow and made to go to bed, so I didn't really hear them.

My dad was at McKay's Crossing, which was halfway between Levin and Wellington. I'm not quite sure how he met my mother, because he didn't dance and my mother liked dancing.

My grandmother was very popular [with the marines] because she had three daughters living at home. My mother was the oldest at 21, and the other two were 18 and 15, on the verge of being the right age for these young marines. My dad said that my grandmother actually encouraged the relationship, and they married in Levin in the Presbyterian church there on 28 August 1943.

Once he survived Saipan and Tinian — those islands — instead of him continuing on up in the Pacific, he was sent back as a combat instructor to Camp Pendleton in California. When the war ended, he got out as soon as he could, and came back to New Zealand, intending to collect his bride and go back to join the police in the States.

One of the interesting asides, and unbeknownst to me, he registered me as an American citizen with the American Embassy here. When I was twenty-three, I went to the embassy — I had married at that stage. I wanted to see my grandmother in the States, and my wife's father was English, so she wanted to see her grandparents in England. We were going to head off for a year, so I went to the embassy and fronted up there with my application forms for our visas, and I would describe the experience as very confusing. The next minute I am whistled into an office, and because I was an American citizen and hadn't registered for the draft for Vietnam service, they didn't know what to do with me. I had to sign a number of papers but anyway, it came back from a court — whatever it was — in the United States that if I gave up my American citizenship then they would take no further action against me. So I was very, very pleased to give up my American citizenship that I didn't know I had anyway.

But anyway, when my dad did come back, he lived for a while with his wife's relatives in Wellington to try and make ends meet and to try and get a job. His first job was actually as a storeman. I can remember him telling me he got $11 a week, and after a year or so they managed to buy their first home in Belmont, Lower Hutt, near Wellington. At one stage he worked at night as a taxi driver to make ends meet, and when they bought their first home they didn't have enough money for furniture, including tables and chairs, so they just sat on apple boxes.

While living in the Wellington area dad played basketball in the town hall with a group of Americans, many of whom were ex-servicemen. Basketball was unheard-of then in New Zealand.

He then had various jobs — stayed around Wellington and the Lower Hutt area. He was a carpet layer and a truck driver and worked for various companies. And then for some unknown reason, he joined the New Zealand prison service. He first worked at Waitako Prison (now Rimutaka Prison) near Upper Hutt. They sold the house in Belmont when he was transferred to Turangi in 1958, and they then lived in prison housing. It was not until 1959 that electricity came to the area and that shows how undeveloped parts of New Zealand was even then. They then moved to Waikune Prison near the National Park, and then to Paremoremo Prison, the maximum security prison for New Zealand at Auckland. He was in charge of B Block. After he retired from Paremoremo, they went to live at Whangamata on the Coromadel Coast, where they had built a home. Eventually, they moved back to Levin, and he saw his last years out in Levin with my mother, where she was born. My mother died there in 1993.

The first marine reunion I remember was in 1968. I can remember vividly the old Paekakariki Pub; that was one of their old watering holes. And Waikato Breweries did a special brew for them with a special label, "Leatherneck Lager." I still have an unopened bottle!

They fascinated me, these guys; they had an aura about them. It was one of confidence; there was no swaggering or brashness like you see in some Americans. They were quiet; and they were polite and friendly. And like I said, it wasn't until they had a few beers that they would reminisce. But it wasn't boasting; it was just reminiscing: "Remember the time that we did such and such." They were confident but in a nice way. They did not have to prove themselves to anyone — they'd already done that.

In 1943, all the [New Zealand] men were overseas, and the women were working on the land and in the services, and there was basically no one here to protect them. We were still settlers and colonials, and unsophisticated compared to the Americans. And the Americans landed here with plenty of money, and dashing uniforms. They were polite, and that went down very well, not only with the younger women but also the older women, who were impressed with their manners.

I can remember my grandmother saying that although they never wanted for anything because they lived on a farm — they had their own meat, and could produce their own butter and what-have-you — but the Americans would roll up in a jeep, and after they left, leave a Jerry can of petrol, which was scarce. There was chocolate and nylons, the things you could not buy. It was an amazing experience in that here they seemed to have everything, but they also had the looks and the manners that seemed to be lacking in our own men, apparently at that time.

My grandmother once made a pertinent comment. They lived on a farm, and it wasn't too far from the coast. It was just beaches for miles along there, and any enemy could have landed there virtually unopposed; and they were expecting the Japanese to arrive any day. When the sirens went, she was to get on a bike, go a mile or two down the road and pick up a farm truck. She then had a predetermined beat to go on and pick these elderly people up, and then take them into the hills where they had caves; and the caves had been stocked with food. So certainly when all these Americans arrived, it was a great relief that there was somebody now to protect us.

When my dad arrived, they had come up from the Pacific [Guadalcanal], and they thought, "Oh, another bloody island!"

He said they couldn't believe it; they came around the heads of Wellington, and there was civilization. He said they simply couldn't believe it; that some of the guys even cried. It was an emotional thing to just come to civilization, because they had been away from it for so long.

They had never heard of New Zealand, knew nothing about New Zealand, didn't know what to expect, and presumed there would be natives. And when my father wrote to his mother and said he had found a woman and that he was going to marry her, she was against it because she expected that he was going to marry some native woman from one of the islands. It wasn't until he actually sent a photograph to show her that she was a white woman that she was satisfied.

As they came in [to the harbor], there was a landing craft or a boat that had "KIWI" on it, and they said, "What the hell is this KIWI?"

They didn't even know what a Kiwi was. So they were pretty igno-rant of New Zealand, but it certainly didn't take them long to come to appreciate what New Zealand had to offer.

My dad's records say that he was on Guadalcanal for six months, New Zealand for eight months, and after Tarawa, was at Camp Tarawa in Hawaii, and then Saipan and Tinian in the Mariana Islands. After that, he went to Camp Pendleton and Camp Elliot in California as a combat instructor.

My dad said that he was rather fortunate when he was on Tarawa, because he didn't go in on the first wave. He went in on the second wave, and as you know, most of the first wave was wiped out. They ground to a halt on the coral. The front [of the landing craft] dropped, and they were all told to get the hell out. They leaped out and found themselves over their heads in water, and he said many of them drowned.

He was in charge of a mortar team of three, and I'm not sure what equipment he had, but he hit the bottom and managed to push off, come up and get some air, and then down again. He reckons that's what saved him; he just kept bobbing all the way in, and he couldn't believe that he got in. He said, "Why me? There were other guys that were more qualified, had better prospects in life, were better educated — they died."

He was a survivor. He survived as a kid fostered out, and he survived as a marine. And some of the stories he told us about some of the things his mother did to him were quite interesting. He really had a hard time; he was pushed from foster home to foster home. I don't think he was abused as such, but certainly not treated very well. So he was a survivor right from the beginning. And the only battle he ever mentioned, and only once or twice in passing, was Tarawa. That seemed to have had the most affect on him.

When I joined the police in 1966 — on one occasion as a young police-man I did a few days' duty down to the Supreme Court. There was an old cop there who had been in the police during the war; he was in the last few years of his career, and when he heard that my dad was an American he said, "Ah, the worst beat to do [during the war] was around Oriental Parade." He said, "I hated doing that because there were American ser-vicemen having sex with the women on the beach, and in the parks." He said it was just terrible.

And then he said, "As you walk around the city, have you noticed the concertina doors that go across the shops?"

You see, a lot of the shops in those days were little alcoves and the shopkeepers put in doors across those alcoves because they would come to work in the morning and find that the alcoves had been used for sex, and they would have to clean the mess up. A lot of the shops, when I started in 1966, still had these metal concertina-sort of mesh-type doors that were meant to stop the American servicemen from having their wicked ways with the New Zealand women in their doorways.

I am proud of my American heritage — proud of my father and what he achieved. My three children are proud, too, to be "quarter American." At one stage my son worked with a Japanese lad whose grandfather was in the Japanese Army during the war. Both grandfathers were on opposing sides, both survived — ironic!

Our heritage here in New Zealand has come from Great Britain and the United States. As a result we have a mix of English, Scottish (including Scandinvian?), Irish and French. Quite a mix but we are pleased to call ourselves Kiwis and to live in New Zealand.

Bibliography

BOOKS

Bergerud, Eric M. *Fire in the Sky: The Air War in the South Pacific*. Boulder: Westview Press, 2000.

Bioletti, Harry. *The Yanks are Coming: The American Invasion of New Zealand, 1942–1944*. Auckland: Century Hutchinson Group, 1989.

Cox, Brian. *Too Young to Die: The Story of a New Zealand Fighter Pilot in the Pacific War*. Auchland: Century Hutchinson, 1987.

Davies, Sonya. *Bread and Roses*. Hong Kong: David Bateman in Association with Fraser Books, 1984.

Dunnigan, James F., and Albert A. Nofi. *The Pacific War Encyclopedia*. N.Y.: Checkmark Books, 1998.

_____. *Victory at Sea: World War II in the Pacific*. N.Y.: William Morrow, 1995.

Edgerton, Robert B. *Warriors of the Rising Sun: A History of the Japanese Military*. New York: W.W. Norton, 1997.

Frank, Richard B. *Guadalcanal: The Definitive Account of the Landmark Battle*. New York: Random House, 1990.

Horn, Alex. *Wings Over the Pacific: The RNZAF in the Pacific Air War*. Auckland: Random Century New Zealand, 1992.

Hutching, Megan. *Against the Rising Sun: New Zealanders Remember the Pacific War*. Auckland: HarperCollins (New Zealand), 2006.

Lowman, David D. *Magic: The Untold Story of U.S. Intelligence and the Evacuation of Japanese Residents from the West Coast During WWII*. Stanford: Athena Press, 2000.

Lundstrom, John B. *Black Shoe Carrier Admiral: Frank Jack Fletcher at Coral Sea, Midway, and Guadalcanal*. Annapolis: Naval Institute Press, 2006.

Masters, A.O. "Cappy." *Memoirs of a Reluctant Batsman: New Zealand Servicemen in the Fleet Air Arm, 1940–1945*. London: Janus Publishing, 1995.

McGee, William L. *Amphibious Operations in the South Pacific*. Vol. 2, *The Solomons Campaign, 1942–1943: From Guadalcanal to Bougainville — Pacific War Turning Point*. Santa Barbara: BMC Publications, 2002.

Miller, Edward S. *War Plan Orange: The U.S. Strategy to Defeat Japan, 1897–1945*. Annapolis: Naval Institute Press, 1991.

Shovel, Sword, and Scalpel: A Record of Service of Medical Units of the Second New Zealand Expeditionary Force in the Pacific (by the officers, NCOs, and men of the units involved). Dunedin, New Zealand, 1945.

Bibliography

Smith, Michael. *The Emperor's Codes: The Breaking of Japan's Secret Ciphers.* N.Y.: Arcade Pub., 2000.

Thomas, John. *Warrior Nation: New Zealanders at the Front, 1900–2000.* Christchurch: Hazard Press, 2000.

van der Vat, Dan. *The Pacific Campaign—World War II: The U.S.–Japanese Naval War, 1941–1945.* N.Y.: Simon & Schuster, 1991.

Waters, S.D. *The Royal New Zealand Navy: Official History of New Zealand in the Second World War, 1939–1945.* Wellington: R.E. Owen, Govt. Printer, 1956.

Williams, H.W. *Dictionary of the Maori Language.* Wellington: Legislation Direct, 2005.

INTERNET SITES

Fleet Air Arm Archives: 1939–1945 http://www.fleetairarmarchive.net/Ships/Index.html.

Hoffman, Lt. Col. Jon T. (USMCR). *Silk Chutes and Hard Fighting: U.S. Marine Corps Parachute Units in World War II.* http://www.nps.gov/archive/wapa/indepth/extContent/usmc/pcn-190-003147-00/sec4.htm.

NGA TOA (MANY WARRIORS): http://www.ngatoa.com/news.php.

New Zealand History Online: http://www.nzhistory.net.nz/war-and-society.

Shaw, Henry I. *First Offensive: The Marine Campaign for Guadalcanal.* http://www.nps.gov/archive/wapa/indepth/extContent/usmc/pcn-190-003117-00/sec1.htm.

Statistics New Zealand: http://www.stats.govt.nz/default.htm.

Index

Index

USS *Bunker Hill* 46
Burnham Military Camp 36
Burns-Phillips 176
Burton, Jack 68

Camp Elliot, California 51, 153, 318, 223
Canada 152; aircrews on British aircraft carriers 40; New Zealand pilots trained in 55, 62, 72, 139
Canterbury, South Island, NZ 36, 55
Carkeek, Huia Tahiwi 119
Carkeek, Louise Heffer, oral history of 119–124
Carrigan, Clifford Charles, oral history of 151–159
Carrigan, Sylvia P. (née Whitehouse), oral history of 151–159
Cassino, Battle of 88
Catalinas *see* "Dumbos"; PBY Catalinas; RNZAF Squadron No. 6
Christchurch, South Island 29, 50, 87, 91; "bicycle city" 166, 219; hospital 29
Coast Watchers 68, 75
Conrad, Bob 110
Cook Island Maori *see* Baudinet, June, oral history of; Savage, Tanya, oral history of
Coral Sea 41
Corsair fighter planes (F4U) flown by RNZAF *see* Lang, E.T., oral history of; Turnbull, Des, oral history of
Cronk, Charles (New Zealand pilot) 65
Crowe, Major Jim 163
Cudby, Joan Hay, oral history of 85–102
Cursey, Archie 24

Davies, Sonya 120–121
Davis, Col. "Cocky" 49
Dean, James 101
Dear John Letters 24, 128
De Havilland Tiger Moth 50, 53, 54, 60, 72
Denton, Jean 218
Depression years 19, 21, 79, 88, 95, 96, 103, 114, 123, 126, 138, 160, 161, 162, 171

De Vall, John 10
Dominion Monarch 139
Draper, Winifred Lea 106
"Dumbos," PBY Catalina 32, 58, 60, 68, 69, 77; see *also* Laird, Charles, oral history of
Duncan, Ngaire Baker, oral history of 106–112
Duniden, South Island 29, 34, 35
Dunlop, Robert Gordon, oral history of 19–28

Edhouse, William John, oral history of 69–78
Elliot, Sir Randle 38
Eltham, North Island 103–105, 171, 174, 176
Empress Augusta Bay, Bougainville 32, 77
Empress of Britain 138
USS *Enterprise* 179
Eparimu, Pipbo 165
Ercole, Johnny 62–64, 167, 169
Espiritu Santo, New Hebrides 55, 66, 74
"essential industry" 28, 60, 108, 117, 131

Fairest, Shirley Anne Winistoerfer, oral history of 208–217
Farland, Merle 31
Featherston 37, 53, 129, 167, 170; see *also* Japanese POWs
Fielding, North Island 39, 50
Fiji 22, 34, 38, 81, 82, 125, 130, 145; soldiers 39; TB hospital in 129
Filariasis (elephantiasis) *see* Tropical diseases
First World War 21, 29, 48, 49, 123, 126, 135, 137, 167, 182, 188, 199, 218
Fisken, Geoffrey Bryson, oral history of 60–68
"Flags of Our Fathers" 161
Fleet Air Arm, British 139, 141
Foley, Archie 140–141
Foley, Colonel 49
Foon, Meng 170
HMS *Formidable* 43
Fort Dorset (Wellington Harbor) 39

228

Index

Index

Nielsen, Gail 84–85
Nissan Island 57–58
Norfolk Island 23–24, 73
North Africa 147, 148, 168
Nouméa, New Caledonia 24, 31
Nye, Walter 174

Oakden, Mrs. 164
O'Brien, Don 204
Office of Navy Public Relations, U.S. 162
Ohakea, North Island 50, 55, 72
Ohakune, North Island, NZ 69, 71, 72
Ohinemutu, North Island 65
Ohura, North Island *see* Skinner, Leonard, oral history of; Watts, Melvin, oral history of
One Tree Hill 71
Onerahi Airbase 72
Opper, Bob 167
Oriental Parade, Wellington 223
Orr, "Bluie" 78
Otago University Medical Corps 30, 35
Otaki, North Island 113, 118, 119, 121; U.S. Marines in 123, 151, 159
Ouenghi, New Caledonia 25

Pa Ariki 199, 203
Paekakariki 41, 42, 81, 173, 175, 221
Pago Pago, Samoa: U.S. Marines in 184–189; *see also* Second Marine Brigade
Pakeha 87, 90, 114, 213
Palmerston North, North Island 40, 41, 60, 195
Papakura 21, 38, 140
Papakura, Ivy 90
Papua New Guinea 42, 72
Pava'ia'i village, Samoa 185–187
PBY Catalinas 32, 60, 63, 77; *see also* Laird, Charles, oral history of
Pearl Harbor 21, 40, 41, 61, 64, 112, 145, 152, 162, 178, 179, 219
Penrhyn Island, Cook Islands 198
Perry, Dave 159
Pescatore, Lou 99
Philippines 42, 195, 196

Pidgin English 31
Pierce, June 149–150
Pink House, New Caledonia 24
Piva airstrip, Bougainville 58
Place, John "Jack" Erskine 104; *see also* Duncan, Ngaire Baker, oral history of
Porirua 156, 157
Porton Plantation 58
Pregnancies 11, 36, 195, 196
President Adams 145
President Coolidge 22, 31
Pukekohe Racecourse 169, 195

Queen Alexandra's Mounted Rifles 48, 80

RAAF Squadron No. 214 & 453 in Singapore 61, 65
Rabaul, New Britain 53, 56, 58, 74, 75, 183
RAF Squadron No. 63 64, 67
RAF Squadron No. 205 60
RAF Squadron No. 243 61, 63, 66
Rarotonga, Cook Islands *see* Baudinet, June, oral history of
Rawhitiroa Hall 103
"Rehab Bursary" 39
RNZAF Squadron #1 (Venturas) *see* Edhouse, William, oral history of
RNZAF Squadron No. 6 (PBYs) 77
RNZAF Squadron No. 8 (Venturas) 78
RNZAF No. 16 Squadron *see* Lang, E.T., oral history of
Roberts, Erastus Winn 100–101
Robinson, "Cobby" 24
Rondell, Fred 195–196
Roosevelt, Eleanor 101, 167, 168
Rotorua, North Island 61, 72, 165
RSA (Returned Servicemen's Club) 28, 123, 157
Ruth, Sergeant 186, 189

St. George Channel 74
Samambula, Fiji 22
Samoa 145
Samoa Hospital 183
Samoan Marines 180–184

231

Index